AF531302

Water Resources Projects and their Environmental Impacts

Published by:

Tilak Wasan

DISCOVERY PUBLISHING HOUSE PVT. LTD.
4383/4B, Ansari Road, Darya Ganj
New Delhi-110 002 (India)
Phone : +91-11-23279245, 23253475, 43596065
E-mail : discoverypublishinghouse@gmail.com
sales@discoverypublishinggroup.com
web : www.discoverypublishinggroup.com

First Edition: **2001**

Reprinted: **2020**

ISBN: 978-81-7141-579-3

Water Resources Projects and their Environmental Impact

Printed at:
Infinity Imaging Systems
Delhi

Dedicated to

BHAI SHRI BABAN PRASAD MISHRA
(Managing Editor, Nava Bharat, Raipur)
—Who taught me journalism,
brotherhood, and commitment to work,
without trying to teach me anything.

FOREWORD

Environmental impact of water resources projects is arguably the most contentious environmental issues of our times; particularly so in India. Whereas one set of people warmly welcome new water resources projects as vanguards of development and progress, another set of people aggressively denounce the projects as harbingers of environmental destruction and poverty. No sooner a new dam or barrage is announced, controversy erupts. As we see from the Narmada and Tehri projects, the controversy keeps snowballing. The construction work proceeds in fits and starts, taking decades and decades, because at every step it encounters protests and counter-protests, legal action and counter-action, bouquets and brickbats. There never seems to be a consensus on whether a water resource project is a net benefactor or a net destroyer.

Over the years, tussles between the governments of different states who share the water of a reservoir, are becoming increasingly more frequent and more fierce, adding yet another frightening dimension to the controversies that shroud water resources projects.

The author has been on several expert panels of Government of India, and has studied not only the environmental impacts of numerous water resource projects but has also acquired an intimate knowledge of the forces and counter-forces that work behind the controversies enveloping these projects. In this book the author has provided the gist of all the documented material on the environmental impact of water resources projects in general and of projects in Krishna, Mahanadi, and Godavari basins in particular. He has also assessed the likely impacts of 'small hydro' which is often perceived as an eco-friendly alternative to large hydro.

I believe the book is a significant contribution to the extant literature on environmental impact of water resources.

Prof. V. T. Patil
Vice-Chancellor
Pondicherry University
Pondicherry

PREFACE

When my *Environmental Impact of Water Resources Projects*, brought out by Discovery Publishing House, New Delhi, some years back, was sold out, we first thought of reprinting it. But the state-of-the-art in this rapidly expanding field of knowledge had already changed. Then we thought of a new edition. But so much had changed, including the heights of so many dams, and depths of so many reservoirs, that a mere new edition would not have done justice to the present status of this field.

So we decided to rewrite the book and the result is now in your discerning hands. As we went through the 1990s there was an ever increasing mention of 'small hydro' whenever there was a discussion on environmental impacts of water resources projects (which was often). And almost always 'small hydro' (including mini and micro hydel projects) were mentioned as people-friendly and eco-friendly substitutes to the so-called anti-people and anti-environment large hydro. In cognizance of this general trend of reasoning, I have included a chapter on small hydro in this book.

I must thank Dr. S.C. Maudgal, Advisor, Ministry of Environment, Government of India, for initiating me into this field of study. And I thank Ms Richa Sharma for helping me through the manuscript.

S. A. Abbasi

CONTENTS

ome up after independence), the frequency as w
des of the adverse environmental impacts of the
arp focus. The adverse impact which was the first
d which always occurred irrespective of the siz
the dam, was the dislocation of the people and
mic problems of rehabilitation. The next obvious im
ogging in the command area which occurred
inevitability soon after an irrigation network
ed. Proliferation of weeds in the command area, cau
lability of stagnant or nearly-stagnant water enric
nt-laden run-off from agricultural fields, was the n
only noticed impact. As the forest cover in the coun
eting fast it was noticed that water resources proje
gst the major culprits; good storage sites for the creati
rs were invariable existing in the forested uplands. W
ng a good chunk of the forest had to go under wat
brought in approach roads and increased human activ
rvoir catchment, resulting in further loss of forests.

nearly four decades after the 'dam boom' had started, w
while major water resources projects have indeed helpe
source management they have also brought in their wak
environmental backlashes.

ation is best summarized by Dr. S.Maudgal, Advisor
f Environment and Forests, Government of India. To quote

ssessment of river valley projects was introduced in India
ecause of the increasing realization that the development
often result in unanticipated undesirable consequences
ay be so drastic as to reduce or even nullify the
nomic benefits for which the project is planned. The
on the design and construction of engineering works,
lue stress on concurrent measures for optimal utilization
tential created, has been the main factor responsible for
the avoidable adverse consequences.

1

INTROD

To the planners and executiv
water resources projects, b
and reservoirs, appeared to be the
predominantly agricultural count
water was the most vital resource
resource in abundance and fre
uncertainities and 'bondage' of nat
year-round use, control the flood
needed power (mainly, it was hoped
and lighting the villages), and wo
for the vigorous growth of a na
aspirations of the Indian people w
Nehru when he called the up-an
modern India'.

Four decades later we find that
forseen, has gone wrong. That so
dimension.

Due to the post-independence spu
dams (83 of the 92 dams in Krishna
in Godavari river basin, and 20 out c

basin have
the magnitu
came into s
realized, a
location of
socio-econ
was water
frightening
commission
by the ava
with nutri
most comm
began dep
were amo
of reservo
the damm
Dams also
in the rese

By now,
know that
in water r
substantia

The sit
Ministry

Impact
in 1978
projects
which n
socio-ec
emphasis
without
of the p
many of

There is a mistaken belief that environmental considerations would put a stop to development. It needs to be categorically stated that such a notion is totally misplaced. Indeed the objective of considering environmental aspects, as part of the development projects, is to achieve:

(a) Sustained development with minimal environmental degradation; and
(b) Prevention of long term adverse environmental side effects by incorporating mitigative measures so that the remedies do not become unmanageable and prohibitive in the long run.

NEED FOR SPECIFIC AND QUANTITATIVE INFORMATION

Several qualitative observations and reports are now available generalising the environmental impact of water resources projects in India (Centre for Science & Environment 1982, 1985; Academy of Gandhian Studies 1990; University of Roorkee 1985, CBIP 1985; please see Chapter 9) but information on individual dam is scarce. Even more scarce are studies in quantitative terms; the magnitudes of physical, chemical, biological, or socio-economic impacts or such benefit-cost analysis which have taken into account environmental benefits/costs have rarely been reported.

THE NUMBER AND DISTRIBUTION OF DAMS

The World Bank has provided financing for dams to over 100 countries and since 1970 alone, it has undertaken over 400 projects involving dams, spread throughout the world.

The distribution of projects involving dams is about 14 per cent in Sub-Saharan Africa, 13 per cent in Latin America and Caribbean, 37 per cent in South Asia, 17 per cent in East Asia and 19 per cent in Europe, the Middle East, and North Africa. Compared to the worldwide processes of dam building, however the World Bank is involved with only a small percentage of all large dam projects (those over 15 metres in height).

According to ICOLD, (International Commission on Large Dams) there are over 35,000 large dams in existence (exclusive of China. Of these, some 11,000 were constructed in 1951-82 period, on an average of 344 dams per year. More recently during the 1975-82 period, the rate of construction dropped to 258 dams per year. In contrast, the Bank may be a major funding agency for about 5 to 10 dams per year, or less than 5 per cent of the average annual construction of dams worldwide.

In the present studies a survey has been conducted to gather and summarize information generated by government departments, pollution control boards, electricity boards, research institutions, and non-governmental organizations on the environmental impacts of water resources projects in the Krishna, Mahanadi and Godavari river basins. The three basins are amongst the most important river basins of India and cover the better part of the Indian peninsula (Fig.1.1). We believe that the depth of information on these basins, reflected in the present studies, is indicative of the status of environmental impact studies on the river basins of the country.

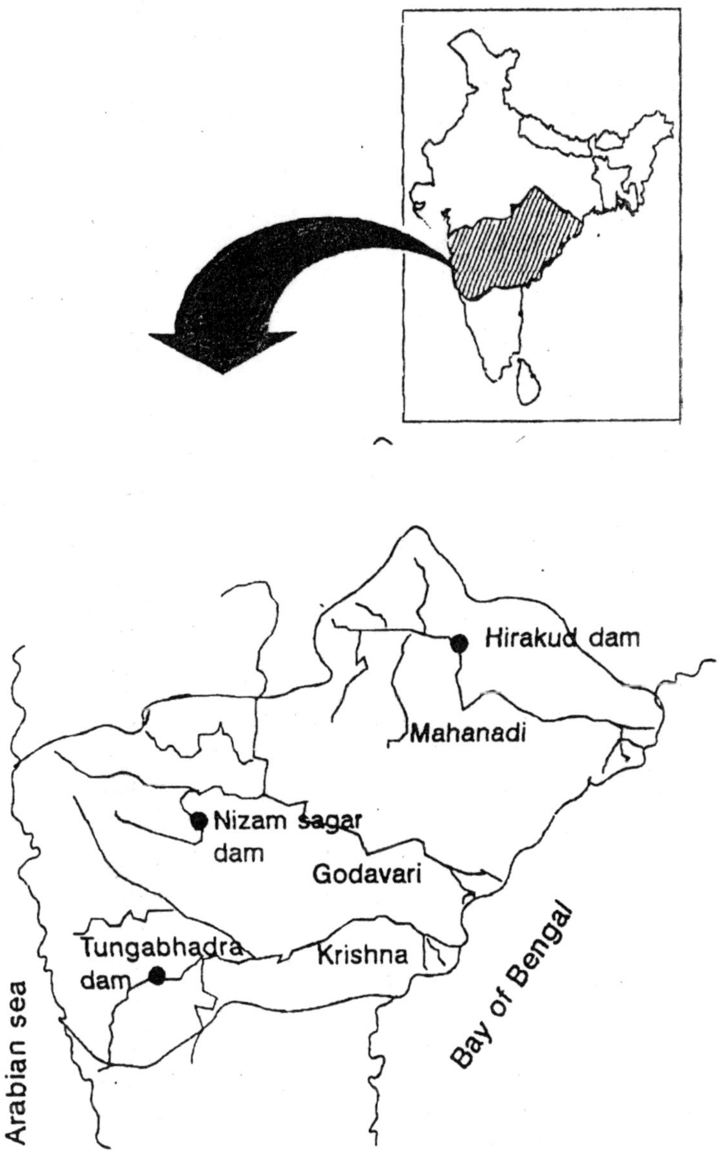

Fig. 1.1: Krishna, Mahanadi and Godavari river basins.

2

RIVERS AND DAMS OF INDIA: *AN OVERVIEW*

Richa Sharma[*]

WATER RESOURCES PROJECTS IN INDIA

India has known the art and science of water management since the civilization dawned on its soil. Numerous ancient texts, inscriptions, local traditions and archaeological remains bear testimony to this fact. Mention of advanced water harvesting systems such as canals, tanks, embankments and wells can be found in *Puranas, Mahabharata, Ramayana* and various other Vedic, Buddhist and Jain texts. Numerous treatises on agriculture and architecture contain detailed information on these (Anon, 1965).

There is a mention of hydrological relationships in the early Hindu texts, written around 800-600 BC. The Vedic hymns, particularly those in *Rig Veda*, contain many notes on irrigated agriculture, river courses, dykes, water reservoirs, well and water lifting structures.

The necessity of protection against the havoc caused by floods and the need for safe water supply for domestic as well as irrigation

[*]M.Sc., M.Phil., Junior Scientist, Centre for Pollution Control and Energy Technology.

usages led to technical ventures by earlier man. These resulted in hydro-technical installations across the rivers. Mention of such sources of irrigation as wells, tanks and canals can be found often in the ancient Indian literature and history (WTC, 1983:1).

As the mankind progressed and towns and cities came up, water was stored in cisterns. For long cisterns used to be rocky i.e. hewn into the rocks. These gradually evolved into masonary structures. By about 2000 BC, mortar began to be used for sealing these cisterns (Garbrecht, 1986). The remains of earliest known cisterns have been discovered in Palestine and Greece. By the middle of the first century AD, covered cisterns with storage volumes of upto 75,000 cubic metres (cum) were being built.

With the development and modifications in the cisterns, all the basic elements of dam construction were known. There is no evidence that the science of dam construction emerged in any one particular place and was taken to others. The earliest known dams to retain water in large quantities were constucted in Jawa (Jordan) during 3000 BC and Wadi Garawi (Egypt) at around 2500 BC.

The earlier great civilizations in the valleys of Nile, Tigris, Euphrates, Indus and Huang rivers, too, had excellent water management system. With the excavation of Harappa and Mohenjodaro in the early 1920s the intricate details of water supply and sewage disposal system of these cultures have come into view. The standard of their hydro-technical infrastructure was not equalled even 2000 years later by the Romans (Garbrecht, 1985).

The farming communities in Baluchistan impounded rainwater for irrigation in third millennium BC *Gabarbunds,* the dams built with stone rubbles, have been discovered in Baluchistan and Kutch whereas brick bunds have been found in Karachi. *Gabarbunds* were probably used for the control of flood waters and for retaining the alluvium coming down the hills (Buller, 1990).

Kautilya's Arthasastra, written in the 3rd century BC, also indicates that rainfall regimes, soil types and irrigation techniques, all these fundamentals of water harvesting systems were not unfamiliar for the people. Evidence of the construction of dams, lakes and irrigation systems by Indians during the time of Chandragupta Maurya (321-297 BC) can be found in archaeological and historical records. The 2nd century AD Junagadh inscriptions provide information about the repair of an embankment, which was destroyed in a flood (Chhabra and Gai, 1981) and restoration of lake Sudarsana which ceased to exist in 9th century AD (Mehta, 1963). One of the largest artificial lakes in India, covering an area of over 65,000 hectares and fed by 365 streams and springs, was built by Bhopal King Bhoja in 11th century AD (Kincaid, 1888). Rajatarangini by Kalhana (Stein, 1961), the 12th century AD account of Kashmir, also reveals notable structures around Dal and Anchar lakes and the Nandi canal which together formed a well-maintained irrigation systems. Similarly, West Bengal's system of overflow irrigation served the double purpose of enriching the soil and supply of water to fields and also checking the dreadful disease of the time, malaria (Willcocks, 1930).

Since India is an agricultural country, creation of higher irrigation potential for increased agricultural yield has been the prime motive force in the development of water resources projects in India. Hydroelectric power generation, flood control, municipal water supply, fisheries and tourism–in that order–have been the other envisaged benefits.

In 1900 the total irrigated area in India was about 1 million hectares. With the appointment of the first Irrigation Commission in 1901 and in pursuance of the recommendations of the Commission several new irrigation projects were undertaken based on damming of rivers. By 1935 the total irrigated area had increased 18 times the 1901 coverage.

During the next decade (1935-45) there was a lull in this activity as the control of irrigation was transferred from the Central control to the Provincial or State governments. Only a further 1.6 million hectares of irrigation potential was created in this decade.

In 1945, Central Water ways. Irrigation and Navigation Commission, later renamed Central Water and Power Commission and still later Central Water Commission (CWC), was set up for assisting the State governments in co-ordinating irrigational activities. By 1950 almost 100 major dams were built. The catalytic role of CWC saw irrigated area expanding to 45.3 million hectares by 1978.

The second Irrigation Commission, set up in 1969, has observed, 'Since independence, the country has made substantial progress in Irrigation Development. The area under irrigation has been nearly doubled of what it was at the time of independence. Even so, about four-fifth of country's cultivated area still depends exclusively on rainfall. The drought conditions in the last four years in several parts of the country and the food shortages have brought into sharp focus the importance of providing greater irrigation facilities. The Irrigation Commission is to go into the question of future irrigation development in the country in a comprehensive manner. Today India ranks second in the world, after China, in terms of net irrigated area (FAO, 1990). Tables 2.1 to 2.4 indicate the size of India's dam building programme.

India has over 1600 dams of which a third lie in Maharashtra. Punjab, Tamil Nadu, Haryana, Rajasthan and Uttar Pradesh have the highest percentage of cultivated land under irrigation. Curiously Maharashtra does not feature in this list; inspite of having the maximum number of dams in the country, only less than half of its cultivated area is irrigated.

According to ICOLD, the International Commission on Large Dams, there are over 35,000 dams in existence (exclusive of China) all over the world. Of these, some 11,000 were constructed during the 1951-82 period, on an average of 344 dams per year. More recently during the 1975-82 period, the rate of construction dropped to 258 dams per year. Hydropower dams or dams with hydropower components make up 4.5 per cent of the total dams involved; the other 55 per cent are primarily irrigation, water supply or flood control dams (Dixon et. al.).

RIVER SYSTEMS OF INDIA

On the basis of catchments, the river basins of India could be divided into three groups, viz.

(i) *Major River Basins*—River basins with catchments of 20,000 sq. km. and above.

(ii) *Medium River Basins*—River basins with catchment area between 20,000 and 2,000 sq. km.

(iii) *Minor River Basins.*—River basins with catchment area below 2000 sq. km.

Besides these, there are the desert rivers, which flow for some distance and are lost in the desert. Division of river basins on the basis of extent of drainage basin is described in Table 2.5. The major river basins cover 83 per cent of the total drainage basin and contribute to 85 per cent of the total surface flow whereas medium and minor river basins share 8 and 9 per cent of the total surface flow. The rivers are well spread over the entire area excepting Thar desert in Rajasthan. Detailed description of these river systems is as follows:

Major river basins

As evident from the Table 2.6 Brahmaputra river originating from Kailash range is the longest followed by Indus and Ganga in that order. River Ganga has the largest catchment area of 10,86,000 sq. km. followed by Brahmaputra.

Medium river basins

West flowing Periyar river, the longest of the lot has the catchment area of 5,398 sq. km. Bhadar river originating from Rajkot and ranking third lengthwise, with 198 km has the maximum catchment area of 7,094 sq. km. followed by Ponnani river in Tamil Nadu with catchment area of 6,186 sq.km.

TABLE 2.1 STATEWISE DISTRIBUTION OF LARGE DAMS (ABSTRACT)

Sl.No.	Name of State	Period								Total
		Upto 1900	1901 to 1950	1951 to 1960	1961 to 1970	1971 to 1980	1981 to 1989	Year of Construction not available	Under construction	
1	2	3	4	5	6	7	8	9	10	11
1.	Andhra Pradesh	3	18	13	17	16	9	9	17	102
2.	Assam	-	-	-	-	-	2	-	1	3
3.	Arunachal Pradesh	-	-	-	-	-	-	-	1	1
4.	Bihar	-	-	12	6	15	23	3	33	92
5.	Gujarat	4	33	64	82	57	57	-	68	365
6.	Goa	-	-	-	-	-	-	3	2	5
7.	Haryana	-	-	-	-	-	-	-	-	-
8.	Himachal Pradesh	-	-	-	1	2	1	-	1	5
9.	Jammu & Kashmir	-	-	-	-	2	1	4	2	9
10.	Karnataka	3	13	7	32	41	38	55	24	213
11.	Kerala	-	1	4	16	7	5	5	16	54
12.	Madhya Pradesh	2	71	38	83	165	207	42	144	752
13.	Maharashtra	18	35	25	143	586	290	91	320	1508
14.	Manipur	-	-	-	-	1	-	1	3	5
15.	Meghalya	-	-	1	3	2	-	-	1	7
16.	Mizoram	-	-	-	-	-	-	-	-	-
17.	Nagaland	-	-	-	-	-	-	-	-	-

{Cont.}...

1	2	3	4	5	6	7	8	9	10	11
18.	Orissa	-	2	3	5	48	72	1	18	149
19.	Punjab	-	-	1	-	-	-	-	1	2
20.	Rajasthan	7	5	30	19	18	18	27	4	128
21.	Sikkim	-	-	-	-	-	-	-	-	-
22.	Tamil Nadu	1	10	10	24	27	9	3	13	97
23.	Tripura	-	-	-	-	1	-	-	-	1
24.	Uttar Pradesh	2	22	17	22	9	7	18	12	109
25.	West Bengal	-	-	1	1	5	1	4	15	27
	Total	40	210	226	454	1002	740	266	696	3634

TABLE 2.2: STATEWISE DISTRIBUTION OF LARGE DAMS (HEIGHT >15 METERS)

Sl.No	Name of State	Period								Total
		Upto 1900	1901 to 1950	1951 to 1960	1961 to 1970	1971 to 1980	1981 to 1989	Year of Construction not available	Under construction	
1	2	3	4	5	6	7	8	9	10	11
1.	Andhra Pradesh	2	14	6	14	12	8	8	15	79
2.	Assam	-	-	-	-	-	2	-	1	3
3.	Arunachal Pradesh	-	-	-	-	-	-	-	1	1
4.	Bihar	-	-	9	6	10	20	3	27	75
5.	Gujarat	1	15	49	66	47	47	-	56	281
6.	Goa	-	-	-	-	-	-	-	2	2
7.	Haryana	-	-	-	-	-	-	-	-	-
8.	Himachal Pradesh	-	-	-	1	2	1	-	1	5
9.	Jammu & Kashmir	-	-	-	-	2	1	4	2	9
10.	Karnataka	1	11	6	13	29	30	14	20	124
11.	Kerala	-	1	4	16	7	4	5	12	49
12.	Madhya Pradesh	1	26	17	41	56	81	20	80	322
13.	Maharashtra	17	22	13	68	313	149	36	223	841
14.	Manipur	-	-	-	-	1	-	-	3	4
15.	Meghalaya	-	-	1	3	2	-	-	-	4
16.	Mizoram	-	-	-	-	-	-	-	-	-

(Cont.)...

1	2	3	4	5	6	7	8	9	10	11
17.	Nagaland	-	-	-	-	-	-	-	-	-
18.	Orissa	-	2	3	4	28	44	-	15	96
19.	Punjab	-	-	1	-	-	-	-	1	2
20.	Rajasthan	3	4	20	9	7	10	9	2	64
21.	Sikkim	-	-	-	-	-	-	-	-	-
22.	Tamil Nadu	1	9	10	24	27	8	3	9	91
23.	Tripura	-	-	-	-	1	-	-	-	1
24.	Uttar Pradesh	2	12	11	13	6	7	10	12	73
25.	West Bengal	-	-	1	1	3	-	1	5	11
	Total	28	116	151	279.	553	412	113	487	2139

TABLE 2.3: STATEWISE DISTRIBUTION OF LARGE DAMS (DAM HEIGHT > 10 METERS < 15 METERS)

Sl.No	Name of State	Period								Total
		Upto 1900	1901 to 1950	1951 to 1960	1961 to 1970	1971 to 1980	1981 to 1989	Year of Construction not available	Under construction	
1	2	3	4	5	6	7	8	9	10	11
1.	Andhra Pradesh	1	4	7	3	4	1	1	2	23
2.	Assam	-	-	-	-	-	-	-	-	-
3.	Arunachal Pradesh	-	-	-	-	-	-	-	-	-
4.	Bihar	-	-	3	-	5	3	-	6	17
5.	Gujarat	3	18	15	16	10	10	-	12	84
6.	Goa	-	-	-	-	-	-	3	-	3
7.	Haryana	-	-	-	-	-	-	-	-	-
8.	Himachal Pradesh	-	-	-	-	-	-	-	-	-
9.	Jammu & Kashmir	-	-	-	-	-	-	-	-	-
10.	Karnataka	2	2	1	19	12	8	41	4	89
11.	Kerala	-	-	-	-	-	1	-	4	5
12.	Madhya Pradesh	1	45	21	42	109	126	22	64	430
13.	Maharashtra	1	13	12	75	273	141	55	97	667
14.	Manipur	-	-	-	-	-	-	1	-	1
15.	Meghalya	-	-	-	-	-	-	-	1	1
16.	Mizoram	-	-	-	-	-	-	-	-	-

(Cont.)...

1	2	3	4	5	6	7	8	9	10	11
17.	Nagaland	-	-	-	-	-	-	-	-	-
18.	Orissa	-	-	-	1	20	28	1	3	53
19.	Punjab	-	-	-	-	-	-	-	-	-
20.	Rajasthan	4	1	10	10	11	8	18	2	64
21.	Sikkim	-	-	-	-	-	-	-	-	-
22.	Tamil Nadu	-	1	-	-	-	1	-	4	6
23.	Tripura	-	-	-	-	-	-	-	-	-
24.	Uttar Pradesh	-	10	6	9	3	-	8	-	36
25.	West Bengal	-	-	-	-	2	1	3	10	16
	Total	12	94	75	175	449	328	153	209	1495

TABLE 2.4: STATEWISE DISTRIBUTION OF LARGE DAMS (HEIGHT > 15 METRES OR STORAGE MORE THAN 60 MILLION CUBIC METRES)

Sl.No	Name of State	Period								Total
		Upto 1900	1901 to 1950	1951 to 1960	1961 to 1970	1971 to 1980	1981 to 1989	Year of Construction not available	Under construction	
1	2	3	4	5	6	7	8	9	10	11
1.	Andhra Pradesh	3	16	6	14	13	8	8	15	83
2.	Assam	-	-	-	-	-	2	-	1	3
3.	Arunachal Pradesh	-	-	-	-	-	-	-	1	1
4.	Bihar	-	-	9	6	10	20	3	30	78
5.	Gujarat	1	15	49	66	47	47	-	56	281
6.	Goa	-	-	-	-	-	-	-	2	2
7.	Haryana	-	-	-	-	-	-	-	-	-
8.	Himachal Pradesh	-	-	-	1	2	1	-	1	5
9.	Jammu & Kashmir	-	-	-	-	2	1	4	2	9
10.	Karnataka	1	12	6	13	29	30	14	20	125
11.	Kerala	-	1	4	16	7	4	5	12	49
12.	Madhya Pradesh	1	26	17	41	56	81	20	80	322
13.	Maharashtra	17	22	13	68	313	149	36	226	844
14.	Manipur	-	-	-	-	1	-	-	3	4
15.	Meghalya	-	-	1	3	2	-	-	-	6
16.	Mizoram	-	-	-	-	-	-	-	-	-
17.	Nagaland	-	-	-	-	-	-	-	-	-

(Cont.)...

1	2	3	4	5	6	7	8	9	10	11
18.	Orissa	-	2	3	4	28	44	-	15	96
19.	Punjab	-	-	1	-	-	-	-	1	2
20.	Rajasthan	3	4	22	9	7	10	9	2	66
21.	Sikkim	-	-	-	-	-	-	-	-	-
22.	Tamil Nadu	1	9	10	24	27	8	3	9	91
23.	Tripura	-	-	-	-	1	-	-	-	1
24.	Uttar Pradesh	2	12	11	15	6	7	10	12	75
25.	West Bengal	-	-	1	1	3	-	1	5	11
	Total	29	119	153	281	554	412	113	493	2154

TABLE 2.5: DIVISION OF INDIAN RIVERS BASED ON THE EXTENT OF DRAINAGE

Category (River)	*No.of River Basin*	*Drainage Basin (km²)*	*Catchment Area (Million km²)*	*Total Run Off 100 Million m³*	*% of Total Run Off*
Major	14	More than 20,000	2.58	11,406	85
Medium	44	Between 2000-20,000	0.24	112	7
Minor+ Desert	55	Less than 2,000	0.30	127	8

The river basin having minimum catchment area is Mandvi whereas Washishthi is the shortest river with length only 48 km and catchment area 2239 sq.km. The detailed description of the medium river basins is given in Table 2.7.

East flowing Ponnaiyar river, the longest with length of 396 km. originating from Kolar in Karnataka has the catchment area of 14,130 sq. km.

Subarnarekha river has the maximum catchment area of 19,296 sq.km. followed by Palar river. Kandleru river is the shortest with length of only 73 km. and Musi river originating from Nellore in Andhra Pradesh has the least catchment area of 2219 sq. km.

Minor and desert river basins

Minor rivers flowing through Goa have the least catchment area of 2,102 sq. km and those flowing through Andhra Pradesh have the maximum catchment area with 44,142 sq. km.

Among the desert rivers Ghaggar river has the least catchment area of 1,309 sq. km. and Luni and others have the maximum catchment area of 80,000 sq. km. Some of the desert and minor rivers along with their catchment areas are presented in Table 2.8.

TABLE 2.6 MAJOR RIVER BASINS

Sl.No.	*Name of river*	*Origin*	*Length (Km.)*	*Catchment Area (sq.km.)*
1.	Brahmaputra	Kailash Range (Tibet)	(2900) 916	(5,80,000) 1,94,413
2.	Indus	Mansarovar (Tibet)	(2880) 1114	(4,68,068) 3,21,289
3.	Ganga	Gangotri (Uttar Kashi)	2525	(10,86,000) 8,61,404
4.	Godavari	Nasik (Maharashtra)	1465	3,12,812
5.	Krishna	Mahabaleshwar (Maharashtra)	1401	2,58,948
6.	Narmada	Amarkantak (Madhya Pradesh)	1312	98,796
7.	Mahanadi	Nazri Town (Madhya Pradesh)	851	1,41,598
8.	Cauvery	Coorg (Karnataka)	800	81,155
9.	Brahmani	Ranchi (Bihar)	799	30,033
10.	Tapi	Betul (Madhya Pradesh)	724	65,145
11.	Pennar	Kolar (Karnataka)	597	55,213
12.	Mahi	Dhar (Madhya Pradesh)	583	34,842
13.	Sabarmati	Aravalli Hills (Rajasthan)	371	21,674
		Total		25,55,463

Note. The figures within brackets indicate the total figures for the river basin in India and neighbouring countries.

Storages existing and proposed

Due to the particular characteristics of the monsoon season, about 80 per cent of the river flows occur in the four or five monsoon months of the year. During this period maximum utilization of the water can be made from the run off of the river with small modifications of regulations which require very little storage.

TABLE 2.7: MEDIUM RIVER BASINS

Sl.No.	*Name of river*	*Origin*	*Length (Km)*	*Catchment Area (sq.km)*
1	2	3	4	5
1.	Periyar	Sivajini Hills (Kerala)	224	5398
2.	Bharathapuzha (also known as Ponnani)	Annamalai Hills (Tamil Nadu)	209	6186
3.	Bhadar	Panchmahals (Gujarat)	135	2770
4.	Shetrunji	Dalkania (Gujarat)	182	5514
5.	Pamba	Devarmalai (Kerala)	176	2235
6.	Vaitarana	Nasik (Maharashtra)	171	3637
7.	Chaliar or Baypore	Elamtalvi Hills (Kerala)	169	2788
8.	Kalinadi	Belgaum (Karnataka)	153	5179
9.	Gangavati or Bedti (in upper reaches)	Dharwar (Karnataka)	152	3902
10.	Ulhas	Raigarh (Maharashtra)	145	3864
11.	Dammanganga	Nasik (Maharashtra)	143	2357
12.	Purna	Dhulia (Maharashtra)	142	2431
13.	Ambika	Dangs (Maharashtra)	142	2715
14.	Dhadhar	Panchmahals (Gujarat)	135	2770
15.	Ozat	Kathiawar (Gujarat)	128	3189
16.	Sharavati	Shimoga (Karnataka)	122	2209
17.	Aji	Rajkot (Gujarat)	106	2139
18.	Netravati	Canara (Karnataka)	103	3657
19.	Savitri	Pune (Maharashtra)	99	2899

(Cont.)...

1	2	3	4	5
20.	Mandvi	Belgaum (Karnataka)	87	2032
21.	Sastri	Ratnagiri (Maharashtra)	64	2174
22.	Washishthi	Ratnagiri (Maharashtra)	48	2239
EAST FLOWING				
23.	Ponnaiyar	Kolar (Karnataka)	396	14130
24.	Subarnarekha	Nagri/Ranchi (Bihar)	395	19296
25.	Baitarni	Keonjhar (Orrisa)	365	12,789
26.	Palar (including tributary Cheyyar)	Kolar (Karnataka)	348	17871
27.	Vaigai	Madurai (Tamil Nadu)	258	7031
28.	Vamsadhara	Kalahandi (Orissa)	221	10,830
29.	Gundlakamma	Kurnool (Andhra Pradesh)	220	8494
30.	Nagavali	Kalahandi (Orissa)	217	9410
31.	Vellar	Chithri Hills (Tamil Nadu)	193	8558
32.	Burhabalang	Mayurbhanj (Orissa)	164	4837
33.	Rushikulya	Phulbani (Orissa)	146	7753
34.	Gundar	Madurai (Tamil Nadu)	146	5647
35.	Kortalaiyar	Chinglepet (Tamil Nadu)	131	3521
36.	Tambraparni	Tirunelveli (Tamil Nadu)	130	5969
37.	Vaippar	Tirunelveli (Tamil Nadu)	130	5288
38.	Swarnamukhi	Koraput (Orissa)	130	3225
39.	Yeleru	Vishakhapatnam (Andhra Pradesh)	125	3809
40.	Pambar	Madurai (Tamil Nadu)	125	3104

{Cont.}...

1	2	3	4	5
41.	Muneru	Nellore (Andhra Pradesh)	122	3734
42.	Musi	Nellore (Andhra Pradesh)	112	2219
43.	Paleru	Nellore (Andhra Pradesh)	104	2483
44.	Sarda	Vishakhapatnam (Andhra Pradesh)	104	2725
45.	Varahanadhi	North Arcot (Tamil Nadu)	94	3044
46.	Kandleru	Vinukonda (Andhra Pradesh)	73	3534

TABLE 2.8: SOME MINOR AND DESERT RIVERS

Sl.No.	*State/Union Territory*	*Catchment Area (Sq. km.)*
MINOR RIVERS		
1.	Gujarat	4,634
2.	Karnataka	2,146
3.	Goa	2,102
4.	Kerala	19,489
5.	West Bengal	10,000
6.	Andhra Pradesh	44,142
7.	Tamil Nadu	21,270
8.	Maharashtra	15,510
DESERT RIVERS		
1.	Luni & Others	80,000
2.	Machhu	2,515
3.	Rupen	4,000
4.	Saraswati	2,935
5.	Banas	8,674
6.	Ghaggar	1,309

Note. Does not include the rivers of Andaman & Nicobar Islands, the rivers draining into other countries and the area of Lakshadweep.

To store the water from the flood season for use in the subsequent seasons there is need for building up of large storage capacity in reservoirs and storage tanks. The storage built up in the projects completed upto end of 6th Plan is about 143 cubic km. From projects under construction another 79 cubic km. is likely to be added making it to 222 cubic km. In addition there are a large number of small tanks etc. which may be assumed to be about 30 cubic km. accounting to in all about 250 cubic km. From projects under consideration another 82 cubic km. would be forthcoming. Details of storage built up, under construction and those under proposal basinwise are given in Table 2.9.

TABLE 2.9 BASIN WISE STORAGE IN INDIA (UNIT-CUBIC KM.)

Sl.No.	*Basin*	*** Annual Flow (Average)*	*Completed Projects*		*Ongoing Projects*		*Total*		*Project under Consideration*	
			Gross Storage	Live Storage	Gross Storage	Live Storage	Gross Storage	Live Storage	Gross Storage	Live Storage
1	2	3	4	5	6	7	8	9	10	11
1.	Indus	73.305	17.814	14.515	3.774	2.441	21.588	16.957	0.308	0.050
2.	(a) Ganga*	501.643	39.574	33.200	17.644	14.729	57.218	47.930	8.922	6.471
	(b) Brahmaputra including Barak etc.	627.867	0.662	0.475	0.950	0.842	1.612	1.318	61.527	46.332
3.	Godavari	118.982	22.404	18.553	15.074	11.955	37.478	30.508	8.177	2.763
4.	Krishna	67.790	41.007	30.186	7.366	6.099	48.373	36.286	0.576	0.423
5.	Cauvery	20.957	8.021	7.181	0.463	0.297	8.485	7.578	0.554	0.482
6.	East flowing rivers between Krishna and Pennar & between Mahanadi and Godavari	23.806	1.191	1.042	4.452	3.659	5.644	4.701	1.345	0.898
7.	East flowing rivers between Pennar and Kanyakumari	17.725	1.375	1.329	0.087	0.077	1.463	1.407	0.035	0.023
8.	Mahanadi	66.879	10.933	8.310	5.505	4.914	16.439	13.224	17.205	11.665
9.	Brahmani & Baitarani	36.227	1.292	1.077	4.390	3.324	5.683	4.401	8.529	6.505

{Cont.}...

1	2	3	4	5	6	7	8	9	10	11
10.	Subarnarekha	10.756	0.398	0.328	2.108	1.329	2.506	1.657	3.726	3.332
11.	Sabarmati	3.812	1.392	1.196	0.391	0.331	1.783	0.152	0.030	0.023
12.	Mahi	11.829	3.021	2.312	2.614	2.192	5.636	4.505	0.220	0.166
13.	West flowing rivers of Kutch, Kathiawar including Luni	15.098	2.903	2.579	1.878	1.630	4.782	4.209	1.936	1.752
14.	Narmada	40.950	3.216	2.806	20.214	14.106	23.431	16.913	0.551	0.463
15.	Tapi	18.000	9.778	8.167	1.200	0.897	10.978	0.906	0.220	0.169
16.	West flowing rivers from Tapi to Tadri including Tadri	108.618	0.958	0.854	2.2314	2.181	3.272	3.037	0.493	0.476
17.	West flowing rivers from Tadri to Kanyakumari	89.250	10.183	8.895	9.382	7.942	19.566	16.838	0.100	0.100
	Total	1853.494	176.131	143.018	99.817	79.054	275.948	222.072	114.461	82.102

* Including tributaries downstream of Farakha.

** The figures include the observed flow and corrected for surface utilization and the effect of actual utilization of groundwater draft not included.

REFERENCES

Anon, (1965). *Irrigation in India through the Ages*, Central Board of Irrigation and Power; New Delhi.

Anon, (1964). *Agriculture in Ancient India,* Indian Council for Agricultural Research, New Delhi, pp. 113-133.

Buller, H. (1990). *Gabarbands in Baluchistan,* Annual Report, Archaeological Survey of India 1903-04. Swati Publication, Delhi, pp. 194-201.

Dixon J.A., Talbot L.M. and Le Moigne Guy (1995). *Dams and Environment,* Consideration in World Bank Projects, The World Bank, Washington, D.C., World Bank Technical Paper 110.

Garbrecht, G. (1985). *Hydrologic and Hydraulic concepts in Antiquity, mimeo.*

Garbrecht, G. (1986). Water Storage in the course of History upto the 16th century, *mimeo.*

Kincaid, W. (1888). *Rambles Among Ruins in Central India,* The Indian Antiquary, Vol. XVII, pp. 348-352.

Mehta, R.N. (1963). *Sudarsan Lake,* in Journal of the Oriental Institute, Baroda, Vol. XVIII, No.1&2, September-December, pp.20-28.

Stein, M.A. (1961). *Kalhana's Rajatarangini: A Chronicle of the Kings of Kashmir (Translated),* Delhi-Patna-Varanasi, Vol. I&II.

Willcocks, W. (1930). *Lectures on the Ancient-System of Irrigation in Bengal and its Application to modern problems,* Calcutta University Readership Lectures, University of Calcutta.

WTC (1983). *Resource Analyses and plan for efficient water management. A case study of Mahi Bank canal command area, Gujarat.* Water Technology Centre. Indian Agricultural Research Institute, New Delhi.

ENVIRONMENTAL IMPACT OF WATER RESOURCES PROJECTS: *A GENERAL INTRODUCTION*

*Richa Sharma**

ENVIRONMENTAL IMPACT OF WATER RESOURCES PROJECTS BASED ON RIVER DEVELOPMENT

The effects of river development schemes on the environment manifest themselves in a number of ways. They are felt upstream, in the storage reservoir, downstream, and often over the whole region. They may be beneficial or detrimental. Dealing with detrimental effects means evaluating the degree to which they are harmful and finding ways of controlling them.

The physical and biological effects of river development schemes arise from the obstacle the dam causes to the natural flow, the climate changes caused by the reservoir interacting with the overlying atmosphere, the effects of the structures on the water in and near the reservoir, and slides and ground tremors caused by the stored water.

* M.Sc., M.Phil., Junior Scientist, Centre for Pollution Control and Energy Technology.

EFFECT OF OBSTACLE CAUSED BY THE DAM

Floating debris

A dam is an obstacle to the passage of trees, ice and other floating debris, fish and shipping.

The effects can be overcome by providing timber chutes, fish ladders or lifts, and shipping locks. Overflow spillways also permit the passage of debris past a dam.

Solid load

A dam reduces or completely blocks the passage of the solid matter conveyed by the river creating varying degrees of disturbance in the natural conditions. Blocking the bed load may disturb the balance of delta areas if natural erosion processes are no longer offset by the arrival of new material. River training works may be necessary to keep the banks stable as was done on the Damieta branch of the Nile.

Reducing the suspended load may deprive arable land of the silt brought down by river floods, an impact brought to sharp focus by the Aswan dam. This is the cost one may have to pay for extended irrigation, but the harm it does may in fact be illusory—silt is not such a good fertiliser as imagined (it contains only 4 per cent by weight of nitrogen available to plants) and chemical fertilizers can be substitued. In addition land formerly fertilized by silt can be cultivated for a greater proportion of the year with controlled and comparatively silt-free applications of irrigation water.

The construction of a dam or barrage across a river channel creates a reservoir which can hold back and retain most of the suspended material normally carried in the water flowing in the river. A water freed from its sediments tends to reacquire the sediment load. This leads to erosion in the channels in the zone immediately downstream. The zone gradually extends downstream until a new equilibrium is reached, when the slope of channel is once more balanced by the reduced suspended load. Such erosion can be corrected (or reduced to some degree) by reconstructing the slope of the channel and/or by changing the discharge from the dam.

Various methods have been used such as building weirs (sometimes also used incidentally for power purposes), spreading flood spillage over a longer period of time, or diverting part of the river flood into an offshoot in times of flood, as is done on the Nile at Aswan.

Settling

A reservoir is a veritable sedimentation tank. The problem of siltation due to water resources development is a global phenomenon. Countries experiencing difficulties include Nepal, Pakistan, Philippines, Burma, Columbia, Egypt, India, Indonesia, Tanzania and Thailand. Twenty-one reservoirs in India have experienced sediment inflows at least 200 per cent higher than anticipated (Ahmad and Singh, 1991). The sediments brought in by the feeder streams and the run-in from the reservoir catchment get an opportunity to settle down in the quiescent waters of the reservoir. This results in two impacts of far-reaching consequences. The first is that the settled sediments reduce the storage capacity of the reservoir. The impact can be strong enough to drastically reduce the reservoir life. For example, the capacity of Nizamsagar reservoir has been reduced to less than half due to sedimentation and sufficient water is not stored any more to irrigate 1100 Km^2 of sugarcane and paddy for which the reservoir was mainly built. The second impact is caused when the de-sedimented water from the reservoir is released into the river downstream and in the irrigation canals. The water tends to reacquire its sediment load and erodes the banks of the river or the canal carrying it. The erosion can play havoc with the canal stability.

The catchment area of Chittaurgarh Irrigation project which consisted of dense natural forests in its upper reaches has been denuded during dam construction. The expected rate of sedimentation is 0.14 million m^3yr^{-1} and the life span of the dam is estimated to be 50 years. The vegetation cover upstream of the dam is poor and it is estimated that after 5 to 10 years a large quantity of silt and sand will be deposited at the head of the dam and in the canal system affecting the fish fauna seriously. A part of this is slowly transferred to the farmers' fields where it will cause congestion of irrigation canals and ditches and a 50 per cent reduction in the life of dam. The canal embankment is devoid of any vegetation cover, therefore it is highly vulnerable to erosion during heavy rainfalls and subject to increased sedimentation (Ahmad and Singh, 1991).

Due to geological and climatic peculiarities, the Himalayan rivers carry some of the highest sediment loads in the World (Bandhopadhyay and Gyawali 1994). The major Himalayan dams like Pong in Himachal Pradesh or Ramganga in Uttar Pradesh have been silted up at a rate four or five times higher than the assumed ones (Bandhopadhyay, 1995).

A turbid layer in the otherwise clear reservoir may flow along the bottom to form a mud lake just in front of the dam capable of blocking the bottom outlets as it hardens, or may remain at mid-depth until it rises to surface near the dam, sometimes entering the intakes or spillway. In some reservoirs, turbidity may extend throughout the reservoir because of the fineness of the material. India will reap the benefit of the Indo-Bhutan Sankosh hydel project by diverting a large volume of the Sankosh river water to the Farakka barrage and consequently clean out siltation of Calcutta port (Down to Earth, 1996).

Nutrient transport

Deposition of suspended nutrients in the reservoir may have consequences for the aquatic biota downstream. It has been blamed for the smaller sardine catches in the Mediterranean off the Nile delta after construction of the High Aswan dam.

On the other hand, however, shallow reservoirs may increase the plankton yield, as in the pool on the Seine river near the town of Troyes.

Retention of small and moderate floods

Small floods have a beneficial effect in that:

(a) they provide ready access to spawning grounds (ponds and lakes) and renew the water in them,
(b) they form small islands used by migrating birds to escape from the predators on the shore,
(c) they prevent the river banks becoming overgrown with trees, and stop mammals destroying the river-side grasses needed to sustain migrating birds, and
(d) they bring nutrients into lakes and ponds.

Water can be released through the dam to stimulate such floods by a proper choice of time, duration and volume released.

Overlarge or untimely releases can cause harm, and the gate operation guidelines drawn up with reference to ecological requirements downstream must be strictly followed to prevent it.

Tidal barriers and barrages

Barriers and barrages constructed in the tidal zone of a river estuary or coastal embankment may be considered as a special case of a barricade.

The characteristics of an estuary may be changed in a variety of ways by a barrage scheme. The inflow of tidal waters may be restricted, leading to effective loss of volume and thereby reduced scouring effect of ebb tides. If this problem is not considered and dealt with, bars may form which handicap navigation. The estuarial regime of salt and fresh water may change from stratified to mixed or vice versa, and this may affect siltation and aquatic life. Wave patterns may also be significantly modified. Upland drainage in terms of both freshwater river run-off and riparian land drainage in the estuary area have to be dealt with. The latter could involve pump schemes. Sewage previously allowed to flow to the sea with limited treatment could require full treatment if liable to be trapped behind a barrage. Docks may be required for shipping access to up-river ports. Fish passes may be required if the estuary is a route for migratory fish, and ice passes if the river carries icefloes in winter. Thought should be given to the effects on flora and fauna previously inhabiting the tidal range which may become permanently inundated.

A barrier differs from a barrage in that it may not be closed permanently or regularly. In the case of the Thames Barrier at Woolwich, the intention is to block only major tidal flood surges from penetrating upstream and flooding London. This may involve closure for a few hours on a few occasions per year. Thus effects on regimes and the environment are only marginal. In other cases of barrier, the environmental effects will approach those of barrages as the frequency of closure increases.

Both barrages and barriers have the effect of preventing some upstream tidal flow. This volume of water rebounds downstream. Coastal protection works need to be raised against this effect.

Effect of Dam on Sea

The large number of dams in operation around the world today could affect the food web structure and bio-geo-chemical cycling of materials in coastal seas. This is the finding of research conducted by scientists at the Hamburg University who studied the effect of Danube river dam on the Black sea ecosystem recently (Science and Technology, *The Hindu*, 1997).

The research supports the fact that man made barriers are trapping vital nutrients suspended in the river water and preventing them from reaching the oceans. Scientists warn that fishes will disappear and rising tides of toxic algae would float across ocean waters if what happened in the Black Sea is repeated in the other major oceans.

The long term data on water and nutrient discharge from the river Danube to the Black Sea revealed a reduction in the dissolved silicate load of the river by about two-thirds since dam constructions in the early 1970s. A concommitant decrease in dissolved silicate concentrations by more than 60 per cent during winter was observed in the Central Black Sea surface waters. The consequent changes in silicon to nitrogen ratio of the Black Sea nutrient load appear to be larger than those caused by eutrophication alone and seem to be responsible for dramatic shifts in phytoplankton species composition from diatoms (siliceous) to coccolithophores and flagellates (non-siliceous).

Human interventions have caused a worldwide increase in river inputs of nitrogen (N) and phosphorus (P) to the coastal seas by more than a factor of four leading to considerable eutrophication and to an increase in the frequency of unusual and/or noxious algal blooms.

The construction of dams in rivers can also cause considerable reductions in nutrient loads owing to the removal of these nutrients in reservoir sediments (the artificial lake effect) whereas this removal might be over compensated by anthropogenic nitrogen and phosphorus inputs downstream of the reservoir, no such compensation has been observed for silicate, for example in the Nile, Dr. Venugopalan pointed out. According to him the Iron Gates hydroelectric dam on the river Danube had captured tiny specks of silicate eroded from soils upstream and carried in the water. For the past 25 years that silicate has settled in sediments on the reservoir floor. He estimates that the dam has so far captured 12 million tonnes of silicate for 15 years' natural supply to the Black Sea turning the sea's biochemistry upside down.

Results published in 'Nature' revealed that water and sediment storage in reservoirs behind the 'Iron Gates' have altered the bio-geochemistry not just of the river and the adjacent coastal waters but also of the entire Black Sea basin (Venkiteswaran, 1997). The observed species shift towards carbonate producing coccolithophores in the coastal waters exert significant control over seawater chemistry. Furthermore, the occurrence of potentially toxic flagellate blooms may become more frequent. Similar effects may be expected for the Central Black Sea where, in contrast to pre-dam conditions silicate depletion appears now to be more frequent.

Today more than 36,000 dams are in operation around the world and more are being constructed at an appreciable rate. Though the observed effects of these dams can be more severe in closed seas (such as the Black Sea) than in rivers feeding into open systems, these effects could be of global consequence.

Effect of flooding on fauna

A new reservoir directly affects the upstream fauna in a number of ways:

(a) many animals die although there may be ways of saving them,
(b) some animals migrate to new areas,
(c) a few animals accommodate to the new environment, particularly amphibians and riparialn fauna,
(d) birds such as water-fowl and waders move into the new water habitat.

The proposed 141 km long canal to be built across the northern part of West Bengal in the Tista river as a part of the Indo-Bhutan Hydel project would spell total doom to the wild life of the area. The canal 60 m wide and 6 m deep with a bed width of 26 m will cut off population of all wild life species from one side to another and will cut off the gene flow and migratory routes of various endangered species, especially the elephant (Down to Earth, 1995).

The Three Gorges dam hydroelectric project in China once promoted as a major money spinner for MNCs is now turning out to be a liability for Beijing as the project, scream the detractors, will spell the doom for the fragile ecosystem of the Three Gorges lake (Down to Earth, 1995).

The removal of trees and shrubs upstream of the Chittaurgarh dam has led to wildlife loss. Disturbances caused by heavy machinery and vehicles, used in dam construction have forced wild life such as sambhar (*Cervus duvaceli*), cheetal (*Axis axis*), Swamp deer (*Cervus duvauceli*), tiger (*Panthera tigris*) to emigrate from the area. There is concern that the forest might lose its deer population entirely. The erection of an 11 km. long and 15 m high dam for water storage in the reservoir is now acting as a major barrier to wild fauna migration (Ahmad and Singh, 1991).

The proposed hydroelectric project across the Rathong Chu river which meanders through Yuksam in West Sikkim, envisages the channelling of the river near the base of Mount Kanchenjunga. Struck by Sikkim's rich flora and several endangered animals like the snow leopard, Himalayan black bear and red panda, the World Wide Fund for nature classified it a priority preservation 'biodiversity hotspot'(Balakrishnan, 1995).

It is sometimes possible to carry out rescue and salvage operations, along the Noah's Ark principle. For instance more than ten thousand tortoises, tapirs, snakes, sloths, armadilloes, etc. were rescued from the Afobaka lake on the Brokopondo in Surinam, whereas zoologists had estimated that there were no large animals left in the area.

An important secondary effect which can arise is that animals displaced from the reservoir area must fit into a new habitat which was previously in equilibrium, a situation which tends to favour shortlived species with high reproduction rates and which are not always the most useful, desirable or attractive. This problem can be common to both forced migration caused by the rising waters of the lake and to the re-establishment of the "rescued" animals in the new habitats.

The creation of a new water body can establish conditions conducive to a large increase in the variety and numbers of birds, particularly water fowl, waders and their predators. The loss of primarily terrestrial habitat is often more than compensated for, by the large increase in water riparian habitat and the restoration and protection of endangered species of water fowl.

The effect of flooding on fauna is generally more pronounced in tropical regions.

Effect on climate

Whether, and to what degree climate can be changed by large reservoirs is the subject of controversy.

The formation of fog by evaporation from a river or lake depends on air humidity, the temperature difference between the water surface and the ambient air, and the salinity of the water. As a very rough rule, the air must be cooler than the water and its relative humidity must be greater than 90 per cent, to create a fog. This means that fog occurs in temperate climates, mainly on winter nights and the early morning.In other climates, shallow reservoirs may make the mist thicker on cool days.

It has been demonstrated experimentally that large reservoirs produce a new microclimate. A change in the rainfall pattern has been detected in Ghana around lake Volta, the peak having shifted from October to July and August, and rain fell for the first time at Aswan when lake Nasser was filled. It is generally accepted that the capacity of large natural lakes in temperate regions for storing heat and cold is the prime cause of the particular microclimates in those areas. Examples are lake Leman, le Bourget lake, Lake Annecy, the Italian lakes and the five Great Lakes.

EFFECTS ON RESERVOIR WATER

Physical and chemical effects

Water temperature

In deep reservoirs, a cold layer underlies a warmer layer of water in summer and knowledge of such thermal layering is essential for an understanding of the effects that deep reservoirs might have on water quality.

In warm seasons, the upper layer of the reservoir (the epilimnion) is heated by sunlight and the warmer inflow, whereas the lower layer (the hypolimnion) remains at around 4°C, representing the maximum density of water. The two layers are separated by a sharp thermal gradient zone, the matalimnion. Temperature changes due to the wind and changes in air temperature are confined to the epilimnion. In colder weather, wind and the lower air and inflow temperature cool down the epilimnion until it is colder than the hypolimnion; vertical currents appear, causing the metalimnion to disappear and the temperature to even out in the body of water (overturn).

At times when there is no stratification, water drawn off from the bottom of the reservoir is provided from the whole vertical slice just in front of the intake, but at other times, the hypolimnion is drawn off first while new inflow into the reservoir stays in the epilimnion. The abstracted water is cold.

A lower water temperature in warm weather is beneficial as regards supply to homes and industry, for thermal power station cooling and fish spawning at the end of summer, but harmful when spawning takes place earlier.

DISSOLVED GAS CONTENT

Oxygen deficit

Oxygen is necessary to sustain aquatic biota and provide a self-purification capacity for the water. Dissolved oxygen penetrates the surface layer (detergent or oil films are obstacles to this process) or is produced by photosynthesis in the phytoplankton from dissolved mineral salts and carbon dioxide.

Biodegradation of dissolved, suspended and deposited organic material depends on oxygen, as does of course respiration of the aquatic biota. Warm water fish needs 4 mg/l to sustain life and reproduce.

If the river is heavily loaded with organic material, the amount of oxygen consumed to degrade it may be more than can be absorbed through the water/air interface, so that the oxygen content quickly falls. Once all the oxygen has been removed in this way, the river reaches an advanced stage of mal-odorous pollution with a scum over the surface, and all aquatic life ceases.

Storing of water in deep reservoirs produces a considerable oxygen deficit in the deeper layers in some periods of the year.

No harm is done if little water is abstracted or spilled in such periods and the oxygen demand downstream is small. The water recovers its normal oxygen content by contact with the atmosphere very quickly. Only large amounts of water released through the dam have detrimental effects because of oxygen depletion.

The oxygen content of water released from deep reservoirs depends on four factors:

1. The extent of thermal layering in the reservoir.
2. The depth of the intakes under the water surface.
3. The amount of organic material present.
4. The amount of decomposition products in the reservoir.

The current practice is to build the intakes with several inlets at different heights so that the water with the highest oxygen content is drawn off. Blowing a stream of oxygen or air through the abstracted water has also been tried.

NITROGEN AND OXYGEN SUPERSATURATION

Water below a spillway may become supersaturated with nitrogen and oxygen. This effect decreases with depth but nitrogen contents of up to 130 per cent have been recorded below high spillways.

The mortality threshold for some fish species appears to be about 120 per cent. The effect was demonstrated on the Columbia and Snake rivers where in 1970, it was estimated that 90 per cent of the young salmon (fry) making their first passage to the sea, died. Fries moving close to the surface were noticeably more affected. Numbers of salmon moving upstream to spawn in the following year were apparently unaffected.

EUTROPHICATION

The condition known as 'eutrophication' (from the Greek 'trephein' to nourish) involves the water and bottom sediments becoming enriched with nutrients to a point where the water quality deteriorates; the nutrient content of the lake rises to a dangerous level, sometimes known as the 'trophic' level.

Until recent times, eutrophication was a slow process, comparable to ageing, affecting natural as well as man-made lakes, but in the last few decades, more widespread use of fertilizers and detergents and growing quantities of waste water have speeded it up. Phosphorus and nitrogen are the main factors.

The first symptoms of eutrophication are:

(i) excessive development of bed plankton and macroscopic plants and weeds near the banks,
(ii) displacement of Salmonidae by Cyprinidae,
(iii) reduced water clarity caused by increase in the number of swimming micro-organisms, and changes in the colour of the water due to the red algae,
(iv) reduced oxygen content near the bottom, accompanied by an increase near the surface,
(v) swimming micro-organisms, and changes in the colour of water due to the red algae,
(vi) reduced oxygen content near the bottom, accompanied by an increase near the surface,
(vii) development of luxuriant weed growth,
(viii) formation of massive amounts of rotting matter on the bed,
(ix) complete disappearance of oxygen in the deeper layers in summer,
(x) appearance of sulphuretted hydrogen, free iron, manganese and ammonium ions,
(xi) appearance of gas bubbles.

By this stage, the lake becomes a 'breeder', causing more pollution from what it has received rather than digesting it.

Impacts of Eutrophication

The impacts of Eutrophication are listed below (Rast and Holland, 1988):

(i) Taste and odour problems can develop in drinking water taken from a eutrophic reservoir even though water is treated prior to its use.

(ii) The water treatment process itself can also become more expensive and time consuming for waters taken from eutrophic water bodies.

(iii) Excessive algae and aquatic plant growths are highly visible and can detract significantly from the aesthetic quality of a water body.

(iv) With dense quantities of algae in a reservoir, the transparency of the water is greatly reduced and the water body can acquire an undesirable 'pea-soup' green colour.

(v) Excessive algal densities can interfere significantly with swimming and other recreational activities.

(vi) Large masses of dead algac can accumulate on beach with negative aesthetic impacts.

(vii) As algae and aquatic plants sink to the bottom of a water body their decay by bacteria can reduce oxygen concentration in bottom waters making it too low to support fish life, resulting in fish kills.

(viii) Excessive levels of iron, manganese and foul smelling hydrogen sulphide in the bottom waters may also occur as a result of oxygen depletion.

(ix) There are also potential negative health impacts, especially in tropical and sub-tropical regions. Cultural eutrophication can aggravate the occurrence of parasitic diseases such as schistosomiasis, onchocerciasis and malaria by enhancing the habitats of the organisms responsible for their transmission to humans.

(x) Eutrophication of water bodies does have some positive aspects. For example in some countries, control cultural eutrophication is used to enhance fish production and other forms of aquaculture for the purpose of producing food. In such cases, the management goal is to maximize this productivity with a minimum of cost and effort.

Development of eutrophication management strategies

A basic practical framework for development of a eutrophication management strategy consists of the following steps (Rast and Holland, 1988):

(i) Identify eutrophication problem and establish management goals.
(ii) Assess the extent of available information about the reservoir.
(iii) Identify available, feasible eutrophication control methods.
(iv) Analyse all costs and expected benefits of alternative management strategies.
(v) Analyse adequacy of existing institutional and regulatory framework for implementing alternative management strategies.
(vi) Select desired control strategy and disseminate plan to interested parties.
(vii) Use institutional mechanisms to minimize future eutrophication problems.

Remedy

1. Purifying the inflow and reduction of nutrient inputs.
2. Agricultural nonpoint source control measures include:
   (i) Conservation tillage
   (ii) Vegetative buffer strips
   (iii) Contour cultivation
   (iv) Correct fertilizer application practices
   (v) Management of livestock manure
3. In Reservoir control measures:

Some treatment procedures can be applied directly to a reservoir,

(i) The harvesting of aquatic plants
(ii) Use of algicides
(iii) Nutrient inactivation in the reservoir

(iv) Artificial oxygenation of bottom waters
(v) The dredging or covering of bottom sediments
(vi) Increasing the water flushing or circulation rates
(vii) Artificial manipulation of in-lake biological communities

4. Use of nutrient rich waters for irrigation or aquaculture purposes.
5. *Building intercepting ditches:* Purification of inflow oxygen injection and building interception ditches have been used for Nantia, Bourget and Annery lakes in France (Rast & Holland, 1988).

DISSOLVED SOLIDS CONTENT

A reservoir can have a complex effect on dissolved solids content of waters, by such mechanisms as oxidation, reduction and ion exchange, but this can often be turned to advantage.

In the simple case of constant high salinity inflow, there is some concentration of salts in the reservoir as evaporation takes place from an increased surface area. However, high salinity inflows are normally in the form of concentrated 'slugs' at a particular time of year. In this case the 'slugs' are diluted by fresher water in the reservoir, and even after allowing for evaporation, effluents are generally at lower salinity levels than inflows. The same applies when one stream forming part of a multiple-tributary system has a high salts concentration.

It has been pointed out that on a global scale, at least 200,000 to 300,000 ha. of irrigated land are lost every year due to salinization and water-logging.

In Pakistan as many as 11 million ha. to 15 million ha. of irrigated land are already suffering from salinization and water logging. Afghanistan, Egypt, Iran, Iraq, Sudan and Syria also have similar problems.

The Chittaurgarh area under Chittaurgarh irrigation project shows high water table indicating that the area is vulnerable to water-logging and salinization because of clay-dominated soils.

A rise in the water table under similar conditions, caused water logging of 45,000 ha of the Sarda canal in Sarda Sahayak Irrigation Project of Uttar Pradesh and of 30,000 ha area in the Gandak canal in Gandak canal irrigation project (Ahmad and Singh, 1991).

A further complicating effect exists where reservoir area groundwaters are saline. At Chowilla Dam site in South Australia substantial seepage flows of highly saline groundwater were predicted, flushed out by the head of fresh impounded reservoir water. The designs incorporated a comprehensive system of relief wells to intercept this flow and prevent it from polluting the river downstream. The seepage was disposed of by pumping to large evaporation ponds.

BIOLOGICAL EFFECTS

Health effects for riparian dwellers

New storage reservoirs and their related water systems have repercussions on the main endemic parasites.

In hot, damp regions, certain of the more chronic and widespread endemic diseases are transmitted through pathogens whose vectors live in fresh water. Such diseases are endemic even before construction of the dam but the reservoir increases the size of the hosts' habitat, thus promoting their expansion.

The main diseases spread in this way are malaria (transmitted through the *Anopheles* mosquito), bilharziasis caused by blood flukes of the genus *Bilharzia* transmitted through a snail, and onchocerciasis, a very widespread disease of Africa and tropical America, transmitted by the bite of a small fly of the *Simuliidae* family.

Anopheles mosquitoes breed in small puddles and swampy areas rather than large lakes, so it is not that the full storage reservoirs behind dams that are responsible for the spread of malaria, but rather the temporary or permanent marginal systems created by seasonal water level fluctuations and human colonization around the edge of the lake promote malaria disease.

Irrigation malaria breaks out in irrigated agricultural areas with large, medium and small dams or tank irrigation projects. High malaria endemicity is recorded in Upper Krishna Irrigation Project in Karnataka and Sardar Sarovar Project on the Narmada in Gujarat (Jain, 1994). A good monsoon and waterlogging from the Indira Gandhi canal combined to create an outbreak of cerebral malaria which quickly spread to epidemic proportions in 1994 and 4,000 people were feared dead. Flood irrigation and stagnant water in the fields breed mosquitoes. Parts of the canal itself have stagnant water as construction is yet not complete. Seepage from the canal has caused massive waterlogging (Jain, 1994).

The Chittaurgrah project is situated in the Tarai region (foothills) which is humid and has a high water table, 0.43 m below ground level. The area is already suffering from waterlogging and flood. The construction of dam and the seepage around it will provide a good breeding ground for mosquitoes and cause malaria, filariasis and poliomyelites epidemics in the area (Ahmad and Singh, 1991).

Bilharziasis, which flourishes in America, Africa and tropical Asia, affects more than 300 million individuals. Conditions are particularly favourable near storage dams and reservoirs as the still or slow moving water promotes the growth of swamp plants on which the snails live. The snails' entire life cycle is aquatic, and they, and through them man, are contaminated in the water. The snails attach themselves to aquatic plants, and are infected through excrement containing eggs, which hatch into larvae living several days inside the snail, after which they emerge into the water and enter human feet, hands or other exposed parts of the body through the skin. Once in the body, the larvae develop into adults, hooking themselves into the liver, intestine and bladder. They lay eggs which are excreted, thus returning to the water for the life cycle to repeat itself.

The larvae and pupae of the fly vector for onchocerciasis live in flowing water, which is better aerated and cooler than stagnant water. As with malaria, it is not the main lake that constitutes the health risk, but the marginal lands and auxiliary water systems.

Ghana between 1958 and 1960, constructed 104 small dams in the north-east part of the country in response to population demand and seasonal hunger. This led to the prevalence of *Schistoma haematobium* infection in the local population tripling from 17 per cent to 51 per cent in 38 surveyed areas with some areas reaching 78 per cent (WHO 1993).

Odei (1982) reported a higher prevalence of schistosomiasis following the creation of new reservoirs with some of the riparian communities recording rates as high as 100 per cent.

The Weija lake was created by the construction of a dam on the river Densu in 1977. The creation of the lake to supply piped water and to support irrigation and fisheries programmes provided ideal conditions for disease transmission. Water related diseases such as guinea worm (dracontiasis) and schistosomiasis were reportedly endemic in and around the river Densu catchment area. Odei (1975) reported that *Bulinus globosus* and *Bulinus truncatus* were the proven host snails of the urinary schistosomiasis, in the river Densu and its tributaries, which existed at a prevalence rate of between 8.3 per cent and 43.3 per cent (Grant 1969).

Migration of disease infected fishermen and peasent farmers, flaws in resettlement programmes, changes in the flow rate of water, proliferation of water weeds and conditions favouring the growth and development of host snails were found to be responsible for tne increasing incidence of schistosomiasis in the lake basin (Ampofo and Zuta, 1995).

Man induced alterations of many South African rivers have created an environment which has abundant food supplies and sufficient flow to allow year-round colonization by filter feeding invertebrates, of which black flies (Simuliidae) are of particular concern (Moor, 1997). The majority of the 39 species of black flies recorded from South Africa (Palmer, 1991) are completely harmless and play an important functional role in the ecology of streams and rivers. There are, however, four species (*Simulium agersi, Simulium nigritarse, Simulium damnosum and Simulium chutteri*) that cause problems of sufficient magnitude to man and his livestock to require remedial intervention. Only one species, *S. chutteri,* under certain circumstances, can attain densities which can be considered to be of plague proportional size.

It is the female blackfly that is in all instances, the blood sucking culprit. It feeds creating large wounds in the victims which often lead to secondary bacterial infection. In sheep, the loss of parts of the ears and, in cattle, badly damaged teats are often encountered following severe outbreaks of blackfly attacks. Blackflies have also been implicated in the mechanical spreading of certain disease bearing organisms. These include Rift-Valley fever virus, Wessels Bron disease and the protozoan *Chlamydia,* which causes blindness in sheep and enzootic abortion in cattle (Bath, 1978) Black flies first became a problem along the Vaal river in the early 1960.

The modified approach taken to keep the black fly population, particularly *S. chutteri*, down to a level where it is no longer a serious threat to riparian livestock is achieved by regulating the flow of the river to almost cease at certain times during spring. This approach of drying out the river bed, by stopping the flow for short intervals and then resuming normal flow again, can, unfortunately, only be carried out within a limited distance downstream of a dam.

The bacterium *Bacillus thuringiensis* var. israclensis ('B.t.i') has proved successful in blackfly population size control along the Vaal and Orange rivers (Car and de moor, 1984; de moor and Car 1986; Palmer, 1993).

The reservoirs created by large dams also have effects on parasitic illnesses not requiring intermediate hosts, such as various types of amoebiasis, and on viral and bacterial diseases, such as typhoid and intestinal infections. The preventive steps are:

(a) before the first filling of the reservoir, clear the area of vegetation; backfill, deepen, impound or drain any areas liable to become swampy through fluctuations in the lake level,
(b) during operation of the scheme, increase and lower the lake level a few centimetres weekly in the egg-laying season,
(c) use pesticides judicially.

The Tennessee Valley Authority used these measures and almost completely eradicated mosquitoes around their dams.

The spraying and spreading of larvicides and pesticides must be repeated at frequent intervals, and the cost may be prohibitive in developing countries. The chemicals must not be toxic for man or the fish forming the staple diet of riparian dwellers.

It might seem cheaper and simpler to treat the disease rather than attempt to destroy the vectors, but unfortunately the available drugs have only a limited effect and in fact are so toxic that they cannot be considered for mass treatment of riverside population.

It is interesting to record that China has now completely stamped out bilharziasis through health education, discipline and increased community awareness.

EFFECTS ON AQUATIC FLORA AND FAUNA

The uncontrolled growth of aquatic plant life in tropical regions may seriously hamper navigation and fishing, provide breeding places for disease-carrying insects, change the chemical composition of the water and block water intakes. The three most troublesome plants are the water lettuce *Pistia stratiotes*, a free floating aquatic herb of the Arum family; a fern *Salvinia molesta* and the worst, the water hyacinth *Eichhornia crassipes.*

In the more temperate regions, the Eurasian aquatic milfoil *Myrcophyllum spicatum L.,* an ornamental aquarium plant, is a great nuisance in shallow lakes. In the absence of suitable means of eradicating it, it is contained by lowering the reservoir level to dry the roots, and spraying selective herbicides by boat or helicopter.

Shallow reservoirs in France are overrun by rushes. But the most serious difficulties from aquatic flora arise from weeds which invade canals downstream of some large reservoirs—the Durance canals below Serre Poncon dam, and the Drac canals below Monteynard for example. The reduction in flow capacity may be large, and there is no known way of overcoming the problem to date.

Reservoirs may also promote considerable development in the aquatic fauna.

For fish, the species composition often changes after a river is dammed. The indigenous fish populations of both North and South Indian man-made reservoirs have changed significantly after their impoundment. Transplanted species have established themselves which were almost nil in 1957-58 in Sathnur reservoir, formed a fishery constituting 25 per cent of the fish landed in 1964-65 and later gradually increased in the catches to occupy a predominant position, reaching 91 per cent in 1975-76. In Stanley reservoir prawns, once abundant on the sandy beds of Cauvery, have disappeared. River Tapti was devoid of major carps prior to its damming but accidental transplantation has resulted in the establishment of *Catla catla* and *Labeo rohita* in the lower stretches of the river. The fish community of Ranaprátap Sagar also appears to be in a state of transition after dam formation. There is a decreasing trend of *Cirrhina mrigala* year after year and the smaller size group is missing. Indications are such that the proper recruitment of *Cirrhina mrigala* is not taking place.

Migratory fishes are of great significance economically and for sporting purposes on many rivers. For these reasons and to minimize ecological changes, fish passes are needed in dams constructed on such rivers. These may take the form of ladders in which the fish swim up steps through a series of connected pools, much as in nature. In the fish lift alternative, the fish enter a bottom chamber and after an interval of time the entrance is shut. The bottom chamber is then filled with water, as in a conduit connecting to an upper chamber at reservoir top water level. The fish swim up and out of the top chamber to the reservoir. Both these systems are efficient for fish migrating upstream to spawn but there is more difficulty in passing spent fish downstream on the way back to the sea.

In association with fish protection works, screens are required to prevent fish entering water passages harmful to themselves and where they could damage or block machinery. The screens may be of steel bars or an electrical system can be used.

Migratory fish can be directed to preferred streams by erecting fish breaks or barriers on other streams. Traps can be incorporated to catch fish temporarily and strip them of spawn for fish hatcheries. Hatcheries can be used to breed fry to stock new reservoirs for sporting purposes.

In the case of catchment diversions, the transfer of unwanted species from one catchment to another should be guarded against, and screens at diversion intakes may be required. A particularly difficult task is the prevention of eel migrations over land saddles close to new reservoirs. The following measures are usually adopted in water resources projects to maintain and rather increase and improve fish quantity and quality.

(i) Fish ladders, fish locks, fish lifts or other special means give positive results.
(ii) In case of certain diversion projects involving dams, tunnels or canal aqueducts, migration of fish species from one river to another can be permitted.
(iii) Continuation of fish resources may be ensured by stocking with young fish.
(iv) Plantation of the upper surface of a reservoir with a flora similar to that existing outwards nearby at the same elevation, can help in preserving population of fish. Such a treatment was tried with success on the Marchlyn Manic dam in North

Wales, UK, to preserve population of salmon, sea-trout, brown trout, eels, and minnows.

(v) Compensation water released through the dam helps in maintaining the fish life downstream.

(vi) Eutrophication can be controlled by clearance of new reservoir areas prior to impounding. Other remedial measures include aeration, purifying inflow and building interception ditches to carry away from the reservoir any land run-off liable to contain traces of fertiliser, particularly compounds of nitrogen and phosphorus.

(vii) In case of barrages, weirs and small diversion dams, under water stone revetments can be made which can create conditions of suitable flora and fauna so vital for the life and growth of fish.

According to Tyson Roberts, an expert with 20 years of research experience on fresh water fish in Thailand and the Mekong basin, the Mekong river rapids are the centres of biodiversity akin to coral reefs in the oceans. The river's ecosystem is described as one of the world's richest in fish biodiversity and productivity. In the past two years alone, fish biologists have added 3 new species to the list of 1,000 indigenous species already known.

The region's experts warn that the dams will deprive biologists of the last chance to study this complex river system in its relatively undisturbed state. Any reduction in the Mekong's flow could affect the river rapids disrupting the riverine food chain and fish habitat. The dams will block *fish migration* routes cutting off spawning and feeding habitat.

Many Mekong species are believed to take annual migrations up and down the largest rivers, including the Mekong mainstream. Schools of *Pangasius kempfii*, a large economically important catfish reaching more than 1 metre in length and weighing more than 15 kg, are believed to travel over 1,000 km. from the South China Sea and Mekong Delta (Rajesh, 1995).

The Three Gorges dam billed as the world's largest water control project on Yangtze river in China will cause damage on important fishing grounds at the mouth of the river Yangtze by cutting short their nitrogen and phosphorus supply because of the siltation (Down to Earth, 1996).

It is suggested that physiographic and hydrologic complexity plays an important role in making rivers suitable for dolphins (Reeves and Leatherwood, 1994). Dams and other artificial constructions degrade dolphin habitat in so far as they reduce such complexity. Research is needed at project sites, both before and after construction of dams, barrages and dikes to document impacts. Specially-designed 'Swimways' may allow upstream and downstream passage by dolphins and can mitigate at least one of the adverse effects of dam projects namely population fragmentation.

Indian sub-continent

(i) Dams and barrages have long been present on rivers of the Indian sub-continent and they have had a major impact on dolphins. The Indus dolphin (*Platanista minor*, also known as Indus susu or bhulan) now exists only as a metapopula tion consisting of four or five artificially isolated sub-populations.

(ii) Barrages built by India along the Nepalese border have left Nepal with only a few sub-populations of Ganges dolphins (*Platanista gangetica*, also known as Gangessusu), confined to upstream ends of Ganges tributaries such as Karnali, Narayani, Koshi and Mahakali.

(iii) Farakka Barrage, constructed near the Indian border with Bangladesh in the early 1970s, mainly to improve navigation in the Hooghly river, partitioned the dolphin population in the lower Ganges.

(iv) China's Yangtze dolphin *Lipotes vexillifer;* (also known as baiji) may be the most endangered cetacean in the world, with an estimated population of less than two hundred.

(v) River bed scouring and altered flow caused by the planned high dam at Three Gorges will degrade about 10 per cent of the habitat currently used by Yangtze dolphins.

South America

South America has two kinds of river dolphins, the Amazon dolphin *Inia geoffrensis;* (also known as boto, tonina or *Bufeo colorado*) and *Sotalia fluviatilis* (known as tueuxi or *Bufeo gris*).

Three large dams (Balbina, Curua-Una, and Tucurui) have already been built in the Brazilian Amazon and several others are planned or under construction.

How dams threaten dolphins

A 1986 international workshop on river dolphins identified a number of potential problems caused by waterway obstruction.

(i) Fragmentation of populations into genetically isolated sub-populations.
(ii) Reduction in prey due to blocked migratory routes.
(iii) Less diversity and smaller biomass of prey in impoundments upstreams of dams due to lowered nutrient availability.
(iv) Downstream effects on prey caused by changes in flow rate, sediment transport, and estuarine salinity.
(v) Limited dispersal of dolphins between river systems due to saline encroachment in estuaries.

Mitigative measures

Dams should be concentrated as near headwaters as possible. Also a series (or 'staircase') of dams on one tributary is usually preferable, from an ecological perspective, to having single dams constructed on several rivers.

Swimway concept

There is a long history of using fishways to permit anadromous fish to maintain their upstream spawning migrations but river-dolphins were neglected because of the lack of their economic value. But now for the sake of preserving biological diversity dolphin swimway concept has gained momentum which can be designed and built at a reasonable cost (Reeves and Leatherwood, 1994).

ACTION ON WATERS OTHER THAN IN THE RESERVOIR

Drying up of rivers

The diversion and drying up of mountain rivers is detrimental to fishing and is an eyesore. It can be remedied by allowing an adequate guaranteed compensation flow through the dam; the amount may be varied in daylight and night hours and from season to season, as required by tourist amenity consieations. The question is particularly acute when natural waterfalls, like Niagara, are bypassed.

Changes in water table

The depth of the water table is changed by storage schemes. It is a simple matter to prevent it rising nearer the ground surface generally at the toes of embankments, which may even be designed to set the level of the water table at the best depth for farming purposes.

River stretches in alluvial plains that are bypassed by the scheme, and deep tailrace canals may, on the other hand, lower the water table. Weirs keep it at an acceptable depth while safeguarding the countryside, water, sports and fishing, and construction of a watertight cutoff parallel to the tailrace prevents ground water draining into it.

Catchment management

In order to protect a new reservoir it is often necessary or desirable to take certain measures in the catchment area. Following impounding of a new reservoir there is frequently additional access and development in the catchment upstream. Uncontrolled deforestation and incautious agricultural development can lead to land erosion problems, particularly on steep land. If not dealt with properly by such measures as controlled re-afforestation and contour ploughing such land erosion can result in rapid siltation of the reservoir as well as loss of good farming soil.

Pollution of reservoirs used for potable water supply must be avoided and controlled access for human beings and the exclusion of large animals may be necessary.

LANDSLIDES

Landslides typify the interaction between the river development scheme and the environment. A reservoir may cause a landslide on the banks, which may partially fill in the reservoir.

The most striking example was at Vajont in the Piava valley in Italy. On the second filling on 9 October 1963, 250 million cubic metres of rock slipped into the 168 million cubic metre reservoir and flung the water over the top of the dam, which stood up without damage. More than 3,000 persons in the valley died.

There are other known examples of smaller slides, and adits are sometimes driven into the reservoir banks to keep a watch on stability. In new reservoir areas with steep sides, a geological and soil mechanics reconnaissance should precede reservoir filling. Any doubtful areas should be thoroughly investigated and analysed taking account of wetting, new water table, and possible rapid drawdown. Zones of probable trouble should be stabilized, drained, or flattened. Slope indicators and other instrumentation such as piezometers should be used for monitoring behaviour of doubtful areas, and in important cases automatic tele-metered warning systems should be incorporated.

INDUCED EARTHQUAKES

The question of whether filling a reservoir will cause earth tremors was first raised in 1934 during construction of the Hoover dam in the USA, but interest was only really awakened among seismologists and dam builders after the earthquakes at Kremasta (1966) and Koyna (1967).

Kremasta dam in Greece is 147m high and impounds 4.8 km of water. The main earthquake in 1966 was of magnitude 6.2 with its focus 20 km under the reservoir.

Koyna dam near Mumbai is 103m high with a reservoir volume of 2.7 km^3. The magnitude of the 1967 earthquake was 6.0 with the focus 9km under the reservoir.

Extensive study during the filling (1959 to 1971) of the Kariba dam (Rhodesia), a 128m high dam with a 175 km reservoir, indicated that the coincidence between reservoir filling and ground motion at Kremasta and Koyna was not chance. Seismic activity under the Kariba reservoir was strikingly parallel to the rise in water level over the five-year filling period and the main earthquake of magnitude occurred when it reached top level for the first time.

Concern about seismic safety of dams has been growing in recent years as it has become evident that the earlier pseudo-static design concept is inadequate (Malla and Weiland, 1993). The most intense public debate on the Tehri dam has centered around the issue of seismicity and dam safety.

The potential of earthquake disaster all along the Himalayan plate boundary has been well known and widely accepted (Khattri, 1987). A debate has been going on for years on the adequacy of present design of the Tehri dam to sustain the dam against the maximum credible earthquakes expected in the area. The occurrence of a major earthquake in 1991 in the upper catchment areas of dam further strengthens the environmental opposition. It may be the case that the feasibility of realising the hydrological dream of storage in the Himalayan rivers will be cut short by seismological realities.

As cited by Khan and Miah (1983) to the hydrological possibilities of storing 400 MAF of water in Brahmaputra basin, they quote from the recommendations of the Geological Survey of India that the Technical Committee on construction of high dams in seismic zones found that only 30 MAF out of a total of 400 MAF i.e. barely 7 per cent would be available as potential storage in Brahmaputra basin. This is an important instance of geological factors limiting the availability of optimal storage volume, independent of the availability of hydrologically feasible storage sites.

By 1976 the correlation between seismic activity and first filling of the reservoir had been recorded in some twenty cases. There are already unambiguous examples in which sensitive instruments for recording earthquake activity were installed some considerable time before construction of the dam as a reference for subsequent events. At Talbingo dam in Australia for example, only one minor earthquake was detected in the 13 years before the reservoir was filled, whereas one hundred tremors of comparable intensity were recorded in the first 15 months afterwards. The strongest tremor occurred just when the reservoir reached its top level, with a magnitude of 3.5. All the foci were shallow, just near the dam.

Most large reservoirs impounded by high dams have not caused any significant earthquake activity on filling, even when they lie in areas of high seismic activity such as California or Mexico. Conditions conducive to induced earthquakes are not therefore clearly understood. However there is sufficient evidence to demonstrate that it is probably true that:

(i) the earthquakes are due to the release of pre-existing stresses which are triggered into instability by the relatively small stresses from the water load, or by weakening of rock by percolating water,
(ii) the earthquakes are shallow, generally less than 10 km deep, compared to many natural earthquakes,
(iii) it cannot be assumed that attempts to control induced seismicity by lowering the water level or moderating the rate of filling after the earthquake sequence has commenced, will be successful or even helpful,
(iv) there remains the possibility that load influenced seismicity can be reduced in some sense by maintaining as slow a rate of filling as practicable, and

(v) it should not be assumed without full study that every seismic swarm near a storage reservoir is a case of load induced seismicity.

Hence, designers of large (more than 100m high) dams or those impounding large (more than 1 km) storage reservoirs must examine the following points:

(a) What is the current state of tectonic stress in the whole region and within the shoreline contour of the proposed reservoir? How does this vary, especially with depth, and how has it varied over recent time, say during the Holocene?
This can be approached by such means as stress measurements on outcrops, and by a detailed geological search for Holocene tectonic movements.

(b) Are there any recent (tertiary or quaternary) volcanic formations in the area?

(c) Are there any nearby active faults, which would be signs of recent tectonic action, especially where they exhibit large displacements (more than 1000ms.), where they are of great length (more than 100 km.), where they are sources of hot springs, where they bring formations of different stiffness into contact with each other, or where they are subject to a non-compressive horizontal stress so that they tend to open?

SOCIAL EFFECTS

Beneficial effects

With the very wide sense of the word 'environment' used here, action on the environment includes all the purposes for which a multiple purpose dam is built in addition to induced effects. All river development schemes are built to produce beneficial effects for society, the main ones being irrigation, land reclamation in river flood plains and tidal areas, domestic and industrial water supply, flood control and improved dry weather flow in rivers, hydro-electricity, navigation, recreational activities, and so on.

Many induced effects may be beneficial. Some are discussed below.

Effects on countrysides, tourism and leisure

The beauty of the new countryside created by storage lakes, especially those in which the water level does not vary to any extent, is a favourable effect on the environment. The same applies where the surrounding area is developed for amenity purposes, and parks and camp sites are increasingly used as a barrier to uncontrolled or excessive building. The dam itself is often a great tourist attraction.

Storage reservoirs near populated areas are increasingly used for water sports and swimming when they can be kept nearly full in the summer season. Unattractive reservoir bank areas affected by drawdown can be limited by subsidiary dams.

Chittaurgarh is a large man made dam situated in the northern region of Shivalik Himalaya with a volume of 100 million m^3, height 15.3 m from deep foundation level and gross catchment area of 194 km^2. So the area can be developed for water sports, tourist lodge, camping sites, huts and shopping centres. Practice of intensive and extensive farming will provide good employment possibilities (Ahmed and Singh, 1991). Besides this the agro-based rural industries, construction, manufacture and distribution of agriculture inputs and outputs, marketing, transport and land improvement etc. will provide additional employment. Development in the area of pharmaceutical, cotton, paper and sugar industries will favour the development of infrastructure facilities e.g. banking, marketing, health care, warehouses, roads and schools (Ahmad and Singh, 1991).

Roads

Road relocation is often an opportunity for considerably improving the existing road system, while dams provide possibilities for cheap road crossings, often a major advantage on wide alluvial plain rivers. Roads may also provide access to otherwise remote areas for emergency activities such as firefighting. This is particularly important in the prevention and control of bush firs, forest fires and conservation of forest regions.

Fisheries development

Large reservoirs generally have a favourable effect on the development of the aquatic fauna. When the Tennessee Valley Authority began building its cascades of storage reservoirs, there was little hope for improved fishing. It was thought that stocks would be abundant for a short time but the reservoirs would afterwards turn into 'biological deserts'. Yet industrial and sport fishing have been continually growing after the fish tonnage increased fifty-fold, while the restocking stations built through fear of natural reproduction in the reservoirs being impossible, have been closed down.

Similar successes have been recorded at Kariba and Lake Nasser, to mention only the larger lakes. Lack of facilities, processing industry and transport do however limit fisheries development in some cases.

The only disappointing results concern the introduction of new species. This policy can however give good results when run by experienced biologists making suitable advance studies.

Fire prevention

New bodies of water created by dams act as barriers to contain and reduce forest and bush fires. This is a particularly important effect in regions with prolonged hot dry summers.

Detrimental effects

Population displacement, the drowning of arable land and archeological sites, and danger to downstream population must be included on the debit side of river development schemes.

Deforestation

Often good storage sites for damming occur in hilly uplands which are thickly forested. Before a reservoir is filled up the entire area to be submerged has to be cleared and forests often become a casualty.

Despite the increased awareness about the need to protect forest cover, little attention is generally paid to this factor when a site is selected for a dam, basically because all forests are state property and no one has to be compensated for them. Even in cost-benefit calculations, forest loss is grossly undervalued and the recurring loss in terms of timber and firewood yield per year and social costs of degradation of environment are never taken into account. Undervaluation of standing forest helps in boosting the cost-benefit ratio for obtaining Planning Commission approval and finance from international agencies like the World Bank. Moreover, the contract for clearing the forest is also undervalued, thus leaving a bigger margin to be shared between the contractors and the forest department.

The forest cover bears the brunt of dam construction in more than one way. In the Himalayan valleys, India, contractors who come to clear the forest which is going to be submerged greedily cut trees even in unaffected area. The forest is also cleared for approach roads, offices, residential quarters and for storage of construction material and rehabilitation.

In September 1987, the Ministry of Environment and Forests (MEF) sanctioned the submergence of over 1,360 hectares of reserved forests for Sardar Sarovar Project under the strict condition that no forest land will be used for rehabilitation. But by June 1990, under pressure from Gujarat and Madhya Pradesh governments, MEF sanctioned the felling of another 2,769 hactares of reserved forest land in Taloda for rehabilitation. With the reduction in forest cover and the entry of people, the pressure on the remaining forest increases. The need for firewood leads, to further denudation. The construction of a dam, therefore, has a multiplier effect.

The 1983-84 annual report of the Department of Environment, Government of India, reveals that the construction of the Idukki dam over the Periyar river in Kerala, India, has hastened the degradation of vegetation and sharply reduced the forest cover. It is estimated that during the period 1951-76, 0.49 million hectares of forest has been lost due to major river valley projects. This is roughly

10 per cent of the area that came under canal irrigation—5.5 million hectares. The construction of Chittaurgarh dam affected a vast area (405 hactare) of natural forests in the Himalayas. The removal of vegetation included the felling of valuable timber and fruits bearing trees and the removal of firewood.

The highest percentage of damaged trees upstream of the dam included Khair (*Acacia catechu*), Impli (*Tamarindus indica*), Jamun (*Syzygium cumini*), Teak (*Tectona grandis*), Shisham (*Dalbergia sissoo*), Chandan (*Santalum album*) etc. The deforestation of these species has caused serious wood scarcity in the area. The construction of the Saryu canal project has also resulted in the denudation of 1,250 hactare of a valuable timber yielding area (Ahmad and Singh, 1991).

The Three Gorges project of China will result in the drowning of 238 km^2 farmland and 50 km^2 orange groves (Chau Kwai-cheong, 1995).

The Bakun dam to be built across the Balui in Malaysia will submerge 695 sq. km. of virgin rain forests and will also inundate the farmlands (Iyer, 1996).

Environmental damages due to the construction of Auburn dam, the most expensive dam in the US history to be built on the American river in California, include the destruction of upto 80.45 km. of deep, richly forested Canyons that provide habitat for wild life and support recreation for 50,000 people a year.

Degree of deforestation involved in the 4,060 MW Indo-Bhutan Sankosh Hydel project will be great deal causing denudation of 700 hactare of prime forest land.

Population displacement

Reservoirs displace a large number of people, the number depending on the reservoir area and the population density. In India, as elsewhere, rehabilitation is the most persistant problem encountered during the development of large dams.

Development related displacement in India can be traced back to Raj days and the construction of the first state owned Yamuna Canal system in 1789.

(i) The construction of the Upper Anicut dam on the Cauvery in 1863 raised the issue of involuntary displacement.
(ii) Colonial administration came out with the Land Acquisition Act in 1894.
(iii) The Tata power company's building of a dam Mulshi Peta in 1920 near Pune displaced 11,000 people, and triggered off the first satyagraha against forcible displacement. (Mitra, 1995).

Since independence, over 1,600 major dams and tens of thousands of medium and smaller irrigation projects have been built with the attendant canal systems and the invariable consequences of water logging and soil salinization. As a result, between 100-120 lakh people have been forcibly displaced (Paranjpye, 1990).

In the absence of firm projectwise data the estimates of the total numbers displaced by planned development interventions from 1951-90 range from a conservative 110 lakhs to an overall figure of 185 lakhs (Fernandes and Thukral, 1989). These figures do not include the sizeable number of people who are not acknowledged as being project affected (i.e. by loss of livelihood caused by natural resource extraction or degradation), those displaced in urban areas and those victimized by the process of secondary displacement. If these are tallied, the number of those displaced since independence would be as high as four crores.

Walter Fernandes estimates that in the recent past the proportion of tribals among those displaced has been increasing (Fernandes, 1991). For example, of the 11.6 lakh persons displaced by 20 representative dams above 50 metres either under construction or being planned in the 1990s 59 per cent are tribals. The figure will obviously increase for dams planned in predominantly tribal areas (Suvarnrekha, Pollavaram, etc.).

The Central Water Commission's 1990 'Register of Large Dams' is also instructive. Of the 32 dams of more than 50 metres height completed between 1951 and 1970 only 9 (22.13 per cent) were in tribal areas. Between 1971 and 1990, 85 additional dams of similar sizes were either completed or were under construction. However, by now not only were they taller and more sophisticated, around 60 per cent of them were in the tribal regions.

A recent official report on the rehabilitation of tribals, based on a comprehensive study of 110 projects, concludes that of 16.94 lakh people displaced by these projects almost 50 per cent (8.14 lakhs) were tribals (GOI, 1993).

Trauma of Displacement

The experience of the post independence period from projects across the country suggests that the long drawn out process of displacement has caused wide-spread traumatic psychological and socio-cultural consequences.

These include the dismantling of production systems, desecration of ancestral sacred zones or graves and temples, scattering of Kinship groups and family systems, disorganization of informal social networks that provide mutual support, weakening of self management and social control, disruption of trade and market links etc.

Essentially, what is established in the acccumulated evidence in the country suggests that except in the rarest of the rare cases, forced displacement has resulted in, what Michael Cernea calls 'a spiral of impoverishments'. In addition there is a loss of complex social relationships which provided avenues of representation mediation and conflict resolution. In essence, the very cultural identity of the community and the individual within it is disrupted causing immense physiological and psychological stress (Cernea, 1991).

The process of displacement is also disempowering since it breaks up socio-political organizations articulating a critique of the project (and of development process itself). Activists of the Tehri Bandh Virodhi Samiti states that there was a conscious strategy of the project authorities and the state government to divide the united resistance to the Tehri project (Kothari, 1996).

The other neglected dimension of displacement is its adverse impact on women. Their trauma is compounded by the loss of access to fuel, fodder and food, the collection of which inevitably requires greater time and effort. Similarly, children are adversely affected since not only is schooling less accessible in most cases there is also a disruption in the traditional socialization processes.

Apathetic Planning

Planners and administrators invariably capitalise on and manipulate the relatively weaker socio-economic and political position of most of the people facing displacement. Their numbers are underestimated, they are treated indifferently and only minimal cash compensation, it at all, is paid. There is an extraordinary unwillingness to grant them clear rights, such as security of tenure on alternative developed land sites.

A graphic and painful example is that of the displaced of Singrauli who are part of the over two lakh people first displaced by the Rihand Dam in 1964 and now face displacement for the incomprehensible fifth time in a single generation.

Some indicative data highlights the severity of the apathy and indifference of official agencies and the government to take responsibility for those who, in an overwhelming number of cases have been forced to forgo their ancestral habitats and have experienced social and cultural disruption in the past four and a half decades of planned development. For example 25 years after the building of the prestigious Bhakra-Nangal Project only 730 out of the 2,108 families displaced in the early 1950s from Bilaspur and Una districts of Himachal Pradesh had been resettled.

A majority of those displaced by other renowned projects like the Hirakud dam in Orissa or the Rihand dam in Uttar Pradesh, have never been officially resettled.

The oustees of the Pong dam in Himachal Pradesh who were displaced in the 1960s had worse in store. Out of the 30,000 families or more that were displaced, only 16,000 were found eligible for compensation and in the end only 3,756 were moved hundreds of miles to a completely different cultural, linguistic and ecological zone in Rajasthan (Bhanot and Singh, 1992).

Official indifference and callousness is also evident in the lack of data regarding the total number of persons displaced by different developmental interventions.

Independent studies of the oustees of Hirakud placed the figure for those displaced at 1,80,000 while official figures were 1,10,000.

Official data for the controversial dam on the Narmada river, the Sardar Sarover Project (SSP) fluctuates between 10,758 families and 30,134 families (Morse et al, 1992). The latest figures of the oustees of the SSP show that since June 1994 the Gujarat government has been able to resettle just 94 families out of the over 41,000 families from all the three states of Gujarat, Madhya Pradesh and Maharashtra (Kothari, 1996).

In case of Tehri dam, direct involuntary displacement will occur for about 80,000 people. Indirectly, another large number of villages would lose parts of land or access road to the nearest towns in the plains.

Because of the Koel karo hydroelectric project about 120 villages were to be submerged over 22,000 ha., displacing over one lakh people of the total and acquisition land, while 10,000 ha. comprise forests (Down To Earth, 1992).

The Tawa dam built on Tawa river in Madhya Pradesh was built for irrigation purposes. Forty-one villages were submerged and almost all inhabitants were adivasis. These adivasi villages which were displaced due to dam have not been rehabilitated and they have hardly received any compensation. There was no attempt to give them alternative land suitable for agriculture, or give them suitable alternative employment. They were not given the minimum conveniences like drinking water, roads, grazing areas which were available to them before and to top all these they were forced to clear forests and rebuild their homes. Some of them who were entitled to compensation got amounts of Rs.150 per acre, Rs. 65 per acre, Rs. 35 per acre and Rs. 18 per acre. The case of Tawa is a unique example of the injustice inherent in displacement of people (Sunil and Smitha, 1996).

After a long struggle and agitation the displaced of the *Bargi dam* have been awarded as part of their rehabilitation the fishing rights on a cooperative basis. The displaced villages formed 54 co-operative societies which were then linked to form a co-operative marketing federation which now looks over the work of the co-operatives. They have raised the wage rate for fishing, given employment to local people and at the end of the year have shown a saving worth Rs. 25 lakhs (Sunil and Smitha, 1996).

The chief obstacle to the process of resettlement is the non-availability of land in Gujarat, where maximum resettlement is planned.

The eleven dam projects on Mekong river in Thailand which will have a total capacity of 14,000 MW, will flood 1,900 sq.km. and displace about 60,000 people (Rajesh, 1995).

Since 1949, some 86,000 water conservancy projects have been undertaken in China involving the resettlement of over 10 million people. Many of the displaced people were resettled in remote border areas far away from their home countries, resulting in widespread adaptation problems and conflicts with the minority groups. In addition, the relocatees were given one payment compensation with no other development oriented assistance. Roughly 30 per cent of the resettlement schemes failed, and because of this bitter experience many people are sceptical of China's competence to resettle the huge number of people who will be affected by the Three Gorges Project (Chan Kwai-Cheong, 1995).

It is a standing practice for the bureaucracy to issue notices for evacuation the moment project is announced, though the actual shifting might not start for years.

A Centre for Social Studies, Surat study shows that most of the oustees in the 19 Gujarat villages facing submission due to SSP had been issued notices as early as 1980. The actual shifting is yet to take place from many villages. The 557 households who had been shifted by 1988 should have been given a total of 1,118 ha. of land, but only 526.5 ha. had actually been handed over (Mitra, 1995).

In some cases, population movements are very extensive—30, 000 persons had to be relocated from the Keban dam area in Turkey, 50,000 from Kariba on the Zambesi, 70,000 from Tsimlian on the Don, and 90,000 for the development of the Volta in Ghana. Tehri dam is estimated to displace nearly a lakh people.

An attempt was made to resettle the Ghanaian population near the reservoir by providing substitute jobs in tourism, irrigation and other new activities. At Kariba, a flourishing industrial fishing industry has replaced the former subsistence fishing.

Some ground realities that continue to be neglected during resettlement are:

In the pre-implementation phase

(i) The desirability and justifiability of the project or developmental intervention itself.

(ii) Consultation with representatives of the local population, particularly and predominantly those who are more vulnerable and the institutionalization of this process.

(iii) The justifiability of reducing or winding down development programmes and resources for the area facing submergence.

(iv) The harassment, intimidation and repression of potential oustees.

(v) If displacement is inevitable, then the full participation of the affected communities in defining a comprehensive rehabilitation package.

In the *Implementation phases* some of the neglected aspects are:

(i) Effects to bribe community leaders with the intention of seeking the consent of the community.

(ii) A wide range of human rights violations including threats, harassment, police actions, firing on peaceful protesters, forced entry into villages and homes, destruction of private property etc,.

(iii) The disruption of nomadic routes which are crucial to the survival of nomadic communities, and

(iv) Land acquisition that in turn displaces those dependent on the acquired land.

The *post-implementation* stage which, for those displaced, is among the most traumatic and undocumented experience, since project authorities move on to the next assignment and government machineries are not oriented to undertake long-term monitoring.

(i) The condition of the displaced in the existing resettlement sites.

(ii) Tracing those who were paid cash compensation and who dispersed over a vast geographical area (as was the case with some of the Pong dam oustees).

(iii) Responsibility for those who were displaced by earlier projects but who continue to face a grim economic and social predicament.

(iv) The displacement caused by the intensive development activity that inevitably follows an initial developmental intervention.

Drowning of arable land and archeological sites

Reservoir basins are often rich in arable land and pasture, sometimes forming the only agricultural potential in the region.

Just as some projects are abandoned because of the size of the population they would displace, other valleys are not developed because of essential agricultural interests. The decision to go ahead with the scheme is only justified if the benefits largely outweigh such upheavals. In some instances however, reclaimed land or land completely or partially protected by the scheme against former devastating floods represents a much larger area than that drowned by the reservoir. The Tennessee Valley Authority reservoirs cover 250,000 hectares but the area protected against river floods on the Ohio and Mississippi downstream is fifteen times larger.

On the question of the drowning of archaeological sites, three projects can be mentioned as examples: at lake Nasser impounded by the High Aswan dam, several monuments, including the Abu Simbel temple, were moved higher up the banks. In Siberia, the Angara rock paintings which would have been drowned by the Bratsk and Oust-Illim reservoir were housed in the local museum. Valuable archeological remains of the second century AD had to be moved out of the reservoir area of Nagarjunasagar dam.

The proposed hydroelectric project across Rathong Chu river in Sikkim is a threat to Yuksam which is a sacred pilgrimage spot. Several Buddhist relics have been unearthed in the area. The Dubdi Gompa monastery which is also an archaeological treasure is close to the site (Balakrishnan, 1991)

DAM BUSTING

A spate of dam busting is sweeping the US after the demolition of Newport Number II dam on the Clyde river in Newport, Vermont. For the last forty years, the dam has been preventing the salmon from reaching its spawning ground. After the dam disappeared with a loud roar and bang within a few weeks, the fish was back jumping in the free running water.

Following this incident which is considered a turning point in the US history of hydroengineering in Maine, several dams on the Rogue river in Oregon and the Snake river in Idaho face a similar fate.

Plans are also on the anvil to dismantle two dams on the Elwha river in Washington state.

Activists in Tasmania want the dam on the Franklin river dismantled so that the pink quartz beaches of Lake Pedder which were submerged by the reservoir be uncovered. And in France, the environmental group SOS Loire has convinced the government to remove the Saint Etienne du vigan dam on the Vienne river to restore passages for migratory fish through the upper Loire Valley.

For dismantling a dam, engineers must consider the entire river system not just the concrete structure itself. Although smaller dams like the Newport Number II may pose relatively lesser problems, costing just about $1 million to be removed within six weeks, large ones would present several problems, and even cause degradation to the environment.

Researches show that once liberated, the sediments in the water may prove to be toxic to fish spawning areas, damaging aquatic species habitats and altering water channels. Careful planned strategy for sediment removal and restoration can minimize the impact of the damage. In long term, environmental gains should outweigh any losses. For instance, report from the Bureau of Reclamation showed that removing the savage Rapids Dam on the Rogue river in Oregon could generate as much as $5 million a year from fishing alone.

INTERBASIN TRANSFER OF WATER

The feasibility plan, prepared by the experts of the National Water Development Agency for linking up the east flowing rivers of the south by a canal along the coast under the national water grid programme has categorized the Mahanadi in Orissa and the Godavari in Andhra Pradesh as surplus rivers to the extent off 280 tmc ft. and 530 tmc ft. respectively, and the Krishna and Pennar in AP and the Cauvery and the Vaigai in Tamil Nadu as deficit rivers.

According to an assessment made by the Central Water Commission the country would face a shortage of 160 cubic km of water by 2050 AD with the requirement by then being 1,300 cubic km as against the present availability of 1,140 cubic km. While an estimated 1,800 cubic km of water is flowing in the rivers in a year on an average, it is being utilized only to the extent of 690 cubic km. Based on this the NWG or national perspective planning contemplated for equitable distribution and optimal utilization, envisages transfer of water from surplus basis to deficit ones, and has two components, the first Himalayan component, aiming at connecting the perennial Himalayan born rivers such as the Ganga, the Yamuna, and the Brahmaputra for the benefit of the drought prone areas in north and the second, Peninsular component, for lining up the east-flowing and west-flowing rivers in the south by two separate canals.

Under the present inter-basin plan of the NWDA which was submitted to the Union Ministry of Water Resources for its approval and follow up, including a central legislation, 395 tmc ft. of water will be diverted from the Mahanadi by a 930 km. long canal so that a quantum of 230 tmc will join the Godavari at Dowlaiswaram. The Godavari is to be linked to the Krishna by three canals the first (300 km.), connecting Ichamballi with Nagarjunasagar, carrying 580 tmc ft. but conveying 501 tmc ft. after wetting the fields en route, the second (270 km.) connecting Ichampalli with Pulichintala carrying 154 tmc ft. but conveying only 57 tmc ft. into the Krishna after meeting the requirements midway, including that of Pulichintala Project proposed by the Andhra Pradesh government, and the third, connecting, Polavaram with Vijayawada (174 km.), carrying 173 tmc ft. but conveying 117 tmc ft. in the end.

The third segment consists of three canals connecting the Krishna with the Pennar. The first canal (564 km.) is to divert 70 tmc ft. from the Alamatti dam and convey 33 tmc ft. after meeting the requirements en route, to the Maddileru stream. The second canal connecting Sri Sailam and the Pennar carries 80 tmc ft. but conveys only 70 tmc after meeting the needs en route, at Adinimmayapalli and the third, connecting Nagarjunasagar with Somasila to carry

430 tmc ft. The fourth segment has a link up canal (535 km.) between Somasila (Pennar) and Grand Anicut (Cauvery) transferrring 302 tmc ft. of water ending up as 135 tmc ft. after meeting the needs en route. Under the last segment (250 km.) about 80 tmc ft. of water of Cauvery will be diverted from the Kattalai regulator to the Vaigai in Tamil Nadu.

The NWDA has also prepared blueprints to connect the west-flowing rivers on the western coast according to which the Pamba in Kerala will be diverted from Achankovil to Vaippur in Tamil Nadu to the extent of 22 tmc ft. all to be used in the drought prone. Tirunelveli, Chidambaranath and Kamarajar districts in Tamil Nadu. The Netravati and Hemavati both in Karnataka are to be connected for 6 tmc for irrigation in Karnataka. The Bedthi and the Wardha, also in Karnataka are to be linked for transfer of 9 tmc into the Tungabhadra near Raichur.

REFERENCES

Afroz Ahmad and Singh P.P. (1991). *Environmental Impact Assessment for Sustainable Development: Chittaurgarh Irrigation Project in Outer Himalayas,* Ambio 20(7); 298-302.

Ampofo J.A and Zuta, P.C. (1995). *Schistosomiasis in the Weija Lake: A case study of the public health importance of man-made lakes,* Lakes and Reservoirs: Research and Management 1; 191-195.

Balakrishnan, M. (1995). *Damned bodyblow.* Down to Earth 6(6); 20-21.

Bandyopadhyay, J. (1990). *Tehri Dam: Challenge before the NF government,* Economic and Politcal Weekly 25(5); 243-244.

Bandyopadhyay, J. and Gyawali, D. (1994) *Himalayan Water Resources: Ecological and Political Aspects of Management,* Mountain Research and Development 14(1); 1-24.

Bandyopadhyay, J. (1995). *Sustainability of Big Dams in Himalayas,* Economic and Politcal Weekly. September 23; 2367-2370.

Bath, G.F. (1978). *The river midge plague.* Karoo Agriculture 1:37-39.

Car, M. and F.C. de Moor (1984). *The response of Vaal River Drift and Benthos to Simulium (Diptera; Nematocera) control using Bacillus thuringiensis var, israelensis (H-14).*

Onderstepoort Journal of Veterinary Research 51; 155-160.

Central Water Commission, 1990. Register of Large Dams in India, New Delhi.

Cernea, M.M. (ed.) (1991). *Involuntary Resettlement Social Research, Policy and Planning in Putting People First: Sociological Variables in Rural Development,* New York: Oxford University Press, 2nd edition 195.

Chau Kwai-cheong (1995). *The Three Gorges Project of China: Resettlement Prospects and Problems.* Ambio 24(2); 98-102.

de Moor, F.C and M. Car (1986). *A field evaluation of Bacillus thuringiensis var israelensis as a biological control agent for Simulium chutteri (Diptera: Nematocera) in the Middle Orange River.* Onderstepoort Journal of Veterinary Research 53;43-50.

de Moor, F.C. (1997). *Regulated rivers: Cause of outbreaks and solution for the control of pest blackfly;* Lakeline; 17(3); 22-23, 40-43.

Down to Earth, Asia and the Pacific 4(10); 8. October 15, 1995.

Down to Earth. *Koel Karo battles on.* 1(2), June 15, 1992.

Down to Earth. 5(14), December 15, 1996.

Fernandes, W. and Thukral, E.G (eds.). (1989). *Development, Displacement and Rehabilitation,* Indian Social Institute, New Delhi.

Fernandas, W. (1991). *Power and Powerlessness: Development Projects and Displacement of Tribals,* Social Action 41; 243-270.

Government of India (1993).Working group on Development and Welfare of Scheduled Tribes during the Eighth Five-year Plan (1990-1995).

Grant, F.C (1969). Report of a survey of endemic diseases in the environs of the Weija to assess the health implications of this new lake. Project Paper; Ghana Water and Sewerage Corporation.

Iyer, M. (1996). *The-dam sham.* Down to Earth 4(17); 38-39.

Jain, R. (1994). *Mosquitoes storm the desert.* Down to Earth 3(13); 5-7.

Khan, A.H and Miah, S. (1983). *'The Brahmaputra River Basin Development'* in Yamen M (ch ed). River Basin Development. Tycooly, Dublin.

Khattri, K.N.(1987). *Great Earthquake Seismicity Gaps and Potential for Earthquake* Disaster Along the Himalayan Plate Boundary; Technophysics,138:79-92.

Kothari, S.(1996). *Whose Nation? The Displced as Victims of Development.* Economic and Political Weekly, June 15, 1996.

Malla, S. and N.Weiland, (1993). *Seismic Safety Assessment of Concrete Dams.* Water Nepal 3(2-3); 59-70.

Mitra, A.(1995). *Development Distress,* Down to Earth, March 31; 31-35.

Morse, B. T. Berger, D.Gamble and H.Brody (1992). *Sardar Sarover: The Report of the Independent Review.* Report commissioned by the World Bank and published by Resource Futures International Inc.

Odei, M.A. (1975). *The prospects of some Water-borne diseases in the area of the proposed Weija Dam Reservoir near Accra.* Ghana Journ. Sci. 15(2); 219-224.

Odei, M.A. (1982). *Schistosomiasis in relation to water resources development.* Summary report on a survey for the distribution of vector snailes and the trematodes of economic importances which they transmit in some water bodies in Ghana Lab.Tech, Rep.100.

Palmer, R.W. (1991). *Description of the larvae of seven species of blackflies (Diptera; Simuliidae) from southern Africa, and a regional checklist of the family.* Journal of the Entomological Society of Southern Africa 54;197-219.

Plamer R.W. (1993). *Short-term impacts of the formulations of Bacillus thuringiensis var. Israelensis de Barjac and the organophosphate temephos, used in blackfly (Diptera: Simuliidae) control, on rheophilic benthic macroinvertebrates in the middle Orange River, South Africa.* South African Journal of Aquatic Sciences 19; 14-33.

Paranjpye, V. (1990). *High Dams on the Narmada: Indian Analysis of the River Valley Projects,* New Delhi: Indian National Trust for Art and Cultural Heritage (INTACH).

Rajesh, N. (1995). *Mekong's miseries.* Down to Earth 3(22); 20-21.

Rao, Malleswara, M. (1997). *Mahanadi, Godavari surplus rivers: Experts. The Hindu,* Aug. 28.

Rast, W and Holland, M. (1988). *Eutrophication of Lakes and Reservoirs. A Framework for Making Management Decisions,* Ambio 17(1); 2-12.

Reeves, R.R. and Leatherwood, S. (1994). *Dams and River Dolphins: Can They Co-exist?* Ambio 23(3); 172-175.

Sunil and Smitha, (1996). *Fishing in the Tawa Reservoir-Adivasis Struggle for Livelihood.* Economic and Political Weekly. April 6, 1996; 870-872.

Thakkar Himanshu, (1995). *Damned-despair.* Down to Earth 4(14); 16.

Venkiteswaran, K.(1997). *How dams weaken the oceans.* Science and Technology, *The Hindu,* July 7.

World Health Organization, (1993). *The Control of schistosomiasis.* Second Report of Expert Committee, WHO *Tech. Ser* 830.

SMALL HYDRO

K.K.Bhatia *
F.I.Khan **
Richa Sharma ***

INTRODUCTION : WHAT IS SMALL HYDRO

As the name implies, small hydro is smaller version of large hydro. But how to quantify the 'largeness' or 'smallness'? In terms of height of impoundment? Storage capacity? Power output? Cost of commissioning?

As yet there is no internationally accepted formal definition of small hydro though it is *generally* taken as power station/plant having output upto 5000 kW. Stations upto output of 1000 kW are often called *micro* and upto 5000 kW as *mini* hydel plants. Indeed equipment technology is available to utilize discharges as small as 200 litres/sec (0.2 cumec), heads down to 1 metre, and a power output of just 1 kW with reasonable cost ! The definitions vary from country to country. In USA even 15,000 kW is considered small hydro development while in France and some other countries 'small' means upto 3,000 kW. It must be clarfied that source of energy from sea waves, coastal tides and ocean water, are not included under

* Scientist—F & Head of Division, NIH, Roorkee.
** Assistant Professor, BITS Pilani.
*** Junior Scientist, CPET, Pondicherry University.

the umbrella of 'small hydro' eventhough hydropower is central to those concepts.

As per Central Electricity Authority and Bureau of Indian Standards, small hydropower stations are classified as follows :

a. Depending on capacity

Name	*Unit size*	*Installation*
Micro	upto 100 kW	100 kW
Mini	101 to 1000 kW	2000 kW
Small	1001 to 6000 kW	15,000 kW

b. Depending on head

Ultra low head	Below 3 metres
Low head	Less than 30 metres
Medium head	Between 30 and 75 metres
High head	Above 75 metres

In Table 4.1 the upper limit of *power generation capacity* set by different countries to define smallness of their hydro projects is given.

TABLE 4.1: UPPER LIMITS OF POWER GENERATION CAPACITIES OF 'SMALL' HYDRO UNITS SET BY VARIOUS COUNTRIES

Countries	*Limits (MW)*
UK (NFFO)	< 5
UNIDO	< 10
India	< 15
Sweden	< 15
Colombia	< 20
Australia	< 20
China	< 25
Philippines	< 50
New Zealand	< 50

Broadly small hydro schemes are of two types—one utilising small discharges but high heads and the second utilising large discharges but smaller heads. These facets also influence the nature of the power generating plants associated with the given site. In high-head units the discharges being small, the physical size of the plant required is also small. In the second type, as the discharges handled are high, the physical size of the generating unit and the power station is consequently quite high. Also for the latter type proper arrangement for entry of water and its discharge is required to be made.

The small hydro development of the first type which is confined mainly to hilly areas is characterized by relatively very simple features of works. The civil works involved comprise a small structure to divert the flow of the hill stream/river, small water conductor system such as a channel, flume or buried conduits, power house building and a small length of transmission line. In these units there is no need for substantial storage and generally run of river (water falls) is utilized. The power is generally consumed near the site of generation thus precluding requirements of long transmission lines.

In the second type, as the heads available are rather low and discharges have to be comparatively larger to be economically viable, their the development can only take place on small rivers, irrigation outlets, canal falls etc. Their power output is generally connected to the larger power grids.

A BRIEF HISTORY

As is the case of most other renewable energy sources which have gained currency during the last two decades, small hydro is not something that has been invented recently but is in fact one of the technologies mankind has been using since centuries (just as it has been using wind energy, biomass energy, geothermal energy and direct solar energy). Watermill which is colloquially known as *panchakki, Gharat, ghatta, water wheel* etc. has been employed since ages in India. It has been estimated that as many as 200,000 sites in India are suitable for installing watermills which can do work equicealent to 2,000 megawatt of power!

The first-ever small hydro unit *for generating electricity* (unlike windmills which used water power directly in getting the work done) was commissioned in India exactly a 100 years ago, in 1897, at Darjeeling. It had a capacity of 130 KW and is operational even this day! Another small hydropower unit of 4.5 MW capacity came up at Sivasamudram, in Karnataka in 1902. It had the express purpose of supplying power to the Kolar gold mines. In the pre-Independence India a substantial proportion of the than installed capacity of 508 MW of hydropower came from small and medium units. After independence the focus was on large projects leading to a total hydropower generation capacity of 21,000 MW. Of these small hydro contributed only about 500 MW.

POTENTIAL OF SMALL HYDRO IN INDIA

Some 2,000 sites have been identified in 13 states in India with a potential of generating about 5,000 megawatt (MW) of power (Table 4.2). Another 1,200 MW of potential has been identified in the 13 Himalayan states for mini hydel units of less than 3 MW capacity (Table 4.3). In addition about 10 MW is proposed to be generated using tail ends of the cooling water systems of thermal power plants (Table 4.4). Furthermore 5,000 MW potential is estimated to be available from yet-to-be identified sites.

ENGINEERING CONSIDERATIONS

Civil works

Civil works form a major part of the total cost of small hydel projects. Therefore, efforts towards reduction in the cost of civil works will play a major role in enhancing the economic viability of these projects. The main components of civil works are: diversion structure, water conductor system, desilting tank, forebay, spillway, penstock, power house, tailrace channel and protection works.

TABLE 4.2: POTENTIAL FOR SMALL HYDROPOWER UNITS IDENTIFIED IN INDIA

State	Number of sites	Capacity (MW)
Arunachal Pradesh	190	111
Bihar	110	134
Gujarat	197	157
Himachal Pradesh	298	1393
Jammu and Kashmir	131	859
Kerala	216	561
Madhya Pradesh	80	238
Maharashtra	122	68
Meghalaya	36	8
Orissa	48	28
Punjab	198	196
Uttar Pradesh	328	1128
West Bengal	69	69
Total	2023	4950

Source: Water Power and Dam Construction, 1995.

Efforts should be made to use the locally available material. The material generally used are reinforced concrete, structural steel, stone masonry brick masonry etc. R&D is going on towards the use of new materials such as ferro-cement and steel fibre reinforced concrete.

GENERATORS

Conventionally hydroelectric A.C. synchronous generators are used. The generator (rotor) should withstand turbine runaway speed i.e. speed attained on sudden load through off. Brushless excitation system generators are used in small hydro power stations which reduce maintenance costs and time. Induction generators need excitation source and as such can only operate when connected to an existing electrical system.

TABLE 4.3: NUMBER OF SITES IDENTIFIED BY UNDP-GEF FOR SMALL HYDEL UNITS IN HILLY REGIONS IN 13 INDIAN STATES

State	*Sites identified*		*Additional sites identified*	*Total sites*
	Numbers	*MW*		
North	415	370	147	562
Jammu and Kashmir	94	112	45	139
Himachal Pradesh	141	152	22	163
Uttar Pradesh	180	106	80	260
East	164	175	--	164
Sikkim	47	48	--	47
West Bengal	49	47	--	49
Bihar	68	80	--	68
North-east	550	465	90	64
Assam	26	28	--	26
Arunachal Pradesh	364	346	--	364
Meghalaya	66	22	14	80
Manipur	66	52	13	79
Nagaland	10	9	42	52
Mizoram	17	7	21	38
Tripura	1	1	--	1
Total	1129	1010	237	1366

PROTECTION, CONTROL AND MANAGEMENT OF EQUIPMENT

A major component in small hydros is for operation and management personnel. These costs can be prohibitive in microhydel. Low cost automation is, therefore, of importance if mini and micro hydels are to function economically. The unit starting and synchronizing can be manual, but emergency shut down must be fool-proof to avoid damage. Development of strategies for simple-to-use or accordingly, dependable and remote control devices for such units is required.

HYBRID SYSTEMS

Hybrid systems may be used to harness and upgrade other available renewable resources which are otherwise unutilized or under utilized.

TABLE 4.4: MINI HYDEL PROJECTS PROPOSED AT THE TAIL-ENDS OF COOLINGWATER SYSTEMS OF THERMAL POWER PLANTS

Power station	*State*	*Capacity proposed (MW)*	*Company unit involved*
Singrauli	Uttar Pradesh	3.00	NTPC
Rihand	Uttar Pradesh	1.50	-do-
Unchahar	Uttar Pradesh	0.25	-do-
Farakka	West Bengal	0.75	-do-
Korba	Madhya Pradesh	1.50	-do-
Anta	Rajasthan	0.20	-do-
Ramagundam	Andhra Pradesh	0.50	-do-
Korba - i	Madhya Pradesh	0.80	MPEB
Korba - ii	Madhya Pradesh	1.00	-do-
Satpura	Madhya Pradesh	1.00	-do-
Parichha - i	Uttar Pradesh	0.50	UPSEB
Parichha - ii	Uttar Pradesh	0.50	-do-

A major cause of low benefit-cost ratio (reported to be 1.68) of isolated small hydro plants is due to poor utilization of power (low head factor). This can be overcome by using surplus off-peak high grade energy in running hybrid systems. For example, a micro-hydel system may operate as base load plant and biomass gasification based electrical generation system as peak load plant. A typical hybrid system incorporating 300 kW micro-hydel and 200 kW biomass gasification based co-generation has come up at Kakroi (Haryana).

INCENTIVES FOR SMALL HYDRO

The Government of India (GOI), through its Ministry of Non-conventional Energy Sources (MNES) is extending multi-dimensional support to the development of mini hydels (upto 3 MW). In tune with the Government's overall thrust on liberalization of economy and private sector participation in power development, small hydro sector has been given the following fiscal incentives.

(i) Schemes involving capital up to Rs 1,000 million need to have prior clearance from the CEA, even if they are single sourced.

(ii) Schemes involving capital upto Rs 500 million need no environmental clearance from Ministry of Environment and Forests (MoEF).

(iii) Income Tax holiday for power.

(iv) Term loans through Indian Rural Energy Development Agency (IREDA) for schemes upto 25 MW.

(v) Concessional customs duty @ 20 per cent to 10 per cent for non-captive use.

For schemes upto 15 MW there is no excise duty for turbines and accelerated depreciation for income tax is under consideration (similar to other new and renewable sources of energy (NRSE) systems).

Additional incentives have been given by MINES for small hydro as follows :

For power schemes of <= 3 MW

(i) Incentives for detailed survey and investigation (DSI) 100 per cent grant-in-aid subject to certain ceilings depending upon the type of schemes.

(ii) Incentives for preparation of detailed project reports (DPRs): grant-in-aid of 50 per cent of the DPR costs subject to certain ceilings depending upon the type of schemes.

(iii) Interest subsidy scheme through financial institutions :

For hilly regions: Rs 11.2 million/MW; applicable project cost - maximum Rs 60 million/MW

For non-hilly regions: Rs 3.83 million/MW; applicable project cost: maximum Rs 40 million/MW

For schemes upto 100 KW

Capital subsidy of Rs 15,000/kW (hilly regions, North-east, and Andaman-Nicobar only)

In addition to the above fiscal incentives, MNES has advised the electricity boards of the concerned states to off-take power from renewables on concessional terms in respect of power wheeling, banking, and buy-back. Following MNES' model guide lines, nine states of India have announced their private sector policy incentive package for small hydro sector (Table4.5). These states have also identified small hydro sites for allotment to private sector for development.

TECHNOLOGIES AVAILABLE

Design of small hydro is not merely the miniaturization of larger hydropower systems—of which the technology has been advanced to near perfection. For this reason R&D on the design of small hydro units is attracting attention, with its aim at cost effectiveness coupled with suitability to the conditions prevailing at different types of sites (Abbasi & Abbasi 1999). Numerous options are available:

Turbine—propeller, Kaplan (Figure 4.1), Francis, cross-flow, or Pelton (Figure 4.2)
Governor—hydraulic, solid-state, or programmable logic controllers
Material for penstocks—steel, concrete, concrete with steel lining, rock tunnel, woodtave, open channel, high density polyethylene, or glass fibre
Civil structures—pre-fabricated material (saving construction time), or locally available material/labour
Design—modular and standardized, or customized
Equipment—off-the shelf or tailor-made
Controls—manually-operated or remotely-supervised

The list of choices could be endless.

More than 10 Indian manufacturers are already in business offering equipment and consultancy. The wide variety of technologies being used is illustrated in Table 4.5.

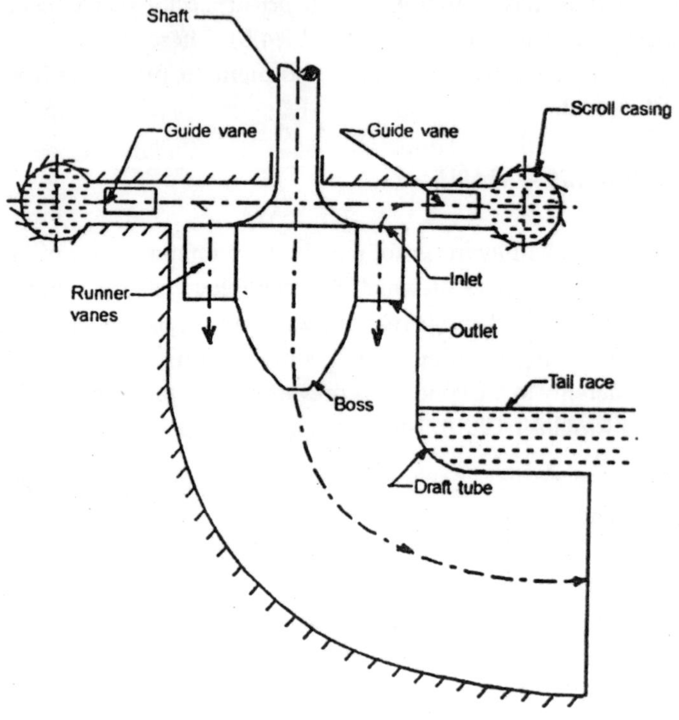

Figure 4.1: Kapalan turbine

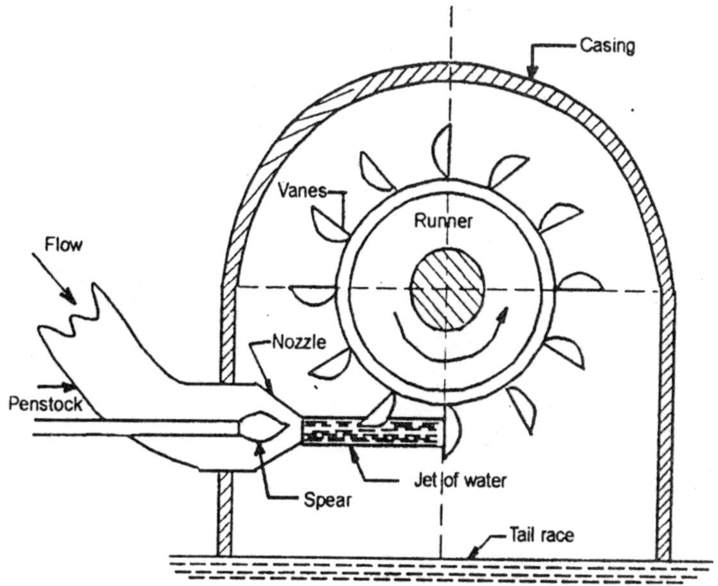

Figure 4.2: Pelton Wheel

THE THRUST IS GREAT...

From the foregoing details it is evident that India is pushing for small hydro with a great sense of dynamism, urgency *and* hope. We are going for the small in a big way!

But is the optimism wholly justified? We, personally, would be very very glad if this large scale use of small hydro proves to be the unmitigated blessing we are hoping it to be.

But we are also apprehensive. Fifty years back when India had gone for medium and large hydro it was with similar (rather higher) expectations. As mentioned in the previous chapters dams seemed to hold promise of helping us in alleviating poverty and build a strong, modern nation. Hydropower promised to give us the *cleanest* possible source of energy—no soot and flyash of thermal power plants, no lurking dangers of nuclear energy, no toxic emissions of petroleum-driven systems. Just water, falling over turbines and then flowing on to agricultural fields to get us bumper harvests! There were other 'bonuses'—fish culture, flood control, sports, recreation, tourism etc. etc. not to mention secure *water* supply alongside *power* supply for industrial growth! Hydropower protects—bigger the prettier—were icons of progress and prosparity.

But, in the 50th year of independence, we talk about large hydropower projects (and dams in general) with mixed emotions. They seemed to have harmed as much as helped us and not a few *believe* that the harm has outweighed the gain by a wide margin. Even in terms of contributing to greenhouse effect dam-based projects rival thermal power projets (Abbasi 1997, Abbasi & Mishra 1997, Abbasi et al 1997). The former do not belch out CO_2 the way thermal power plants do but nevertheless contribute to greenhouse effect by releasing large quantities of methane.

Now we are pinning great hopes on small hydro. *Small hydropower projects do not suffer from the drawbacks of medium and large projects* is the refrain. The apprehension of these authors are: How can we be so sure? The environmental impacts of <u>any</u> activity become apparent only when the activity is carried out over significantly large areas and/or on a significantly large scale. Be it biomass energy, solar energy, geothermal energy, or solid-waste energy it *looks* benign when used sporadically in small units here or there but the perspective changes drastically when any of these options are used continuously, widely, and/or on a large scale (Abbasi & Abbasi, 1997).

Would the situation be better if small hydro is put to widespread use? Let us look at the *expectations* and try to see how realistic they are and where the likely pitfalls are. Presented below, in italics, are a set of arguments culled mainly from a recent review authored by Dr B.S.K.Naidu, Executive Director of Indian Renewable Energy Development Agency, New Delhi (Naidu, 1997). The counter arguments are presented below each of the main arguments.

Small hydro is more consistent compared to other renewables like wind, solar, biomass with regard to its availability for power generation... even run-off-the river schemes can have small pondage to meet the daily peak requirement of power.

If wind energy depends on wind, and solar on sun-shine, hydro energy too *depends* on availability of water. During summer when power needs are generally higher than rest of the year, all hydropower schemes *can* suffer from loss of capacity utilization if the water level in the storage reservoir falls (which often *does* happen). A run-of-the-river scheme would be even more succeptible to water availability, whether it has facility of a storage pond or not. Shallow reservoirs and ponds—such as the one that accompany small hydro—are likely to dry up quicker than deeper reservoirs used in large hydropower projects. Lastly it is not quite correct to club biomass with wind, solar, and hydro as examples of 'inconsistent sources' because it is very easy and inexpensive to store biomass energy by just stockpiling the biomass when it is available aplenty for using it later. Water for use in generating hydropower or the wind or solar energy can not be stored away in godowns as biomass can be.

It (small hydro) needs little investment, affordable by private houses
Yes. So does wind, solar etc.

Short gestation, enabling quicker electricity and financial returns
True. But numerous conventional and non-conventional energy sources <u>also</u> have this attribute.

Small hydro is significant for off-grid, rural, in farflung isolated communities having no chances of grid extension for years to come.

Again, wind, solar, biomass and other sources are <u>equally</u> relevant in such situations.

(a) Levelized cost of generation from small hydro would be less than half that of thermal;
(b) *real capital investment is less than that of thermal (power plants);*

TABLE 4.5: TECHNOLOGIES BEING USED IN THE WORLD BANK PROJECTS FINANCED BY INDIAN RENEWABLE ENERGY DEVELOPMENT AGENCY

Name of the project	*Capacity (KW)*	*Net Head (M)*	*Civil Works*			*E & M Works*			
			Type of scheme	*Water conductor system*	*Gate/ valve*	*Turbine*	*Control*	*Power house*	*Generation vòltage(KV)*
1	2	3	4	5	6	7	8	9	10
Andhra Pradesh :									
Gundur BC-II	2 x 2150	8.5	Canal	Open	Gates	S type kaplan	Digital	RCC+S	11
		drop	channel	-do-	-do-				11
Lock in Sula	2 x 2000	12.2	-do-	-do-	-do-	-do-	-do-	-do-	3.3
Karnataka:						S type semi-	-do-	-do-	3.3
Mala Prabha	2 x 1200	10	Canal	-do-	-do-	kaplan			
				drop		-do-	-do-	RCC+M	3.3
Shiva	2 x 1500	8.3	-do-	-do-	BV	S type kaplan	-do-	RCC+S	3.3
Dhupdal	2 x 1400	4.8	Dam	Pens-	Gates	-do-	-do-	-do-	3.3
			toe	tock	+ BV	-do-	-do-	-do-	3.3
Shahpur-1	1 x 1300	6.2	Canal	-do-	-do-	-do-	-do-	-do-	3.3
				drop		-do-	-do-	-do-	3.3
Shahpur-2	1 x 1300	6.2	-do-	-do-	-do-	Francis	-do-	-do-	3.3
Shahpur-3	1 x 1300	6.2	-do-	-do-	-do-	S type kaplan	-do-	-do-	11
Shahpur-4	1 x 1300	6.2	-do-	-do-	-do-	S type semi-	-do-	-do-	3.3

{Cont.}...

1	*2*	*3*	*4*	*5*	*6*	*7*	*8*	*9*	*10*
Shahpur-5	1 x 1400	9.8	-do-	-do-	-do-	kaplan			
Anveri	2 x 750	22	-do-	-do-	Gates	-do-	-do-	-do-	3.3
Hemavathy	4 x 4000	16	Dam toe	Pens- tock	Gates + BV	-do-	-do-	-do-	3.3
Maddur	2 x 1000	13.2	Canal	-do- drop	Gates				
Mudhol	1 x 1000	13.1	-do-	-do-	-do-				
Deverebalekare	2 x 1000	10.9	Dam toe	Penstock	-do-				
Kerala:									
Western Kallar	1 x 3000 + 2 x 1000	66	R-O-R	-do-	Gates + BV	Francis	-do-	-do-	6.6
Karikkayam	2 x 7500	20	-do-	Penstock	-do-	Vertical kaplan	-do-	-do-	11
Ullungal	2 x 3500	10	-do-	Penstock	-do-	S type kaplan	-do-	RCC+M	6.6
Boothathankettu	4 x 4000	9.5	Dam toe	-do-	Gates	S type kaplan	-do-	-do-	11
Kuthungal	3 x 7000	134	R-O-R	Pressure tunnel	-do-	Francis	-do-	-do-	11
Tamil Nadu:									
Periyar Vaigai	3 x 2200	17	Canal	Open drop	-do- channel	S type semi- kaplan	-do-	-do-	11

(c) *on the basis of* project life cycle costs *in real terms... small hydro becomes several times cheaper than the thermal option...*

Even if we accept all the assumptions/presumptions that have led to the above-mentioned results *vis-a-vis* cost of small hydro compared to thermal power, it tells nothing about cost of small hydro relative to medium and large hydro. By using conventional wisdom about the economics of scale one would imagine small hydro to be significantly costlier *per kilowatt of energy generated.* Furthermore the positive attribute, that small hydro can provide power in remote and hilly localities, carries with it the logistic problems of providing support for maintenance and trouble-shooting in remote areas.

ENVIRONMENTAL IMPACTS

The argument most often put forward to support the case of small hydro is: *it is environmentally benign.*

But is it? Or would it remain so once it is used extensively? What is the *existing* evidence with which we can assume that small hydropower plants shall have no, or significantly less, adverse environmental impacts?

According to the authors it would be good if large-scale use of small hydro turns out to be free (or mostly free) from the environmental problems we have found with medium and large-scale hydropower projects. But there is little concrete evidence to give up worrying. In his review mentioned above, Naidu (1997) writes:

Small hydro projects are generally environment friendly and non-polluting. They do not involve serious deforestation, rehabilitation, and submergence. However, depending on the site and the layout of the scheme, trees may have to be removed in marginal areas. This is invariably compensated by afforestation of equivalent area or double the area of degraded forest. These projects do not involve construction of dams and therefore, generally no rehabilitation problems arise. However, in case of formation of small pondages and also any removal of habitation along the diversion canals, etc. suitable arrangements are made in consultation with the government authorities. Pollution and related negative effects are not expected in hydro projects. However the projects pass through the pollution clearance mechanisms of the state governments and also the forest clearance in case of involvement of forest lands. The effect on the downstream water supply and drainage is one of the important concerns which is addressed during the SHP design. The dry area of the stream of canal from the diversion structure till the tail race vis-a-vis *the water needs of habitat for drinking and irrigation and effects on aquatic and fish life are to be studied in detail. Necessary compensatory measures like provision of separate drinking water, irrigation lines, fish ladders, etc. are to be incorporated in the design to mitigate such impacts.*

Due to the environmentally-benign nature of these small schemes and to reduce the time involved in clearance procedures, MoEF has exempted hydel projects with an outlay of less than Rs 500 million from environmental clearance.

This passage is liberally peppered with *however*. There is optimism but the basis for it is not given. The mitigation measures—rehabilitation, compensatory afforestation, provision for fish ladders etc.-are the ones always mentioned by the proponents of larger hydropower projects as well. But we all know that their effectiveness in practice has been far below the expectations.

Of particular concern is the observation (quoted above) that, due to the environmentally benign nature of these small schemes ... MoEF has exempted hydel projects ... of less than Rs 500 million from environmental clearance ... Aren't we taking the environmentally benign nature for granted?

These authors are worried (and would be extremely glad to be proved wrong) that once a large number of small hydropower schemes become operational their adverse environmental impacts shall come to the fore.

To these authors it appear that environmental problems per kilowatt generated by small hydel power projects may not be significantly less than those we associate with larger hydel projects (Abbasi 1991, Abbasi & Abbasi 1997, Abbasi & Nipancy 1993, Abbasi et al 1989). Among the factors to consider in making a comparison are the reach of river habitat affected by the interruption of water flow, barriers to animal movement in the water, water loss from evaporation, wilderness quality of the sacrificed portion of river, and the amount of access road needed. With smaller dams, storage is an increasingly important problem and could lead to the necessity for constructing more low-head systems than anticipated. The problems of siltation and eutrophication which are common with major reservoir are likely to be even more serious with smaller and shallower bodies of water created by mini and micro projects. Lastly the emission of greenhouse gases are as likely to occur from shallow reservoirs—which are similar to paddy fields known to contribute substantially to methane emissions (Lindan and Bollich 1993, Wang et al 1993)—as from large reservoirs, if not more. All in all, the environmental impacts of smaller and dispersed hydropower projects are not likely to be insignificant. It is a moot point whether they would be as severe as of 'known devils' - large hydropower projects.

REFERENCES

Abbasi, S.A., and Abbasi, N. (1998). *Environmental impact of non-conventional energy sources,* International Journal of Energy-Environment Economics, USA, 3-1-50.

Abbasi, S.A. (1997). *Wetlands of India—ecology and threats, Vol I : endangered wetlands of peninsular India,* Discovery Publishing House, New Delhi, 279 pages.

Abbasi, S.A. and Mishra, P.K. (1997). *Wetlands of India—ecology and threats, Vol II : the ecology and the exploitation of lake Chilka,* Discovery Publishing House, New Delhi, 253 pages.

Abbasi, S.A., Bhatia, K.K.S. and Abbasi, N. (1997). *Wetlands of India—ecology and threats Vol III : the ecology and the wetlands of Kerala,* Discovery Publishing House, New Delhi, 317 pages.

Abbasi, S.A. and Abbasi, N. (1997). *Water and water pollution,* Enviromedia, Karad, 218 pages.

Abbasi, S.A. (1991). *Environmental impact of water resources projects,* Discovery Publishing House, New Delhi, 201 pages.

Abbasi, S.A. and Nipaney, P.C. (1993). *World's worst weed - control and utilization,* International Book Distributors, Dehradun, 258 pages.

Abbasi, S.A., Nipaney, P.C. and Soni, R.(1989). *Simulation of the impact of acid rain and alkaline wastewater discharge on pond biota,* International Journal of Environmental Studies (UK), 35; 97-103.

Lindan, C.W. and Bollich, P.K. (1993). *Methane emissions from Louisiana first and ratoon crop rice.* Soil Science, 156 (1), 42-48.

Naidu, B.S.K. (1997). *Small hydro in India: environment friendly alternative energy source* TERI Information Monitor on Environmental Science 1 (2); 81-93.

Wang, Z.P., Lindan, C.W., Delaune, R.D. and Partick (Jr) W.H. (1993). *Methane emission and entrapment in flooded rice soils as effected by soil properties,* Biology and fertility of soils, 16, 163-168.

5

KRISHNA, MAHANADI AND GODAVARI RIVER BASINS

THE KRISHNA RIVER BASIN

River Krishna is one of the major rivers in Southern India and has a basin draining in three states: Maharashtra, Karnataka and Andhra Pradesh. River Krishna originates at Mahabaleshwar in Satara district at an altitude of 1.4 Km above mean sea level (MSL) in the Western ghats. Average annual flow of Krishna is 67,790 million m^3. It flows in easternly direction through Satara and Sangli in Kolhapur districts of Maharashtra; Belgaum, Bijapur, and Gulbarga districts of Karnataka, and Mehbubnagar, Kurnool, Guntur and Krishna districts of Andhra Pradesh meeting the Bay of Bengal at Machalipattam. These areas are covered in a run of 1,401 Kms encompassing a drainage area of 258,948 sq Km; of which 26.8 per cent lies in Maharashtra, 43.8 per cent in Karnataka and 29.4 per cent in Andhra Pradesh. At its origin Krishna receives plentiful rainfall varying from 3,800 mm to 6350 mm. The rainfall dwindles to about 500 mm towards the plains.

Krishna has a large number of tributaries, the major ones are Koyna, Venna, Warna and Panchaganga (which meet in Maharashtra), Bhima and Ghataprabha (which meet in the Karnataka) and Tungabhadra (which meets in Andhra Pradesh).

MAJOR WATER RESOURCES PROJECTS ACROSS KRISHNA RIVER

The oldest dam across Krishna is at Khadakwasla which was completed in 1879. Of the 95 odd dams constructed in the Krishna basin so far, nearly half are earth/gravity dams. The average height above foundation of the dams is 28.76 m with the highest, 143m, occurring in the Srisailam dam. The average gross storage capacity (gsc) of the dams is 657 million m^3; the most voluminous being the Nagarjunasagar dam with a gsc of 11557.7 million m.

The salient features of the dams across Krishna and its tributaries are:

1. Khadakwasla Dam

Khadakwasla Dam is constructed across the Mutha river, one of the tributaries of Bhima river, in Maharashtra for irrigation and water supply. Salient features are:

Type	- Masonry with earth backing
Area of catchment	- 501.8 Km^2
Rainfall	- Min.40 cm; Max.635 cm
Height above lowest foundation	- 31.79 m
Length of the dam	- 373 m
Gross storage capacity	- 85,900,000 m^3
Effective storage capacity	- 56,000,000 m^3
Volume content of dam	- 730,000 m^3
Year of completion	- 1879

2. Dhupdal Weir

Dhupdal Weir is constructed on Ghataprabha river in Karnataka for flood control and power generation. Salient features are:

Area of catchment	- 2797.2 Km^2
Maximum discharge of canal	- 65.09 m/s
Year of completion	- 1894
Length of barrage/Anicut	- 2084.98 m

TABLE 5.1: KRISHNA RIVER BASIN

Sl.No.	Name of the Dam	Year of Commissioning	Height above lowest Foundation (meters)	Gross storage capacity (m^3)	Functions/I/p/ws/FC/R
1	2	3	4	5	6
1.	Khadakwasla Dam	1879	31.79	85,900,000	Irrigation and water supply
2.	Dhupdal Weir	1894			Power generation and diversion
3.	Madagamasur Tank	1908	24.4	54,630,000	Irrigation
4.	Vani Vilasa Sagar Dam	1910	43.31	8,500,000,000	Irrigation
5.	Osman Sagar Project	1920	37	3,28,640,000	Water supply and flood control
6.	Himayat Sagar Project	1926	34	216,600,000	Irrigation and water supply
7.	Bhatghar Dam	1927	57.91	672,670,000	Irrigation and water supply
8.	T.G.Hally Reservoir	1933	38.1	93,400,000	Water supply
9.	Anjanapura Tank	1936	21.33	39,760,000	Irrigation
10.	Dindi Dam	1943	24	73,900,000	Irrigation and Hydropower
11.	Tungbhadra Dam	1953	49	3,764,000,000	Irrigation and Hydropower
12.	Bhadra Dam	1953	80.36	2,023,000,000	Irrigation and Hydropower
13.	Radhanagari Dam	1954	42.68	236,810,000	Irrigation and Hydropower
14.	Bullapura Tank	1954	16.46	680,000	Irrigation
15.	Tunga Anicut	1956	18.13	-	Irrigation
16.	Prakasham Barrage	1957	4.27	-	Irrigation
17.	Rajolibunda Division Scheme	1960	-	-	Irrigation
18.	Areshankar Dam	1960	19.2	7,220,000	Irrigation
19.	Bhairavanitippa Dam	1961	20	711,253,000	Irrigation

{Cont.}...

1	2	3	4	5	6
20.	Tadavalga Tank	1961	10.8	1,840,000	Irrigation
21.	Nakhanpur Tank	1961	13.76	2,530,000	Irrigation
22.	Musi Dam	1963	30	136,144,000	Irrigation
23.	Koyna Dam	1964	103	2,797,400,000	Hydropower
24.	Basavapattana Dam	1964	14.6	1,370,000	Irrigation
25.	Dharma Reservoir	1964	20.12	22,240,000	Irrigation
26.	Vir Dam	1965	35.82	278,330,000	Hydro power and Irrigation
27.	Sulkod Tank	1965	10.98	1,340,000	Irrigation
28.	Yellur Tank	1965	15.5	420,000	Irrigation
29.	Ghod Dam	1965	29.6	216,300,000	Irrigation
30.	Hangi Tank	1965	12.81	1,410,000	Irrigation
31.	Hokarani Tank	1966	11.88	1,210,000	Irrigation
32.	Bavaleshwara Tank	1967	14.62	19,050,000	Irrigation
33.	Kurnoor Dam	1968	23.7	35,240,000	Irrigation
34.	Aigali Tank	1969	15.2	2,300,000	Irrigation
35.	Kuppagadi Tank	1969	11.27	1,840,000	Irrigation
36.	Bellikindi Tank	1970	11.9	1,110,000	Irrigation
37.	Mangalore Tank	1970	16.4	1,590,000	Irrigation
38.	Chittawadagi Tank	1971	12.05	5,690,000	Irrigation
39.	Havithinal Tank	1972	10.75	1,580,000	Irrigation
40.	Malaprabaha Dam	1973	40.23	1,068,000,000	Irrigation
41.	Panchshet Dam	1973	60.04	303,000,000	Irrigation and water supply

{Cont.}...

1	2	3	4	5	6
42.	Nagarjuna Sagar Project	1974	125	11,557,700,000	Irrigation and Hydropower
43.	Kundwan Tank-I	1974	13.05	2,170,000	Irrigation
44.	Bharatagi Tank	1975	13.1	2,800,000	Irrigation
45.	Borkhal Dam	1976	35.05	175,150,000	Irrigation
46.	Kanholi Dam	1976	21.1	22,213,000	Irrigation
47.	Dhom Dam	1977	50	382,270,000	Irrigation
48.	Hidkal Dam (Ghatprabha Project)	1977	62.48	1,444,140,000	Irrigation and Hydropower
49.	Hangnipangaon Dam	1977	14.53	45,510,000	Irrigation
50.	Ekkundi Tank	1977	11.17	1,910,000	Irrigation
51.	Balakundi Tank	1978	14.3	7,450,000	Irrigation
52.	Kolkewadi Dam	1979	64	36,220,000	Irrigation
53.	Jigagwani Tank	1979	11.93	4,040,000	Irrigation
54.	Narihalla Reservoir	1979	31	22,940,000	Irrigation and Water Supply
55.	Kadliwadi Tank	1980	10.62	2,450,000	Irrigation
56.	Hulikunta Tank	1980	20.27	2,720,000	Irrigation
57.	Ujjani Dam	1981	56	3,140,000,000	Irrigation
58.	Bommanahalli Tank	1981	12.7	2,540,000	Irrigation
59.	Kulgi Aheri Tank	1981	13.53	1,430,000	Irrigation
60.	Katral Tank	1981	1.22	2,880,000	Irrigation
61.	Chikkangaon Tank	1981	15.95	1,070,000	Irrigation
62.	Itagi Dam	1982	15.25	860,000	Irrigation

{Cont.}...

1	2	3	4	5	6
63.	Kanvikervinkoppa Tank	1982	16.77	430,000	Irrigation
64.	Narayanpur Dam	1982	29.72	1,071,000,000	Irrigation
65.	Gowdahally Tank	1983	13.73	2,390,000	Irrigation
66.	Manikdho Dam	1984	51.8	308,060,000	Irrigation and Hydropower
67.	Sri Sailam Hydro Electric Project	1984	143	8,722,000,000	Hydropower
68.	New Irrigation Tank at Hosahalli	1985	16.76	3,240,000	Irrigation
69.	Biggerahalla Tank	1986	15.16	630,000	Irrigation
70.	Dinsi Tank	1986	17.1	930,000	Irrigation
71.	Parunde Dam	U/C	20.02	1,020,000	Irrigation
72.	Chaskman Dam	U/C	46.28	318,170,000	Irrigation and Hydropower
73.	Nira Deodhar Dam	U/C	46.15	156,060,000	Irrigation
74.	Dimbhe Dam	U/C	70.1	382,220,000	Irrigation and Hydropower
75.	Pimpalgaon Dam	U/C	14.53	12,660,000	Irrigation
76.	Changliar Tank	U/C	14.79	1,800,000	Irrigation
77.	Ankarmanhal Tank	U/C	16.83	1,540,000	Irrigation
78.	Gobbur Tank	U/C	10.3	3,020,000	Irrigation
79.	Upper Hinala Tank	U/C	18.27	6,500,000	Irrigation
80.	Aherijumbagi Dam	U/C	10.29	1,728,000	Irrigation
81.	Krishyal Tank	–	10.92	1,610,000	Irrigation
82.	Mukherlhihal Tank	–	10.41	1,450,000	Irrigation

{Cont.}...

1	2	3	4	5	6
83.	Nagathan Tank	–	10.67	2,770,000	Irrigation
84.	Ragasamudra Tank	–	22.7	5,000,000	Irrigation
85.	Ronihal Tank	–	13.1	1,350,000	Irrigation
86.	Kanher Dam (Krishna Irrigation Project)	U/C	50.34	286,000,000	
87.	Almatti Dam	U/C	48.8	6,430,000,000	Irrigation and Hydropower
88.	Hippargi Barrage	U/C	26	170,000,000	Irrigation
89.	New Irrigation Tank at Huvinabhevi	–	11	1,830,000	Irrigation
90.	Warna Dam	U/C	88.8	963,970,000	Irrigation
91.	Warasgaon Dam	–	69	30,400,000	Irrigation
92.	Vir Baji Pasalkar	U/C	27.2	374,000,000	Irrigation

3. Madagamasur Tank

Madagamasur tank is constructed across the river Kumudavathy near Hirekerur in Karnataka mainly for irrigation purposes. The salient features of the tank are:

Type	- Earthen
Height above lowest foundation	- 24.4 m
Length of the dam	- 564 m
Gross storage capacity	- 54,630,000 m^3
Year of completion	- 1908

4. Vani Vilasa Sagar Dam

The Vani Vilasa Sagar Dam is constructed across the Vedavati river, one of the tributaries of Tungabhadra river in Karnataka for irrigation. Its salient features are:

Type	- Masonry
Area of catchment	- 5,374 Km^2
Rainfall	- 61 cm
Height above lowest foundation	- 43.31 m
Length of the top of the dam	- 406 m
Gross storage capacity	- 850,000,000 m^3
Effective storage capacity	- 797,100,000 m^3
Year of completion	- 1910

5. Osman Sagar Project

The Osman Sagar Project is constructed across the Musi river in Andhra Pradesh for water supply and flood control. Salient features are:

Type	- Gravity dam
Height above lowest foundation	- 37 m
Length of crest	- 1,920 m.
Gross storage capacity	- 328,640,000 m^3
Effective storage capacity	- 317,790,000 m^3
Year of completion	- 1920

6. Himayat Sagar Project

The Himayat Sagar Project is constructed in Andhra Pradesh across Issa river, one of the tributaries of Krishna. It is a dual purpose dam meant for irrigation and water supply. Salient features are:

Type	- Gravity dam
Gross storage capacity	- 216,600,000 m^3
Effective storage capacity	- 204,300,000 m^3
Height above lowest foundation	- 34 m
Length of the dam	- 1,402 m
Year of completion	- 1926

7. Bhatghar Dam

Bhatghar Dam is constructed across the Yelwandi river, sub-river of Nira in Krishna basin and is a dual purpose project for power generation and irrigation. Its salient features are:

Type	- Masonry gravity
Rainfall	- Min.100cm., Max., 650 cm
Area of catchment	- 332 Km^2
Height above lowest foundation	- 57.91 m
Length of the dam	- 1,626 m
Volume content of the dam	- 672,000 m^3
Gross storage capacity	- 672,670,000 m^3
Live storage capacity	- 665,590,000 m^3
Year of completion	- 1927

8. T.G. Hally Reservoir

T.G. Hally reservoir is constructed across the river Kumudavath near Bangalore in Karnataka. Its salient features are:

Type	- Gravity and masonry
Height above lowest foundation	- 38.1 m
Length of the dam	- 448.06 m
Gross storage capacity	- 93,400,000 m^3
Effective storage capacity	- 90,610,000 m^3
Year of completion	- 1933

9. Anjanapura tank

Anjanapura Tank is constructed across the river Kumudavathy near Shimoga in Karnataka. Salient features are:

Type	- Earthen
Height above lowest foundation	- 21.33 m
Length of the dam	- 1,794 m
Gross storage capacity	- 39,760,000 m^3
Effective storage capacity	- 27,360,000 m^3
Volume content of the dam	- 777,700 m^3
Year of completion	- 1936

10. Dindi Dam

Dindi Dam is constructed across the river Dindi near Mahaboob Nagar city in Andhra Pradesh for irrigation purpose. Salient features of the dam are:

Type	- Gravity and masonry
Height above lowest foundation	- 24 m
Length of the dam	- 2,329 m
Gross storage capacity	- 73,900,000 m^3
Effective storage capacity	- 68,510,000 m^3
Year of completion	- 1943

11. Tungabhadra Dam

River Tungabhadra is a major river of Karnataka state. The river is formed by the confluence of the rivers, Tunga and Bhadra in Shimoga district, after originating in the picturesque and dense forests of Western Ghats. The Tungabhadra Project is a dual purpose project for power as well as irrigation. Salient features are:

Type	- Masonry Dam with central spillway section, Earthen dam and composite dam on the left side.
Area of catchment	- 27,853 Km^2
Height above lowest foundation	- 49 m

Gross storage capacity	- 3,764,000,000 m^3
Live storage capacity	- 3,307,000,000 m^3
Length of the dam	- 701 m
Volume content of the Dam	- 1,156,000 m^3
Year of completion	- 1953

12. Bhadra Dam

Bhadra dam is built across the Bhadra river and serves the dual purpose of irrigation and hydropower generation. Salient features are:

Type	- Composite dam.
Area of catchment	- 1,968 Km
Gross storage capacity	- 2,023,000,000 m^3
Live storage capacity	- 1,785,000,000 m^3
Length of the top of the dam	- 440.3 m
Height above lowest foundation	- 80.63 m
Volume content of the dam	- 682,420 m
Year of completion	- 1953.

13. Radhanagari Dam

Radhanagari dam is constructed across one of the tributaries of Krishna, Bhogawati in Maharashtra. This is a dual purpose project meant for irrigation and hydropower generation. Salient features are:

Type	- Gravity
Area of catchment	- 110 Km^2
Rainfall	- 635 cm to 760 cm
Height above lowest foundation	- 42.68 m
Length of the dam	- 1,143 m
Gross storage capacity	- 236,810,000 m^3
Effective storage capacity	- 220,000,000 m^3
Total volume content	- 368,000 m^3
Year of completion	- 1954

14. Bullapura Tank

Bullapura tank is constructed across the river Krishna in Karnataka for irrigation purpose. Its salient features are:

Type	- Earthen
Height above lowest foundation	- 16.46 m.
Length of the dam	- 116.5 m
Gross storage capacity	- 680,000 m^3
Effective storage capacity	- 640,000 m^3
Year of completion	- 195 m

15. Tunga Anicut

Tunga Anicut is constructed across the river Tunga in Karnataka for irrigation. Salient features are:

Type	- Gravity dam
Area of catchment	- 2,321 Km^2
Height above lowest foundation	- 18.13 m
Maximum discharge capacity of spillways	- 7,358 m^3/s
Length of the dam	- 543.75 m
Year of completion	- 1956

16. Prakasham Barrage

Location	- Near Vijayawada city
Type	- Concrete construction
Area of catchment	- 251,358 Km
Full reservoir level	- 23.52 m
Length of barrage	- 1,036 m
Height above lowest foundation	- 4.27 m
Year of completion	- 1957

17. Rajolibunda Anicut

Rajolibunda Diversion Scheme consists of the construction of Rajolibunda Anicut in the river Tungabhadra for irrigation. Salient features are:

Area of catchment - 35.320 Km^2
Mean annual rainfall in the catchment - 105.1 cm
Maximum discharge of canal - 23.79 m/s
Year of completion - 1960

18. Areshankar Dam

Areshankar dam is constructed across one of the tributaries of Krishna in Karnataka near Almatti for irrigation. Salient features are:

Type - Gravity
Height above lowest foundation - 19.2 m
Length of crest - 1,188 m
Gross storage capacity - 7,220,000 m^3
Year of completion - 1960
Ultimate benefit area - 1,240 hectares

19. Bhairavanitippa Dam

Bhairavanitippa dam is constructed across the river Hagari-near Anantapur in Andhra Pradesh for the purpose of irrigation. The salient features of the dam are:

Type - Gravity/Earthen
Height above lowest foundation - 20 m
Length of the dam - 2,234 m
Gross storage capacity - 711,253,000 m^3
Effective storage capacity - 65,270,000 m^3
Year of completion - 1961

20. Tadavalga Tank

Tadavalga tank is constructed across the river Bhima near Indi in Karnataka for irrigation purpose. The salient features of the tank are:

Type - Earthen dam
Height above lowest foundation - 10.8 m
Length of the dam - 1,253 m

Gross storage capacity - 1,840,000 m^3
Effective storage capacity - 1,800,000 m^3
Volume content of dam - 101,000 m^3
Year of completion - 1961

21. Nakhanpur Tank

Nakhanpur tank is constructed across Bhima river near Bijapur in Karnataka for irrigation purpose. Its salient features are:

Type -
Height above lowest foundation - 13.76 m
Length of the dam - 951 m
Gross storage capacity - 2,530,000 m^3
Effective storage capacity - 2,500,000 m^3
Volume content of dam - 151,000 m^3
Year of completion - 1961

22. Musi Dam

Musi dam is constructed across the Musi river, one of the tributaries of Krishna in Andhra Pradesh for irrigation. Salient features are:

Type - Gravity dam
Gross storage capacity - 136,144,000 m^3
Height above lowest foundation - 30 m
Length of the dam - 463 m
Volume content of dam - 220,000 m^3
Ultimate benefit area - 240 Hectares
Year of completion - 1963

23. Koyna Dam

Koyna Hydro Electric Project—Stage I and II consists of the construction of Koyna Dam in Maharashtra across the river Koyna, one of the tributaries of Krishna for Hydropower generation. Salient features are:

Type - Gravity
Rainfall - 389.4 cm
Area of catchment - 891 Km

Gross storage capacity - 2,797,400,000 m^3
Effective storage capacity - 2,640,000,000 m^3
Height above lowest foundation - 103 m
Length at the top of the dam - 805 m
Volume content of dam - 1,555,000 m^3
Year of completion - 1964

24. Basavapattana Dam

Basavapattana dam is constructed across the river Ghataprabha, one of the tributaries of Krishna in Karnataka mainly for irrigation purpose. The salient features are:

Type - Earthen
Height above lowest foundation - 14.6 m
Length of the dam - 90 m
Gross storage capacity - 1,370,000 m^3
Effective storage capacity - 1,200,000 m^3
Volume content of dam - 27,230 m^3
Year of completion - 1964

25. Dharma Reservoir

Dharma reservoir is built across river Dharma near Hanagal in Karnataka for irrigation purpose. The salient features are:

Type - Earthen
Height above lowest foundation - 20.12 m
Length of the dam - 1448.2 m
Gross storage capacity - 22,240,000 m^3
Effective storage capacity - 22,240,000 m^3
Year of completion - 1964

26. Vir Dam

Vir Dam is constructed across Nira river one of the tributaries of Bhima river present in Maharashtra. This is a dual purpose project for hydro power generation as well as irrigation. Salient features are:

Type - Earth-cum-Gravity

Rainfall - 107 cm
Area of catchment - 1,756 Km^2
Gross storage capacity - 278,330,000 m^3
Effective storage capacity - 266,250,000 m^3
Height above lowest foundation - 35.82 m
Length of the dam - 3503 m
Volume content of the dam - 1,770,000 m^3
Year of completion - 1965

27. Sulkod Dam

Sulkod dam is constructed across Krishna river near B.Bagewadi, in Karnataka for irrigation purpose. The salient features are:

Type - Earthen
Height above lowest foundation - 10.98 m
Length of the dam - 890m
Gross storage capacity - 1,340,000 m^3
Effective storage capacity - 900,000 m^3
Volume of the dam - 99,430 m^3
Year of completion - 1965

28. Yellur Tank

Yellur tank is constructed across the river Krishna near Belgaum in Karnataka for irrigation purpose. Salient feature of the tank are:

Type - Earthen
Height above lowest foundation - 15.5 m
Length of the dam - 393 m
Gross storage capacity - 420,000 m^3
Effective storage capacity - 380,000 m^3
Volume content of the dam - 95,220 m^3
Year of completion - 1965

29. Ghod Dam

The Ghod dam is constructed across one of the tributaries of Bhima river, the Ghod river in Maharashtra for irrigation.

Type - Earthen dam

Height above lowest foundation	- 29.6 m
Length of the dam	- 2,519 m
Gross storage capacity	- 216,600,000 m^3
Effective storage capacity	- 154,800,000 m^3
Volume content of dam	- 1,190,000 m^3
Year of completion	- 1965

30. Hangi Dam

Hangi dam is built across Bhima river near Sindagi in Karnataka for irrigation purpose. The main features of the dam are:

Type	- Earthen
Height above lowest foundation	- 12.81 m
Length of the dam	- 785 m
Gross storage capacity	- 1,410,000 m^3
Effective storage capacity	- 1,400,000 m^3
Volume content of the dam	- 153,880 m^3
Year of completion	- 1965

31. Hokarani tank

Hokarani tank is constructed across Krishna river near Muddebihal city in Karnataka for irrigation purpose. The salient features of the tank are:

Type	- Earthen
Height above lowest foundation	- 11.88 m
Length of the dam	- 876.9 m
Gross storage capacity	- 1,210,000 m^3
Effective storage capacity	- 1,100,000 m^3
Volume content of the dam	- 95,720 m^3
Year of completion	- 1966

32. Bavaleshwara Tank

Bavaleshwara tank is constructed across the river Bhima in Karnataka for irrigation purpose. Its salient features are:

Type	- Earthen
Height above lowest foundation	- 14.62 m

Length of the dam	- 1,207 m
Gross storage capacity	- 19,050,000 m^3
Effective storage capacity	- 1,300,000 m^3
Volume content of the dam	- 197,000 m^3
Year of completion	- 1967

33. Kurnoor Dam

Kurnoor dam is constructed across the river Bori in Maharashtra near Osmanabad for irrigation. Salient features are:

Type	- Earthen dam
Height above lowest foundation	- 23.7 m
Length of the dam	- 1,206 m
Ultimate benefit area	- 3,640 Hectares
Gross storage capacity	- 35,240,000 m^3
Effective storage capacity	- 32,670,000 m^3
Volume content of the dam	- 450,000 m^3
Year of completion	- 1968

34. Aigali Tank

Aigali tank is constructed across the river Krishna near Athani in Karnataka for irrigation purpose. The salient features of the tank are:

Type	- Earthen
Height above lowest foundation	- 15.2 m
Length of the dam	- 526.5 m
Gross storage capacity	- 2,300,000 m^3
Effective storage capacity	- 1,300,000 m^3
Volume content of the dam	- 108,970 m^3
Year of completion	- 1969

35. Kuppagadi Tank

Kuppagadi tank is constructed across Krishna river, in Karnataka mainly for irrigation purpose. The salient featues are:

Type	- Earthen
Height above lowest foundation	- 11.27 m

Length of the dam - 969 m
Gross storage capacity - 1,840,000 m^3
Effective storage capacity - 1,600,000 m^3
Volume content of the dam - 71,700 m^3
Year of completion - 1969

36. Bellikindi Tank

Bellikindi tank is constructed across the river Malaprabha, one of the tributaries of Krishna river in Karnataka. The main purpose of the tank is to assist in irrigation. Its salient features are:

Type - Earthen
Height above lowest foundation - 11.9 m
Length of the dam - 486 m
Gross storage capacity - 1,110,000 m^3
Volume content of the dam - 98,410 m^3
Year of completion - 1970

37. Mangalore Tank

Mangalore tank is constructed across Krishna river near Bagalkat city in Karnataka mainly for irrigation purpose. Its salient feature are:

Type - Earthen
Height above lowest foundation - 10.4 m
Length of the dam - 124 m
Gross storage capacity - 1,590,000 m^3
Effective storage capacity - 1,300,000 m^3
Volume content of the dam - 30,210 m^3
Year of completion - 1970

38. Chittawadagi Tank

Chittawadagi tank is constructed across the river Mala prabha near Hunagund in Karnataka. The purpose of the tank is to assist in irrigation. Salient features of the tank are:

Type - Earthen
Height above lowest foundation - 12.05 m

Length of the dam - 1,660 m
Gross storage capacity - 5,690,000 m^3
Effective storage capacity - 5,100,000 m^3
Volume content of the dam - 155,970 m^3
Year of completion - 1971

39. Havithinal Tank

Havithinal tank is constructed across Bhima river near Bijapur city in Karnataka for irrigation purpose. Main characteristics of the tank are:

Type - Earthen
Height above lowest foundation - 10.75 m
Length of the dam - 739.1 m
Gross storage capacity - 1,580,000 m^3
Effective storage capacity - 1,200,000 m^3
Volume content of the dam - 10,500 m^3
Year of completion - 1972

40. Malaprabha Dam

River Malaprabha is a tributary of Krishna basin. Malaprabha dam meant for irrigation is across this river. Salient features are:

Type - Straight gravity masonry dam.
Rainfall - Min 51 cm, Max 508 cm.
Area of catchment - 2,176 Km^2
Gross storage capacity - 1,068,000,000 m^3
Live storage capacity - 866,600,000 m^3
Year of completion - 1973
Height above lowest foundation - 40.23 m
Length of the dam - 154.33 m

41. Panshet Dam

Panshet Dam is constructed across a local stream in Maharashtra near Poona. It is a dual purpose dam for irrigation and water supply. Salient features are:

Type - Earthen dam

Gross storage capacity	- 303,000,000 m^3
Effective storage capacity	- 256,000,000 m^3
Volume content of the dam	- 2,061,000 m^3
Height above lowest foundation	- 60.04 m
Length of the dam	- 765 m
Year of completion	- 1973

42. Nagarjunasagar Dam

Nagarjunasagar Dam is meant for both irrigation and hydropower generation. Its salient features are:

Type	- Earth-cum-gravity
Area of catchment	- 215,192 Km^2
Gross storage capacity	- 11,557,700,000 m^3
Live storage capacity	- 6,919,776,000 m^3
Irrigable area	- 0.81 million hectares.
Height above lowest foundation	- 125 m
Length of the dam	- 4,865 m
Volume content of the dam	- 7,960,000 m^3
Year of completion	- 1974

43. Kundwan Tank-I

Kundwan tank-I is constructed across the river Bhima near Indi city, in Karnataka to assist in Irrigation. Salient features of the tank are:

Type	- Earthen
Height above lowest foundation	- 13.05 m
Length of the dam	- 1137 m
Gross storage capacity	- 2,170,000 m^3
Effective storage capacity	- 1,700,000 m^3
Volume content of dam	- 104,000 m^3
Year of completion	- 1974

44. Bharatagi Tank

Bharatagi tank is built across the river Bhima near B.Bagewadi city in Karnataka for irrigation purpose. The main features of the tank are:

Type	- Earthen
Height above lowest foundation	- 13.1 m
Length of the dam	- 1,164.28 m
Gross storage capacity	- 2,800,000 m^3
Effective storage capacity	- 2,200,000 m^3
Volume content of dam	- 78,620 m^3
Year of completion	- 1975

45. Borkhal Dam

This is the second dam across Krishna river at Borkhal in Satara district. Its salient features are:

Type	- Earthen Dam in the main gorge and masonry spillways
Gross storage capacity	- 175,150,000 m^3
Live storage capacity	- 129,520,000 m^3
Height above lowest foundation	- 35.05 m
Length at the top of the dam	- 3341.8 m
Benefits of Krishna projects	- Irrigation 70,256 ha
Date of completion	- May 1976

46. Kanholi Dam

Kanholi Dam is constructed across Krishna river near Nagpur in Maharashtra to assist in irrigation. Salient features of the dam are:

Type	- Earthen
Height above lowest foundation	- 21.1 m
Length of the dam	- 1,375 m
Gross storage capacity	- 22,213,000 m^3
Effective storage capacity	- 20,485,000 m^3
Volume content of dam	- 115,300 m^3
Year of completion	- 1976

47. Dhom Dam

The first point from its origin where Krishna has been dammed is at Dhom in Wai Taluka in Satara District. Dhom is just 25 km from the source of Krishna and was commissioned in 1978. Salient features are:

Type	- Earthen Dam in the main gorge and masonry
Rainfall	- Min 101 cm, Max 635 cm
Area of catchment	- 217.56 Km^2
Gross storage capacity	- 382,270,000 m^3
Live storage capacity	- 331,100,000 m^3
Maximum Height	- 50 m
Length of the dam	- 2,478 m
Volume content of the dam	- 6,335,000 m^3
Year of completion	- 1977

48. Ghataprabha Project

The Ghataprabha project consists of the construction of Hidkal Dam across the river Ghataprabha one of the tributaries of Krishna in Karnataka. This project is a dual purpose one for power generation as well as irrigation. Salient features are:

Type	- Composite dam
Area of catchment	- 1,412 Km^2
Gross storage capacity	- 1,444,140,000 m^3
Effective storage capacity	- 1,316,720,000 m^3
Height above lowest foundation	- 62.48 m
Volume content of dam	- 140,720 m^3
Length of the dam	- 44.81 m
Year of completion	- 1977

49. Hingnipangaon Dam

Hingnipangaon dam is built across the river Bhagawat near Borshi in Maharashtra for irrigation. Salient features of the dam are:

Type	- Earthern
Height above lowest foundation	- 21.87 m
Length of the dam	- 2,193 m
Gross storage capacity	- 45,510,000 m^3

Effective storage capacity - 31,970,000 m^3
Volume content of dam - 740,000 m^3
Year of completion - 1977

50. Ekkundi Tank

Ekkundi tank is built across the river Krishna near B.Bagewadi city in Karnataka for irrigation. Main characteristics of the tank are:

Type - Earthen
Height above lowest foundation - 11.17 m
Length of the dam - 990 m
Gross storage capacity - 1,910,000 m^3
Effective storage capacity - 1,700,000 m^3
Volume content of the dam - 82,280 m^3
Year of completion - 1977

51. Balakundi Tank

Balakundi tank is constructed across the river Malaprabha near Hunagund in Karnataka for irrigation. Salient features of the tank are:

Type - Earthen
Height above lowest foundation - 14.3 m
Length of the dam - 1,687 m
Gross storage capacity - 7,450,000 m^3
Effective storage capacity - 6,400,000 m^3
Volume content of the dam - 236,640 m^3
Year of completion - 1978

52. Kolkewadi Dam

Koyna Hydro Electric Project-Stage III consists of the construction of Kolkewadi Dam across Boladwadi stream in Maharashtra for hydropower generation. Salient features are:

Type - Gravity
Area of catchment - 25.38 Km^2
Gross storage capacity - 36,220,000 m^3

Effective storage capacity - 11,220,000 m³
Height above lowest foundation - 64 m
Length at the top of the dam - 492 m
Volume content of dam - 576,000 m³
Year of completion - 1979

53. Jigagwani Tank

Jigagwani tank is built across Bhima river near Sindagi city in Karnataka for irrigation. Main characteristics of the tank are:

Type - Earthen
Height above lowest foundation - 11.93 m
Length of the dam - 150.4 m
Gross storage capacity - 4,040,000 m³
Effective storage capacity - 3,800,000 m³
Volume content of the dam - 14,590 m³
Year of completion - 1979

54. Narihalla Reservoir

The Narihalla Reservoir is a dual purpose project for irrigation and water supply. It is constructed across the Narihalla river which is a tributary of Tungabhadra. Salient features are:

Type - Earth dam
Area of catchment - 429 Km²
Gross storage capacity - 22,940,000 m³
Live storage capacity - 20,870,000 m³
Height above lowest foundation - 31 m
Length of the dam - 55.47 m
Year of completion - 1979

55. Kadliwadi Tank

Kadliwadi tank is constructed across Bhima river near Sindagi city in Karnataka for irrigation. Salient features of the tank are:

Type - Earthen
Height above lowest foundation - 10.62 m
Length of the dam - 1210 m

Gross storage capacity - 2,450,000 m^3
Effective storage capacity - 2,200,000 m^3
Volume content of the dam - 85,000 m^3
Year of completion - 1978

56. Hulikunta Tank

Hulikunta tank is constructed across Narihalla river near Sandur in Karnataka for irrigation. The salient features are:

Type - Earthen
Height above lowest foundation - 20.27 m
Length of the dam - 416 m
Gross storage capacity - 2,720,000 m^3
Effective storage capacity - 2,570,000 m^3
Volume content of the dam - 159,843 m^3
Year of completion - 1980

57. Ujjani Dam

In Maharashtra the Ujjani Dam is constructed across the Bhima river for irrigation purpose. Salient features are:

Type - Earthen-Gravity dam
Rainfall - 69 cm
Area of catchment - 14,850 Km^2
Gross storage capacity - 3,140,000,000 m^3
Effective storage capacity - 1,440,000,000 m^3
Height above lowest foundation - 56 m
Length of crest - 574 m
Length of the dam - 2,534 m
Volume content of the dam - 1,793,000 m^3
Year of completion - 1981

58. Bommanahalli Tank

Bommanahalli tank is built across Krishna river near B.Bagewadi in Karnataka for irrigation purpose. Salient features of the tank are:

Type - Earthen
Height above lowest foundation - 12.7 m

Length of the dam - 904 m
Gross storage capacity - 2,540,000 m^3
Effective storage capacity - 2,000,000 m^3
Volume content of the dam - 59,500 m^3
Year of completion - 1981

59. Kulgi Aheri Tank

Kulgi Aheri tank is constructed across river Bhima near Bijapur in Karnataka for irrigation. Salient features of the tank are:

Type - Earthen
Height above lowest foundation - 13.53 m
Length of the dam - 583 m
Gross storage capacity - 1,430,000 m^3
Effective storage capacity - 1,300,000 m^3
Volume content of the dam - 34,950 m^3
Year of completion - 1981

60. Katral Tank

Katral tank is built on river Bhima near Bijapur in Karnataka with the main purpose of assisting in irrigation. Salient features of the tank are:

Type - Earthen
Height above lowest foundation - 1.22 m
Length of the dam - 1,430 m
Gross storage capacity - 2,880,000 m^3
Effective storage capacity - 2,200,000 m^3
Year of completion - 1981

61. Chikkangaon Tank

Chikkangaon tank is built across Bhima river near Basava kalyam in Karnataka to assist in irrigation. The salient features of the tank are:

Type - Earthen dam
Height above lowest foundation - 15.95 m
Length of the tank - 357.76 m^3

Gross storage capacity	- 1,070,000 m^3
Effective storage capacity	- 940,000 m^3
Volume content of tank	- 79,000 m^3
Year of completion	- 1981

62. Itagi dam

Itagi dam is constructed across Krishna river near Khanapur in Karnataka for irrigation. Salient features of thedam are:

Type	- Earthen
Height above lowest foundation	- 15.25 m
Length of the dam	- 701.4 m
Gross storage capacity	- 860,000 m^3
Effective storage capacity	- 860,000 m^3
Volume content of the dam	- 126,000 m^3
Year of completion	- 1982

63. Kanvikervinkoppa Tank

Kanvikervinkoppa tank is built acorss Krishna river near Belgaum city in Karnataka for irrigation. Main features of the tank are:

Type	- Earthen
Height above lowest foundation	- 16.77 m
Length of the tank	- 498 m
Gross storage capacity	- 430,000 m^3
Effective storage capacity	- 430,000 m^3
Volume content of tank	- 128,900 m^3
Year of completion	- 1982

64. Narayanpur Dam

Type	- Masonry in gorge and earth in flanks
Area of catchment	- 47,850 Km^2
Irrigable area	- 5,82,739 Hectares.
Gross storage capacity	- 1,071,000,000 m^3
Live storage capacity	- 868,000,000 m^3
Height above lowest foundation	- 29.72 m
Length of the dam	- 10,637.52 m

Volume content of dam	- 2,050,000 m^3
Year of completion	- 1982

65. Gowdahally Tank

Gowdahally tank is built across K.K. Halla river near Mysore in Karnataka for irrigation. Main characteristics of the tank are:

Type	- Earthen
Height above lowest foundation	- 13.73 m
Length of the tank	- 731.5 m
Gross storage capacity	- 2,390,000 m^3
Effective storage capacity	- 2,330,000 m^3
Volume content of tank	- 270,400 m^3
Year of completion	- 1983

66. Manikdoh Dam

Manikdoh dam is constructed across the river Kukadi, one of the tributaries of Bhima river in Maharashtra, for irrigation and hydropower generation. Salient features are:

Type	- Gravity
Gross storage capacity	- 308,060,000 m^3
Effective storage capacity	- 283,070,000 m^3
Height above lowest foundation	- 51.8 m
Length of the dam	- 930 m
Volume content of dam	- 596,000 m^3
Year of completion	- 1984

67. Shrishailam Dam

Shrishailam project is for hydropower generation. Its salient features are:

Type	- Straight gravity dam in stone masonry and concrete
Area of catchment	- 206,242 Km^2
Gross storage capacity	- 8,722,000,000 m^3
Live storage capacity	- 5,974,845,000 m^3
Height above lowest foundation	- 143 m
Length of the dam	- 512 m

Volume content of the dam - 1,953,000 m^3
Year of completion - 1984

68. Hosahalli Irrigation Tank

New Irrigation tank at Hosahalli is constructed across the tributary of Tungabhadra for irrigation in Karnataka. Salient features are:

Type - Earthen
Gross storage capacity - 3,240,000 m^3
Effective storage capacity - 2,940,000 m^3
Volume content of dam - 436,840 m^3
Height above lowest foundation - 16.76 m
Length of crest - 532 m
Length of the dam - 868.68 m
Year of completion - 1985

69. Biggerahalla Tank

Biggerahalla tank is constructed across the river Tungabhadra near Chikkamagalore city in Karnataka for the purpose of irrigation. Salient features of the tank are:

Type - Earthen
Height above lowest foundation - 15.16 m
Length of the tank - 450 m
Gross storage capacity - 630,000 m^3
Effective storage capacity - 5,80,000 m^3
Year of completion - 1986

70. Dinsi Tank

Dinsi tank is built across Krishna river near Gulbarga city in Karnataka to assist in irrigation. The main features of the tank are:

Type - Earthen
Height above lowest foundation - 17.1 m
Length of the tank - 360 m
Gross storage capacity - 930,000 m^3
Effective storage capacity - 840,000 m^3
Volume content of the tank - 80,050 m^3

Year of completion	- 1986

71. Parunde Dam

Parunde dam is being constructed across Nira river near Junnar in Maharashtra to assist in irrigation. Main features of the dam are:

Type	- Earthen
Height above lowest foundation	- 20.02 m
Length of the dam	- 345 m
Gross storage capacity	- 1,020,000 m^3
Effective storage capacity	- 880,000 m^3
Year of completion	- Under construction

72. Chaskman Dam

Chaskman dam is being constructed across the river Bhima near Khed in Maharashtra. It has dual purpose of assisting in irrigation and hydropower generation. Salient features of the dam are:

Type	- Earthen/Gravity
Height above lowest foundation	- 46.28 m
Length of the dam	- 1045 m
Gross storage capacity	- 318,170,000 m^3
Effective storage capacity	- 210,990,000 m^3
Volume content of dam	- 2,903,000 m^3
Year of completion	- Under construction

73. Nira Deodhar Dam

Nira Deodhar dam is being built across the river Nira near Bher in Maharashtra for irrigation and hydropower generation. Salient features of the dam are:

Type	- Earthen
Height above lowest foundation	- 46.15 m
Length of the dam	- 1,608 m
Gross storage capacity	- 1,560,600,000 m^3
Effective storage capacity	- 1,507,940,000 m^3
Volume content of dam	- 1,860,000 m^3
Year of completion	- Under construction

74. Dimbhe Dam

Dimbhe dam is being constructed across Ghod river near Ambegaon in Maharashtra for irrigation and hydropower generation. Salient features of the dam are:

Type	- Gravity/Masonry
Height above lowest foundation	- 70.1 m
Length of the dam	- 852 m
Gross storage capacity	- 382,220,000 m^3
Effective storage capacity	- 353,910,000 m^3
Volume content of the dam	- 1,252,000 m^3
Year of completion	- Under construction

75. Pimpalgaon Dam

Pimpalgaon dam is being built across the river Bhogawati near Barshi in Maharashtra for irrigation. Main characteristics of the dam are:

Type	- Earthen
Height above lowest foundation	- 14.53 m
Length of the dam	- 2,552 m
Gross storage capacity	- 12,660,000 m^3
Effective storage capacity	- 9,960,000 m^3
Volume content of the dam	- 695,000 m^3
Year of completion	- Under construction

76. Changliar Tank

Changliar tank is being built across the river Krishna near Bidar in Karnataka for the purpose of irrigation. Salient features are:

Type	- Earthen
Height above lowest foundation	- 14.79 m
Length of the dam	- 306 m
Gross storage capacity	- 1,800,000 m^3
Effective storage capacity	- 1,650,000 m^3
Volume content of the dam	- 13,320 m^3
Year of completion	- Under construction

77. Ankarmanhal Tank

Ankarmanhal tank is being constructed across the river Narihalla near Sandur in Karnataka for irrigation. The salient features of the tank are:

Type	- Earthen
Height above lowest foundation	- 16.83 m
Length of the tank	- 277.35 m
Gross storage capacity	- 1,540,000 m^3
Effective storage capacity	- 1,230,000 m^3
Volume content of the dam	- 850,830 m^3
Year of completion	- Under construction

78. Gobbur Tank

Gobbur tank is being built across the river Krishna near Glubarga city in Karnataka for irrigation. The main features of the tank are:

Type	- Earthen
Height above lowest foundation	- 10.3 m
Length of the dam	- 1,525 m
Gross storage capacity	- 3,020,000 m^3
Effective storage capacity	- 2,390,000 m^3
Volume content of the dam	- 119,320 m^3
Year of completion	- Under construction

79. Upper Hinala Tank

Upper Hinala tank is being constructed across the river Tungabhadra near Raichur city in Karnataka for irrigation. Salient features of the tank are:

Type	- Earthen
Height above lowest foundation	- 18.27 m
Length of the tank	- 1,935 m
Gross storage capacity	- 6,500,000 m^3
Effective storage capacity	- 5,700,000 m^3
Volume content of the dam	- 377,830 m^3
Year of completion	- Under construction

80. Aherijumbagi Dam

Aherijumbagi dam is being constructed across Krishna river near Bijapur city in Karnataka for irrigation. Salient features of this dam are:

Type	- Earthen
Height above lowest foundation	- 10.29 m
Length of the dam	- 1,062 m
Gross storage capacity	- 1,728,000 m^3
Effective storage capacity	- 1,500,000 m^3
Volume content of the dam	- 98,040 m^3
Year of completion	- —

81. Krishyal Tank

Krishyal tank is being constructed across Krishna river near B.Bagewadi city in Karnataka for irrigation purpose. Main features of the tank are:

Type	- Earthen
Height above lowest foundation	- 10.92 m
Length of the tank	- 806 m
Gross storage capacity	- 1,610,000 m^3
Effective storage capacity	- 1,400,000 m^3
Volume content of the tank	- 79,690 m^3
Year of completion	- —

82. Mukherlhihal tank

Mukherlhihal tank is being built across the river Krishna near B.Bagewadi city in Karnataka to assist in irrigation. Salient features of the tank are:

Type	- Earthen
Height above lowest foundation	- 10.41 m
Length of the tank	- 852 m
Gross storage capacity	- 1,450,000 m^3
Effective storage capacity	- 1,200,000 m^3
Volume content of the tank	- 57,000 m^3
Year of completion	- —

83. Nagathan Tank

Nagathan tank is being constructed across Bhima rivernear Bijapur city in Karnataka for irrigation purpose. Salient features of the tank are:

Type	- Earthen
Height above lowest foundation	- 10.67 m
Length of the tank	- 1,128.5 m
Gross storage capacity	- 2,770,000 m^3
Effective storage capacity	- 2,400,000 m^3
Volume content of the tank	- 119,170 m^3
Year of completion	- —

84. Ragasamundra Tank

Ragasamundra tank is being built across Krishna river near Badami city in Karnataka to assist in irrigation. Salient features of the tank are:

Type	- Earthen
Height above lowest foundation	- 22.7 m
Length of the tank	- 297 m
Gross storage capacity	- 5,000,000 m^3
Effective storage capacity	- 4,310,000 m^3
Volume content of the tank	- 90,160 m^3
Year of completion	- —

85. Ronihal Tank

Ronihal tank is constructed across Krishna river near B.Bagewadi in Karnataka for irrigation. Salient features of the tank are:

Type	- Earthen
Height above lowest foundation	- 13.1 m
Length of the tank	- 720 m
Gross storage capacity	- 1,350,000 m^3
Effective storage capacity	- 1,200,000 m^3
Volume content of the tank	- 81,650 m^3
Year of completion	- —

86. Kanher Dam

Kanher Dam is constructed (Krishna irrigation project) across the river Venna in Maharashtra for irrigation. Salient features are:

Type	- Earth-cum-gravity
Area of catchment	- 20,461 Km^2
Rainfall	- Min 101 cm, Max 635 cm
Gross storage capacity	- 286,000,000 m^3
Effective storage capacity	- 271,680,000 m^3
Height above lowest foundation	- 50.34 m
Length of the dam	- 1,954 m
Volume content of the dam	- 6,308,000 m^3
Year of completion	- Under construction

Upper Krishna Project

The Upper Krishna Project in Karnataka state comprises construction of two dams across Krishna River. The Upper Dam which will impound bulk of storage requirements, will be constructed at Almatti, where the river cuts across a hill range and a good site for a large storage Dam is available. The lower dam which will serve mainly as a diversion Dam is situated at Narayanpur. In addition to these two Dams, a barrage will be constructed across Krishna river at Hippargi which will afford lift irrigation. Salient features are:

87. Almatti Dam

Type	- Spillway and non-spillway portion is of masonry and left flank is of earthen dam.
Area of catchment	- 35,925 Km^2
Irrigable area	- 2,06,387 Hectares
Gross storage capacity	- 6,430,000,000 m^3
Live storage capacity	- 6,095,000,000 m^3
Height above lowest foundation	- 48.8 m
Length of the dam	- 1,565 m
Volume content of dam	- 1,350,000 m^3
Year of completion	- Under construction

88. Hippargi Barrage

Catchment area	- 22,699 sq. Km
Lift Irrigation land	- 54,227 m. hectares.
Gross storage capacity	- 170,000,000 m^3
Live storage capacity	- 138,740,000 m^3
Height above lowest foundation	- 26 m
Length of the dam	- 5,463 m
Volume content of dam	- 29,980,000 m^3
Year of completion	- Under construction

89. Huvinabhevi Irrigation Tank

New irrigation tank at Huvinabhevi is constructed across the tributary of Krishna for irrigation in Karnataka. Salient features are:

Type	- Earthen
Gross storage capacity	- 1,830,000 m^3
Volume content of dam	- 1,620,000 m^3
Height above lowest foundation	- 11 m
Length of crest	- 545 m

90. Warna Dam

Warna Dam is constructed across the river Warna in Maharashtra for irrigation. Salient features are:

Type	- Composite earthen dam with masonry
Area of catchment	- 301 Km^2
Rainfall	- 687 cm
Gross storage capacity	- 963,970,000 m^3
Effective storage capacity	- 780,000,000 m^3
Height above lowest foundation	- 88.8 m
Length of the dam	- 1,580 m
Volume content of the dam	- 21,219,000 m^3
Year of completion	- Under construction

91. Warasgaon Dam

Warasgaon dam is constructed across the Mosi river in Maharashtra near Poona for irrigation. Salient features are:

Type	- Earthen.
Gross storage capacity	- 30,400,000 m^3
Volume content of dam	- 718,000 m^3
Height above lowest foundation	- 69 m
Length of crest	- 788 m

92. Vir Baji Pasalhar Dam

Vir Baji Pasalhar Dam is being constructed across Mosi river near Velhe in Maharashtra for irrigation. Main characteristics of the dam are:

Type	- Gravity
Height above lowest foundation	- 27.2 m
Length of the dam	- 780 m
Gross storage capacity	- 374,000,000 m^3
Effective storage capacity	- 275,000,000 m^3
Volume content of the dam	- 739,000 m^3
Year of completion	- Under construction

The other major water resources development projects in Krishna River Basin are:

93. Sunkesula Dam and

94. Kistna Dam in Andhra Pradesh and

95. Khodshi Weir in Karnataka.

THE MAHANADI RIVER BASIN

Mahanadi river originates from a pond near Pharsiya village in Raipur district of Madhya Pradesh, flowing east and draining into the Bay of Bengal after a run of 851 Km. The basin extends over an area of about 1,41,589 Km^2 of which 53.1 per cent lies in Madhya Pradesh, 46.5 per cent in Orissa and the rest in Bihar and Maharashtra. Before reaching the plains of coastal Orissa, Mahanadi flows for 23 Km through a narrow gorge near Tikarpara village. Below Naraj it splits into two branches, the Kathjuri (Devi) and the Birupa. Further down another branch called the Kuakhai is formed. Mahanadi has a maximum discharge of 44,7000 cusec. Its annual flow is 66,879 million m³. The principal tributaries of the river are Seonath, Hasdeo, Mand, Jonk, Ib, Ong and Tel-the last two join the river downstream Hirakund Reservoir. Table 5.2 describes the main characteristics of the tributaries.

Mahanadi river basin has a tropical climate with average annual rainfall of 155cm. The basin geology is characterised by precambrian rocks of the Eastern Ghats, composed of rock types such as khondalites, charnockites, leptynites, granites, and gneisses, palimestones, sandstones and shales of the Gondwana series, and coastal tracts underlain by recent deltaic alluvium of the river with littoral deposits. Some of the richest mineral belts of the sub-continent, including iron ore, coal, limestone, dolomite, bauxite, lead and copper deposits occur in the basin.

TABLE 5.2: THE TRIBUTARIES OF MAHANADI

River	*Source*	*Length in Km.*	*Catchment in Km²*	*Annual flow in million m³*
Left Bank				
The Seonath	Kotgal	383	30,761	13,073
The Hasdeo	North of Sarhat	333	9,803	5,389
The Mand	—	241	5,237	3,246
The Ib	Raigarh	251	12,447	9,003
Right Bank				
The Jonk	Khariar	196	3,673	1,850
The Ong	Hill	204	5,182	2,220
The Tel	Koraput	296	22,818	11,716

Data taken from Rao (1979)

Major water resources projects across Mahanadi river

Mahanadi river is much less regulated than Krishna and Godavari rivers with only 28 dams in its basin compared to 95 in Krishna basin and 74 in Godavari basin. Hirakud reservoir—one of the largest in India—is situated in this basin. The 28 dams in Mahanadi are on an average, 26.33 m high above the foundation and have an

TABLE 5.3: MAHANADI RIVER BASIN

Sl.No.	*Name of the Dam*	*Year of Commissioning*	*Height above lowest Foundation (metres)*	*Gross storage capacity (m^3)*	*Functions/I/p/ws/FC/R*
1	2	3	4	5	6
1.	Rudri-Pick-Up Weir	1915	—	312,000,000	Irrigation
2.	Tandula Dam	1921	25	312,000,000	Irrigation
3.	Murramsilli Dam	1929	26	165,338,000	
4.	Hirakud Dam	1957	59	8,100,000,000	Irrigation Flood control
5.	Hasdeo Barrage	1968	—		Irrigation
6.	Dudhwa Tank	1972	25	287,600,000	Irrigation
7.	Karanjkote Dam	1977	15.55	1,954,000	Irrigation
8.	Mahanadi Reservoir Project	1978	32	909,000,000	Irrigation and Hydropower
9.	Ravi Shankar Sagar Project	1978	32	909,320,000	Irrigation
10.	Sundar Project	1978	20	47,000,000	—
11.	Kodabhal Dam	1982	18.4	9,000,000	Irrigation
12.	Kinkari Dam	1982	17.68	16,000,000	
13.	Talasara Dam	1983	21	19,050,000	Irrigation
14.	Chattenjore Dam	1983	10.97	1,265,000	Irrigation
15.	Jharbandha Dam	1984	19.08	13,307,500	Irrigation
16.	Liar Dam	1984	16	1,152,000	Irrigation

{Cont.}...

1	*2*	*3*	*4*	*5*	*6*
17.	Sarafgarh Dam	1986	25	13,750,000	Irrigation
18.	Pendrawan Dam	1986	16	4,200,000	Irrigation
19.	Runagaon Dam	1987	13.41	529,000	Irrigation
20.	Ghurlijore Dam	—	12.19	2,179,000	Irrigation
21.	Upper Jonk Dam	U/C	24.81	81,000,000	Irrigation
22.	Hasdeo Bango Dam	U/C	86	3,047,000,000	—
23.	Sondur Reservoir Project	—	38	198,000,000	—

average gross storage capacity of 673 million m^3. The major dams in Mahanadi basin are listed in Table 5.3.

1. Rudri Pick-up Weir

Rudri Pick-up Weir is constructed in Mahanadi for irrigation. Salient features are:

Area of catchment	- 3,658 Km^2
Mean annual rainfall in the catchment	- 189.2 cm
Year of completion	- 1915

2. Tandula Dam

Tandula Dam is constructed across Tandula and Sukha rivers in Madhya Pradesh for irrigation. Salient features are:

Type	- Earthen dam
Gross storage capacity	- 312,000,000 m^3
Effective storage capacity	- 102,040,000 m^3
Height above lowest foundation	- 25 m
Length of crest	- 4,420 m
Volume content of the dam	- 2,609,000 m^3
Year of completion	- 1921

3. Murram Silli Dam

Murram Silli dam is constructed across the river Silaria near Raipur in Madhya Pradesh. Main features of the dam are:

Type	- Earthen
Height above lowest foundation	- 26 m
Length of the dam	- 2591 m
Gross storage capacity	- 165,338,000 m^3
Effective storage capacity	- 161,710,000 m^3
Year of completion	- 1929

4. Hirakud Dam

Sixteen miles from end to end, Hirakud is the world's longest mainstream dam over the river Mahanadi and one of the major dams of India. It is situated at 21°32'N and 83°52'E which is about 15 Km upstream of Sambalpur town. It is a multipurpose dam meant for irrigation, flood control (down stream delta) and power generation. The total catchment area of the Mahanadi at its mouth is about 1,33,120 sq Km out of which Hirakud Catchment is 83,395 sq Km. The catchment of the river can be broadly classified as upland plateau. It is an undulating up land tract, sloping generally from North to South and much broken up by rugged ranges of hills. Elevation falls from R.L. 173.73 M (570 ft) at North to R.L. 146.34 M (480 ft) at Sambalpur. A number of channels leading to river Mahanadi traverse this area in all directions as a result of the undulations. Isolated hills rising abruptly from the plains are a common sight and a large portion of the area is cut off by ravines and ridges interspersed with plains. The Bargarh plain is the most fertile part of the plateau. The Seonath, the Jonk, the Hasdeo, the Mand and the Ib are the principal tributaries of Mahanadi above the Dam.

Monsoon in the catchment is generally from middle of June to end of September. Maximum average rainfall over the catchment above Hirakud is 1,804 mm (71.03 inches) and minimum is 889 mm (34.99 inches). The mean annual rainfall is of the order of 1,370 mm (53.9 inches). The salient features of the Hirakud dam are:

Type	- Composite (earth, masonry and concrete)
Gross storage capacity	- 8,100,000,000 m^3
Live storage capacity	- 5,822,000,000 m^3
Length of crest	- 4,800 m
Height above lowest foundation	- 59 m
Rainfall	- 137 cm
Volume content of the dam	- 25,100,000 m^3
Irrigation	- 2,64,288 Ha
Year of completion	- 1957

5. Hasdeo Barrage

Hasdeo Barrage is present in Hasdeo river. Salient features are:

Area of catchment	- 7,723 Km^2
Mean annual rainfall	- 150.5 cm
Year of completion	- 1968
Purpose	- Multipurpose

6. Dudhawa Tank

The Dudhawa Tank is constructed across Mahanadi in Madhya Pradesh for irrigation. Salient features are:

Type	- Earthen dam
Gross storage capacity	- 287,600,000 m^3
Effective storage capacity	- 283,550,000 m^3
Height above lowest foundation	- 25 m
Length of the dam	- 2,906 m
Volume content of dam	- 2,281,000 m^3
Year of completion	- 1972

7. Karanjkote Dam

Karanjkote dam is built across Tel nalla near Bhavanipatna in Orissa for the purpose of irrigation. Salient features of the dam are:

Type	- Earthen
Height above lowest foundation	- 15.55 m
Length of the dam	- 3,506 m
Gross storage capacity	- 1,954,000 m^3
Effective storage capacity	- 1,783,000 m^3
Volume content of dam	- 82,400 m^3
Year of completion	- 1977

8. Mahanadi Reservoir Project

The Mahanadi Reservoir Project in Raipur District of Madhya Pradesh is a dual purposed one for power generation as well as irrigation. Salient features are:

Type	- Masonry, earth and rockfill.
Area of catchment	- 3,670 Km^2
Rainfall	- 143 cm
Gross storage capacity	- 909,000,000 m^3
Live storage capacity	- 766,000,000 m^3
Year of completion	- 1978

9. Ravi Shankar Sagar Project

Ravi Shankar Sagar Project is constructed across Mahanadi in Madhya Pradesh for irrigation, water supply and hydroelectric power generation. Salient features are:

Type	- Earthen, Rockfill, gravity dam
Gross storage capacity	- 909,000,000 m^3
Effective storage capacity	- 766,000,000 m^3
Height above lowest foundation	- 32 m
Length of crest	- 1,830 m
Length of the dam	- 2,919 m
Volume content of the dam	- 200,000 m^3 (Masonry and concrete) 2500,000 m^3 (earth)
Ultimate benefit area	- 12,800 hectares
Year of completion	- 1978

10. Sundar Project

Sundar dam is constructed across the river Sundar near Nawapara in Orissa to assist in irrigation. Salient features of the dam are:

Type	- Earthen
Height above lowest foundation	- 20 m
Length of the dam	- 2,700 m
Gross storage capacity	- 47,000,000 m^3
Effective storage capacity	- 44,400,000 m^3
Year of completion	- 1978

11. Kodabhal Dam

Kodabhal dam is located in the sub-basin of Tel river near Bhavaniptana in Orissa. The main purpose of the dam is to assist in irrigation. Salient features of the dam are:

Type	- Earthen
Height above lowest foundation	- 18.4 m
Length of the dam	- 159 m
Gross storage capacity	- 9,000,000 m^3
Effective storage capacity	- 6,850,000 m^3
Volume content of the dam	- 201,600 m^3

Year of completion - 1982

12. Kinkari Dam

Kinkari dam is built across the river Mahanadi near Raigarh in Madhya Pradesh for the purpose of irrigation. Main features of the dam are:

Type - Earthen
Height above lowest foundation - 17.68 m
Length of the dam - 367 m
Gross storage capacity - 16,000,000 m^3
Effective storage capacity - 15,000,000 m^3
Year of completion - 1982

13. Talasara Dam

Talasara dam is built acros Ib Nalla near Sundargarh in Orissa for irrigation. Main features of this dam are:

Type - Earthen
Height above lowest foundation - 21 m
Length of the dam - 72.5 m
Gross storage capacity - 29,050,000 m^3
Effective storage capacity - 16,600,000 m^3
Volume content of the dam - 507,750 m^3
Year of completion - 1983

14. Chhatenjore Dam

Chhatenjore dam is constructed across the river Mahanadi near Sundargah in Orissa for irrigation. Salient features of the dam are:

Type - Earthen and gravity
Height above lowest foundation - 10.97 m
Length of the dam - 865.76 m
Gross storage capacity - 1,265,000 m^3
Effective storage capacity - 968,000 m^3
Volume content of the dam - 24,352 m^3
Year of completion - 1983

15. Jharbandha dam

Jharbandha dam is built across Ong river near Padampur in Orissa for irrigation. Salient features of the dam are:

Type	- Gravity and masonary
Height above lowest foundation	- 19.08 m
Length of the dam	- 97.8 m
Gross storage capacity	- 13,307,500 m^3
Effective storage capacity	- 10,070,000 m^3
Volume content of the dam	- 10,510 m^3
Year of completion	- 1984

16. Liar Dam

Liar dam is built across the Tel nalla near Bhavanipatna in Orissa to assist in irrigation. Salient features of the dam are:

Type	- Earthen
Height above lowest foundation	- 16 m
Length of the dam	- 533 m
Gross storage capacity	- 1,152,000 m^3
Effective storage capacity	- 895,000 m^3
Volume content of the dam	- 177,000 m^3
Year of completion	- 1984

17. Sarafgaarh Dam

Sarafgaarh dam is constructed across the river Ib near Sundargarh in Orissa for irrigation. Salient featues are:

Type	- Earthen
Height above lowest foundation	- 25 m
Length of the dam	- 60 m
Gross storage capacity	- 13,750,000 m^3
Effective storage capacity	- 12,200,000 m^3
Volume content of the dam	- 236,650 m^3
Year of completion	- 1986

18. Pendrawan Dam

Pendrawan dam is constructed across Tel nalla near Rajkhar iar in Orissa for irrigation. Salient features of the dam are:

Type	- Earthen
Height above lowest foundation	- 16 m
Length of the dam	- 475 m
Gross storage capacity	- 4,200,000 m^3
Effective storage capacity	- 2,949,000 m^3
Volume content of the dam	- 143,000 m^3
Year of completion	- 1986

19. Runagaon Dam

Runagaon dam is built across river Mahanadi near Sundargarh in Orissa to assist in irrigation. Salient features of the dam are:

Type	- Earthen and gravity
Height above lowest foundation	- 13.41 m
Length of the dam	- 688.85 m
Gross storage capacity	- 529,000 m^3
Effective storage capacity	- 429,000 m^3
Volume content of the dam	- 138,260 m^3
Year of completion	- 1987

20. Ghurlijore Dam

Ghurlijore dam is constructed across Mahanadi near Sundar garh in Orissa for irrigation. Main features of the dam are:

Type	- Earthen and Gravity
Height above lowest foundation	- 12.19 m
Length of the dam	- 1,127.76 m
Gross storage capacity	- 2,179,000 m^3
Effective storage capacity	- 2,059,000 m^3
Volume content of the dam	- 56,230 m^3
Year of completion	—

21. Upper Jonk Dam

Upper Jonk dam is being constructed across river Jonk near Nawapara in Orissa for irrigation. Salient features of the dam are:

Type	- Earthen
Height above lowest foundation	- 24.81 m
Length of the dam	- 627 m

Gross storage capacity - 81,000,000 m^3
Effective storage capacity - 65,000,000 m^3
Volume content of the dam - 690,000 m^3
Year of completion - Under construction

22. Hasdeo Bango Dam

Hasdeo Bango dam is being constructed across river Hasdeo near Bilaspur in Madhya Pradesh to assist in irrigation. Main features of the dam are:

Type - Earthen and gravity
Height above lowest foundation - 86 m
Length of the dam - 2,688 m
Gross storage capacity - 3,417,000,000 m^3
Effective storage capacity - 3,047,000,000 m^3
Year of completion - Under construction

23. Hasdeo Project Phase III

Hasdeo Project Phase III comprises the construction of Hasdeo dam across one of the tributaries of Mahanadi, the Hasdeo river. Salient features are:

Type - Masonry in gorge, earth in saddle
Area of catchment - 6.737 Km^2
Rainfall - 150.5 cm
Gross storage capacity - 3,417,000,000 m^3
Live storage capacity - 3,047,000,000 m^3
Height above lowest foundation - 86 m
Year of completion - Under construction.

24. Sondur Reservoir

The Sondur Reservoir project is constructed across one of the tributaries of Mahanadi in Madhya Pradesh for irrigation. Salient features are:

Type - Earthen cum gravity dam

Gross stroage capacity	- 198,000,000 m^3
Effective storage capacity	- 179,000,000 m^3
Height above lowest foundation	- 38 m
Length of the dam	- 3,405 m
Volume content of the dam	- 100,000 m^3 (Masonry and Concrete) 2,100,000 m^3 (earth)
Year of completion	- Under construction

Other major water resources projects which are present in the Mahanadi River basin are:

25. Uttei Project

26 . Ong Project

27 . Birupa–Weir and

28 . Mahanadi Delta Irrigation Scheme

THE GODAVARI RIVER BASIN

Godavari river originates in Trimbakeshwar, Nasik district in Maharashtra State. After traversing some 1965 Km it joins the Bay of Bengal in Andhra Pradesh. It has a catchment area of 312, 812 sq Km of which 69.3 per cent lies in Maharashtra. Its main tributaries are Pravara, Parna, Penganga and Waingana. Average annual flow of Godavari river is 118,982 million m^3.

There are many pilgrimage centres on the banks of Godavari, out of which Trimbakeshwar, Nasik, and Paithan are the major ones where lakhs of people gather on special festivals and Sinhastha Mela. Many important cities and villages are situated on the banks of the river utilising the river water.

Godavari discharges 92 Km^3 of water annually into the Bay of Bengal, which is one-fourth of that of the Ganges. The basin include major geological formations such as the Tertiary Deccan Traps (48 per cent), Archean granites (39 per cent), precambrian and Gondwana sedimentary rocks (11 per cent) and recent alluvials (2 per cent).

The mean rainfall over the basin is 1,185 mm yr^{-1} and the mean elevation is 420 m.

MAJOR WATER RESOURCES PROJECTS ACROSS GODAVARI RIVER

There are 74 major water resources projects in the Godavari river basin based on dams (Table 5.4) of which the oldest is Ramappa dam commissioned in 1,213. More than half of the dams are earthen. The average height above foundation of the dams is 30.53 m and average gross storage capacity of the dammed reservoirs is 278.34 million m^3. Wilson dam, the seventh oldest dam in the basin, is also the deepest going 82.35 m from the top to the foundation while *Ekamba tank* is the shallowest with its height above foundation barely 11m. Dasmanthapur dam is the least voluminous of the reservoirs in the Godavari basin, its gross storage capacity, 0.441 million m^3 is over 8,000 times lesser than that of Balimela reservoir which is the most voluminous.

1. Ramappa Dam

Ramappa dam is built across the river Manair, near Warangal in Andhra Pradesh. The main features of this thirteenth century dam are:

Type	- Earthen
Height above lowest foundation	- 17 m
Gross storage capacity	- 152,939,000 m^3
Effective storage capacity	- 82,477,000 m^3
Year of completion	- 1213

2. Bhatodi Dam

Bhatodi dam is constructed across the river Mahalungi near A'Nagar in Karnataka for irrigation. Salient features of the dam are:

Type	- Gravity
Height above lowest foundation	- 15.24 m
Length of the dam	- 706 m
Gross storage capacity	- 1,050,000 m^3
Effective storage capacity	- 570,000 m^3
Year of completion	- 1892

3. Waghadi Dam

Waghadi dam is constructed across Kalwan river, which is one of the tributaries of Godavari in Maharashtra, to assist in irrigation. Salient features are:

Type	- Earthen dam
Gross storage capacity	- 17,100,000 m^3
Height above lowest foundation	- 32 m
Length of crest	- 1,255 m
Volume content of the dam	- 132,000 m^3
Year of completion	- 1911

4. Mopad Dam

Mopad dam is constructed across Maneru river near Nellore in Andhra Pradesh for irrigation purpose. The salient features of the dam are:

Type	- Earthen
Height above lowest foundation	- 28 m
Length of the dam	- 1,663 m
Gross storage capacity	- 59,800,000 m^3
Effective storage capacity	- 59,800,000 m^3
Year of completion	- 1921

5. Alair Dam

Alair dam is constructed across the Alair stream in Andhra Pradesh for irrigation. Salient feature are:

Type	- Gravity
Gross storage capacity	- 16,187,000 m^3
Height above lowest foundation	- 30 m
Volume content of the dam	- 66,000 m^3
Year of completion	- 1922

6. Pocharam Dam

Pocharam dam is constructed in Aylair stream for irrigation in Andhra Pradesh. Salient features are:

Type	- Gravity

TABLE 5.4: GODAVARI RIVER BASIN

Sl.No.	Name of the Dam	Year of Commissioning	Height above lowest Foundation (metres)	Gross storage capacity (m^3)	Functions/I/p/ws/FC/R
1	2	3	4	5	6
1.	Ramappa Dam	1213	17	152,939,000	Irrigation
2.	Bhatodi Dam	1892	15.24	1,050,000	Irrigation
3.	Waghadi Dam	1911	32	17,100,000	Irrigation
4.	Mopad Dam	1921	28	59,800,000	Irrigation
5.	Alair Dam	1922	30	16,187,000	Irrigation
6.	Pocharam Dam	1922	31	51,537,000	Irrigation
7.	Bhandardara Dam (or) Wilson Dam	1926	82.35	312,400,000	Irrigation
8.	Mulshi Lake	1927	50.6	522,760,000	Hydropower
9.	Nizam Sagar Reservoir	1931	38	841,481,000	Irrigation
10.	Upper Manair Dam	1950	31	62,337,000	—
11.	Koli Sagar Dam	1955	16	86,094,000	Irrigation
12.	Kaddam Dam	1958	43	215,800,000	Irrigation
13.	Jalaput Dam	1960	60.67	970,630,000	Hydropower
14.	Sindhaphana Dam	1963	19.05	2,600,000	Irrigation
15.	Gangapur Reservoir	1965	36.59	215,800,000	Irrigation
16.	Mahasangvi Dam	1965	16.98	6,750,000	Irrigation

{Cont.}...

1	*2*	*3*	*4*	*5*	*6*
17.	Ambhora Dam	1965	17.2	2,237,000	Irrigation
18.	Siddheswar Dam	1968	38.26	250,820,000	Irrigation
19.	Manar Dam	1968	27	139,000,000	Irrigation
20.	Yeldari Dam	1968	51.2	934,310,000	Irrigation and Hydropower
21.	Upper Sileru Dam	1968	30.48	127,700,000	Hydropower
22.	Guntawada Dam	1968	37	122,740,000	Hydropower
23.	Terna Dam	1970	15	22,910,000	Irrigation
24.	Masaajog Dam	1970	14.17	2,705,000	Irrigation
25.	Mula Dam	1972	46.65	736,250,000	Irrigation
26.	Manyarwadi Dam	1972	15.35	1,890,000	Irrigation
27.	Basalpur Dam	1972	17.85	1,530,000	Irrigation
28.	Bhojapur	1972	29.65	21,620,000	Irrigation
29.	Bavalgaon Tank	1973	16.62	1,880,000	Irrigation
30.	Karanjwan (Upper Godavari Project)	1974	42.92	175,580,000	Irrigation
31.	Palkhed Dam	1975	21.65	21,240,000	Irrigation
32.	Pawna Dam	1975	38.1	305,000,000	Irrigation, Water Supply and Hydropower
33.	Jayakwadi Project Paithan Reservoir	1976	43	2,910,000,000	Irrigation and Navigation

{Cont.}...

1	*2*	*3*	*4*	*5*	*6*
34.	Ghatkhed Dam	1976	19.47	1,680,000	
35.	Tongalphodi Dam	1976	16.8	1,440,500	Irrigation
36.	Kalkaqam Dam	1976	17.4	2,122,000	Irrigation
37.	Gondvihir Dam	1977	15.7	2,380,000	Irrigation
38.	Pakka Dam	1977	11.79	883,000	Irrigation
39.	Balimela Dam	1977	70	3,610,000,000	Hydropower
40.	Sri Rama Sagar Dam	1977	43	317,200,000	Irrigation and Hydropower
41.	Forebay Dam	1978	67	4,070,000	Irrigation
42.	Ekamba Tank	1979	11.21	1,810,000	Irrigation
43.	Bhivapur Dam	1979	17.9	4,000,000	Irrigation
44.	Waghad Dam	1979	45.6	76,480,000	Irrigation
45.	Satneer Dam	1980	15.58	1,540,000	Irrigation
46.	Sonal Dam	1980	19.6	20,770,000	Irrigation
47.	Medipally Tank	1981	15.08	—	Irrigation
48.	Ozarkhed Dam (Upper Godavari Project)	1982	36.3	67,950,000	Irrigation
49.	Manjra Dam (Dhanegaon)	1982	25.6	251,920,000	Irrigation
50.	Isapur Dam	1982	47	1,254,000,000	Irrigation
51.	Parsodi Dam	1982	20.55	1,113,000	Irrigation
52.	Shokdari Dam	1982	30.36	5,204,000	Irrigation

{Cont.}...

1	*2*	*3*	*4*	*5*	*6*
53.	Dasamanthapur Dam	1982	18.2	441,000	Irrigation
54.	Malkangiri Dam	1982	16.7	296,000	Irrigation
55.	Tegampur Tank	1983	15.18	4,040,000	Irrigation
56.	Upper Wainganga Dam	1984	43	507,000,000	—
57.	Lower Manair Dam (Pochampad project)	1986	42	680,458,000	Irrigation and water supply
58.	Lower Thrina Dam	1988	19	14,826,000	Irrigation
59.	Jayakwadi project Majalgaon Dam	U/C:1988	32	453,640,000	Irrigation and Hydropower
60.	Wainganga Dam	-	11.4	15,000,000	—
61.	Lendi Dam	U/C	27	7,345,000	Irrigation
62.	Godavari —Barrage	U/C	51.64	38,990,000	Irrigation
63.	Donkarayi Dam (Lower Sileru Hydroelectric Scheme)	U/C	71	470,000,000	Navigation Hydropower
64.	Neopur Dam	U/C	16.60	11,380,000	Irrigation
65.	Upper Wardha Dam	U/C	52	790,000,000	Irrigation

{Cont.}...

1	*2*	*3*	*4*	*5*	*6*
66.	Lower Wardha Dam	U/C	20	274,000,000	Irrigation
67.	Punegaon Dam	U/C	25.53	20,390,000	Irrigation
68.	Pedda Vagu Dam	U/C	16	15,800,000	Irrigation
69.	Singur Dam	U/C	33.49	846,710,000	Irrigation and water supply
70.	Upper Manar	U/C	30.9	107,980,000	Water supply

Gross storage capacity - 51,537,000 m^3
Effective storage capacity - 51,500,000 m^3
Height above lowest foundation - 31 m
Length of crest - 640 m
Year of completion - 1922

7. Bhandardara Dam or Wilson Dam

Bhandardara Dam, also called Wilson Dam, is constructed across Pravara river in Maharashtra for irrigation.

Type - Gravity
Area of catchment - 122 km^2
Rainfall - 356 cm
Gross storage capacity - 312,400,000 m^3
Height above lowest foundation - 82.35 m
Length of crest - 507 m
Volume content of the dam - 336,000 m^3
Effective storage capacity - 307,310,000 m^3
Length of the dam - 2,717 m
Year of completion - 1926

8. Mulshi Lake Dam

Mulshi lake dam is constructed across the river Mula near Puna in Maharashtra with the main purpose of hydropower generation. Salient features of this dam are:

Type - Gravity
Height above lowest foundation - 50.6 m
Length of the dam - 1,908 m
Gross storage capacity - 522,760,000 m^3
Year of completion - 1927

9. Nizam Sagar Reservoir

Nizam Sagar Reservoir is constructed across Manjira river in Andhra Pradesh. It is a dual purposed dam for irrigation and hydro power generation. Salient features are:

Type - Earthen cum Gravity dam

Gross storage capacity - 841,481,000 m³
Effective storage capacity - 724,910,000 m³
Height above lowest foundation - 38 m
Volume content of the dam - 868,000 m³
Length of the dam - 5,682 m
Year of completion - 1931

10. Upper Manair Dam

Upper Manair dam is constructed across the river Manair Kundliar near Kamareddi in Andhra Pradesh. The salient features of the dam are:

Type - Rockfill and Earthen
Height above lowest foundation - 31 m
Length of the dam - 3,200 m
Gross storage capacity - 62,337,000 m³
Year of completion - 1950

11. Koli Sagar Dam

Koli Sagar dam is constructed across Pada vaggu stream in Andhra Pradesh for irrigation purpose. The salient features of the dam are:

Type - Gravity and Masonry
Height above lowest foundation - 16 m
Length of the dam - 274 m
Gross storage capacity - 86,094,000 m³
Effective storage capacity - 38,214,000 m³
Volume content of the dam - 76,000 m³
Year of completion - 1955

12. Kaddam Dam

Across the Kaddam river, one of the tributaries of Godavari in Andhra Pradesh, Kaddam dam is constructed for irrigation. Salient features are:

Type - Composite dam with masonry wall in bed side
Area of catchment - 2,590 Km²

Rainfall - 102 cm
Height above lowest foundation - 43 m
Gross storage capacity - 215,800,000 m^3
Live storage capacity - 137,100,000 m^3
Length of the dam - 2,101 m
Volume content of the dam - 908,000 m^3
Year of completion - 1958

13. Jalaput Dam

Jalaput dam is constructed across the river Sileru near Jalaput in Orissa for hydropower generation. Salient features of the dam are:

Type - Gravity and masonry
Height above lowest foundation - 60.67 m
Length of the dam - 805 m
Gross storage capacity - 970,630,000 m^3
Effective storage capacity - 892,600,000 m^3
Year of completion - 1960

14. Sindhphana Dam

Sindhphana dam is constructed across the river. Sindhphana in Maharashtra for irrigation. Salient features are:

Type - Earthen dam
Gross storage capacity - 12,600,000 m^3
Effective storage capacity - 10,810,000 m^3
Height above lowest foundation - 19.05 m
Length of the dam - 1,937 m
Volume content of the dam - 12,593,000 m^3
Year of completion - 1963

15. Gangapur Reservoir

The Gangapur Reservoir is constructed near Gonpur village in Nasik District of Maharashtra State on Godavari river for irrigation. Salient features are:

Type - Earthen dam
Gross storage capacity - 215,800,000 m^3

Effective storage capacity - 203,800,000 m^3
Height above lowest foundation - 36.59 m
Volume content of the dam - 4,350,000 m^3
Length of the dam - 3,902 m
Year of completion - 1965

16. Mahasangvi Dam

Mahasangvi dam is constructed across the river Manjra near Mahasangvi in Maharashtra for irrigation. Main features of the dam are:

Type - Earthen
Height above lowest foundation - 16.98 m
Length of the dam - 945 m
Gross storage capacity - 6,750,000 m^3
Effective storage capacity - 5,880,000 m^3
Volume content of the dam - 6,748,000 m^3
Year of completion - 1965

17. Ambhora Dam

Ambhora dam is constructed across Mahalungi river near Sanganamer in Maharashtra for irrigation. Salient features of the dam are:

Type - Earthen
Height above lowest foundation - 17.2 m
Length of the dam - 625 m
Gross storage capacity - 2,237,000 m^3
Effective storage capacity - 1,897,000 m^3
Volume content of the dam - 198,000 m^3
Year of completion - 1965

18. Sidheswar Dam

Sidheswar dam is constructed across the river Purna for irrigation. Salient features are:

Type - Earthen dam
Gross storage capacity - 250,820,000 m^3

Effective storage capacity	- 80,940,000 m^3
Height above lowest foundation	- 38.26 m
Length of the dam	- 6,658 m
Volume content of the dam	- 1,006,000 m^3
Year of completion	- 1968

19. Manar Dam

Manar dam is constructed across the Manar river for irrigation in Maharashtra near Nanded. Salient features are:

Type	- Earthen dam
Gross storage capacity	- 139,000,000 m^3
Effective storage capacity	- 128,700,000 m^3
Height above lowest foundation	- 27 m
Length of crest	- 1,859 m
Length of the dam	- 2,592 m
Volume content of the dam	- 1,557,000 m^3
Year of completion	- 1968

20. Yeldari Dam

Yeldari dam is constructed across the river Purna in Maharashtra for irrigation as well as Hydropower generation. Salient features are:

Type	- Earthen Gravity Dam (Masonry Dam)
Rainfall	- 70 cm
Gross storage capacity	- 934,310,000 m^3
Live storage capacity	- 809,660,000 m^3
Height above lowest foundation	- 51.2 m
Length of crest	- 3,270 m
Length of the dam	- 4,432 m
Volume content of the dam	- 1,400,000 m^3
Year of completion	- 1968

21. Upper Sileru Dam

Upper Sileru dam is constructed across the Sileru river in A.P. for hydro-power generation. Salient features are:

Type	- Earthen dam
Height above lowest foundation	- 30.48 m
Length of crest	- 625 m
Length of the dam	- 625 m
Gross storage capacity	- 127,700,000 m^3
Effective storage capacity	- 93,200,000 m^3
Year of completion	- 1968.

22. Guntawada Dam

Guntawada dam is built across river Sileru near Visakhapatnam in Andhra Pradesh mainly for hydropower generation. Its salient features are:

Type	- Gravity and Masonry
Height above lowest foundation	- 31 m
Length of the dam	- 625 m
Gross storage capacity	- 122,740,000 m^3
Effective storage capacity	- 88,220,000 m^3
Year of completion	- 1968

23. Terna Dam

Terna dam is constructed across the river Thirna near Kalamanuri in Maharashtra for irrigation. Salient features of the dam are:

Type	- Earthen
Height above lowest foundation	- 15 m
Length of the dam	- 2,651 m
Gross storage capacity	- 22,910,000 m^3
Effective storage capacity	- 18,630,000 m^3
Volume content of the dam	- 186,000 m^3
Year of completion	- 1970

24. Masaajog Dam

Masaajog Dam is constructed across the tributary of Manjra which is in turn is the tributary of Godavari in Maharashtra for irrigation. Salient features are:

Type	- Earthen dam

Gross storage capacity	- 2,705,000 m^3
Effective storage capacity	- 2,495,000 m^3
Height above lowest foundation	- 14.17 m
Lenght of the dam	- 1,136 m
Volume content of the dam	- 159,000 m^3
Year of completion	- 1970

25. Mula Dam

Mula dam is constructed across the Mula river in Maharashtra for irrigation (Dhyaneshvar Sagar).

Type	- Earthen dam
Rainfall	- Min 51 cm, Max 508 cm
Area of catchment	- 2,274 Km^2
Gross storage capacity	- 736,250,000 m^3
Live storage capacity	- 60,882,000 m^3
Height above lowest foundation	- 46.65 m
Length of crest	- 2,820 m
Length of the dam	- 2,856 m
Volume content of the dam	- 7,561,000 m^3
Year of completion	- 1972

26. Manyarwadi Dam

Manyarwadi dam is constructed across Sindphana river near Manyarwadi in Maharashtra for irrigation. Salient features of the dam are:

Type	- Earthen
Height above lowest foundation	- 15.35 m
Length of the dam	- 953 m
Gross storage capacity	- 1,890,000 m^3
Effective storage capacity	- 1,735,000 m^3
Year of completion	- 1972

27. Basalpur Dam

Basalpur dam is built across the river Wardha near Basalpur in Maharashtra to assist in irrigation. Main characteristics of the dam are:

Type	- Earthen
Height above lowest foundation	- 17.85 m
Length of the dam	- 402 m
Gross storage capacity	- 1,530,000 m^3
Effective storage capacity	- 1,420,000 m^3
Volume of the dam	- 72,000 m^3
Year of completion	- 1972

28. Bhojapur Dam

Bhojapur dam is constructed across the Mahalungi river for irrigation. Salient features are:

Type	- Earthen dam
Gross storage capacity	- 21,620,000 m^3
Effective storage capacity	- 10,610,000 m^3
Height above lowest foundation	- 29.65 m
Length of crest	- 34 m
Length of the dam	- 733 m
Volume content of the dam	- 812,000 m^3
Year of completion	- 1972

29. Bavalgaon Tank

Bavalgaon tank is built across the river Godavari near Aurad city in Karnataka for irrigation purpose. Salient features of the tank are:

Type	- Earthen
Height above lowest foundation	- 16.62 m
Length of the dam	- 410 m
Gross storage capacity	- 1,880,000 m^3
Effective storage capacity	- 1,880,000 m^3
Year of completion	- 1973

30. Karanjwan Dam (Upper Godavari Project)

Karanjwan Dam is constructed across the river Kadwa in Maharashtra for irrigation. Salient features re:

Type	- Earth-cum-gravity
Rainfall	- 137 cm.

Area of catchment	- 249 Km^2
Gross storage capacity	- 175,580,000 m^3
Effective storage capacity	- 166,220,000 m^3
Height above lowest foundation	- 42.92 m
Length of the dam	- 2,483 m
Volume content of the dam	- 1,702,000 m^3
Year of completion	- 1974

31. Palkhed Dam

Across the Kadwa river, which is the tributary of Godavari Palkhed dam is constructed for irrigation. Salient features are:

Type	- Earthen Gravity dam
Gross storage capacity	- 21,240,000 m^3
Effective storage capacity	- 21,240,000 m^3
Height above lowest foundation	- 21.65 m
Length of crest	- 3,570 m
Length of the dam	- 3,870 m
Volume content of the dam	- 610,000 m^3
Year of completion	- 1975

32. Pawna Dam

Pawna dam is constructed across the river Pawna (tributary of Mula/Mutha/Bhima)—in Maharashtra for irrigation, water supply and hydropower generation. Salient features are:

Type	- Earth-cum-gravity
Area of catchment	- 113 km^2
Height above lowest foundation	- 38.1 m
Gross storage capacity	- 305,000,000 m^3
Effective storage capacity	- 274,000,000 m^3
Length of the dam	- 1,329 m
Volume content of the dam	- 145,000 m^3 (Concrete and masonry)
	- 2,320,000 m^3 (Earth)
Year of completion	- 1975

33. Jayakwadi Reservoir

Jayakwadi Reservoir is known as Paithan Reservoir. It is an irrigation project on Godavari river at Paithan in Maharashtra state. The salient features of Jayakwadi reservoir stage-I are as follows:

Type	- Earth-cum-gravity
Rainfall	- 101.6 cm
Area of catchment	- 21,750 Km^2
Height above lowest foundation	- 43 m
Gross storage capacity	- 2,910,000,000 m^3
Effective storage capacity	- 2,170,000,000 m^3
Length of the dam	- 10,209 m
Volume content of the dam	- 13,330,000 m^3
Year of completion	- 1976

34. Ghatkhed Dam

Ghatkhed dam is built across the river Wardha near Ghatkhed in Maharashtra. Salient features of the dam are:

Type	- Earthen
Height above lowest foundation	- 19.47 m
Length of the dam	- 440 m
Gross storage capacity	- 1,680,000 m^3
Effective storage capacity	- 1,570,000 m^3
Volume content of the dam	- 191,000 m^3
Year of completion	- 1976

35. Tongalphodi Dam

Tengalphodi dam is constructed across river Purna near Dahigaon in Maharashtra for irrigation. Main characteristics of the dam are:

Type	- Earthen
Height above lowest foundation	- 16.8 m
Length of the dam	- 645 m
Gross storage capacity	- 1,440,000 m^3
Effective storage capacity	- 1,160,000 m^3
Volume content of the dam	- 137,000 m^3
Year of completion	- 1976

36. Kalkaquam Dam

Kalkaquam dam is constructed across Godavari near Sunabeda in Orissa for irrigation. Main features of the dam are:

Type	- Earthen
Height above lowest foundation	- 17.40 m
Length of the dam	- 445 m
Gross storage capacity	- 2,122,000 m^3
Effective storage capacity	- 1,980,000 m^3
Volume content of the dam	- 139,000 m^3
Year of completion	- 1976

37. Gondvihir Dam

Gondvihir dam is constructed across the river Purna near Malhora in Maharashtra to assist in irrigation. Main characteristics of this dam are:

Type	- Earthen
Height above lowest foundation	- 15.7 m
Length of the dam	- 1,400 m
Gross storage capacity	- 2,380,000 m^3
Effective storage capacity	- 2,090,000 m^3
Volume content of the dam	- 293,000 m^3
Year of completion	- 1977

38. Penti Pakka Dam

Penti Pakka Dam is constructed across the Godavari river in Maharashtra for irrigation. Salient features are:

Type	- Earthen Dam
Gross storage capacity	- 883,000 m^3
Effective storage capacity	- 535,000 m^3
Height above lowest foundation	- 11.79 m
Length of crest	- 240 m
Length of the dam	- 638 m
Year of completion	- 1977

39. Balimela Dam

Balimela Dam project of Andhra Pradesh and Orissa is constructed across the river Sileru for hydropower generation. Salient features are:

Type	- Earthen dam
Rainfall	- 140 cm
Area of catchment	- 4,910 Km^2
Gross storage capacity	- 3,610,000,000 m^3
Effective storage capacity	- 2,676,000,000 m^3
Height above lowest foundation	- 70 m
Length at the top of the dam	- 1,823 m
Volume content of the dam	- 13,856,000 m^3
Year of completion	- 1977

40. Srirama Sagar Dam

Srirama Sagar Dam is constructed across the river Godavari in the Pochampad village of Andhra Pradesh for the purpose of both irrigation and hydropower generation. Salient features are:

Type	- Masonry and Earth dam
Rainfall	- 88 cm
Area of catchment	- 91,750 Km^2
Height above lowest foundation	- 43 m
Gross storage capacity	- 3,172,000,000 m^3
Effective storage capacity	- 2,322,000,000 m^3
Length of the dam	- 14,600 m
Volume content of the dam	- 11,060,000 m^3
Year of completion	- 1977

41. Forebay Dam

Lower Sileru Hydro Electric Scheme consists of the construction of Forebay dam across the Sileru river in Andhra Pradesh about 15 Km away from Donkarayi for Hydropower generation. Salient features are:

Type	- Earthen dam

Rainfall - 193 cm
Area of catchment - 6 Km^2
Gross storage capacity - 4,070.000 m^3
Effective storage capacity - 4,020,000 m^3
Height above lowest foundation - 67m
Length at the top of the dam - 564m
Volume content of the dam - 2,669,000 m^3
Year of completion - 1978

42. Ekamba Tank

Ekamba tank is constructed across Godavari river near Auradcity in Karnataka for irrigation. Main features of the tank are:

Type - Earthen
Height above lowest foundation - 11.21 m
Length of the dam - 899 m
Gross storage capacity - 1,810,000 m^3
Effective storage capacity - 1,700,000 m^3
Volume content of the tank - 67,580 m^3
Year of completion - 1979

43. Bhivapur Dam

Bhivapur dam is built across the river Wardha near Bhivapur in Maharashtra for irrigation. Main characteristics of the dam are:

Type - Earthen
Height above lowest foundation - 17.9 m
Length of the dam - 1,176 m
Gross storage capacity - 4,000,000 m^3
Effective storage capacity - 3,440,000 m^3
Volume content of the dam - 125,000 m^3
Year of completion - 1979

44. Waghad Dam

Waghad dam is constructed across Kalwan river near Dinderi for irrigation purpose. Salient features of the dam are:

Type - Earthen

Height above lowest foundation - 45.6 m
Length of the dam - 952 m
Gross storage capacity - 76,480,000 m^3
Effective storage capacity - 70,000,000 m^3
Volume content of the dam - 1,783,000 m^3
Year of completion - 1979

45. Satneer Dam

Satneer dam is built across the river Wardha near Satnoer in Maharashtra to assist in irrigation. Main characteristics of the dam are:

Type - Earthen
Height above lowest foundation - 15.58 m
Length of the dam - 1,246 m
Gross storage capacity - 1,540,000 m^3
Effective storage capacity - 1,460,000 m^3
Volume content of the dam - 202,000 m^3
Year of completion - 1980

46. Sonal Dam

Sonal dam is constructed across the river Aran Mahanadi in Maharashtra. This dam is meant for irrigation. Salient features are:

Type - Earthen dam
Gross storage capacity - 23,984,000 m^3
Height above lowest foundation - 19.6 m
Length of the dam - 1,164 m
Gross storage capacity - 20,770,000 m^3
Effective storage capacity - 16,370,000 m^3
Volume content of the dam - 698,000 m^3
Year of completion - 1980.

47. Medipally Tank

Medipally tank is constructed across the river Godavari near Aurad city in Karnataka to assist in irrigation. Salient features of the tank are:

Type - Earthen
Height above lowest foundation - 15.08 m
Length of the dam - 427.2 m
Effective storage capacity - 1,590,000 m^3
Year of completion - 1981

48. Ozarkhed Dam

The Upper Godavari Project consists of the construction of the Ozarkhed Dam across the river Unanda in Maharashtra state. The salient features of this dam, which is meant for irrigation are:

Type - Earthen dam
Area of catchment - 182 Km^2
Height above lowest foundation - 36.3 m
Gross storage capacity - 67,950,000 m^3
Effective storage capacity - 60,320,000 m^3
Length of the dam - 3,266 m
Volume content of the dam - 2,662,000 m^3
Year of completion - 1982

49. Manjra Dam

Manjra Dam is constructed across the Manjra river which is tributary Kaij of Godavari in Maharashtra for irrigation. Salient features are:

Type - Earthen gravity dam
Rainfall - 77.4 cm
Area of catchment - 2,373 Km^2
Gross storage capacity - 251,920,000 m^3
Effective storage capacity - 174,980,000 m^3
Height above lowest foundation - 25.6 m
Length of crest - 4,250 m
Length of the dam - 4,669 m
Volume content of dam - 2,450,000 m^3
Year of completion - 1982

50. Isapur Dam

Isapur dam is constructed across the river Penganga near Nanded in Maharashtra for irrigation. The main features of the dam are:

Type - Earthen and gravity
Height above lowest foundation - 47 m
Length of the dam - 4,120.1 m
Gross storage capacity - 1,250,000,000 m^3
Effective storage capacity - 951,000,000 m^3
Volume content of the dam - 6,337,000 m^3
Year of completion - 1982

51. Parsodi Dam

Parsodi dam is constructed across the river Wardha near Parsedi in Maharashtra for irrigation. Main characteristics of the dam are:

Type - Earthen
Height above lowest foundation - 20.55 m
Length of the dam - 176 m
Gross storage capacity - 1,113,000 m^3
Effective storage capacity - 1,073,000 m^3
Volume content of the dam - 63,000 m^3
Year of completion - 1982

52. Shokdari Dam

Shokdari dam is constructed across river Wardha near Shokdari in Maharashtra for irrigation. Salient features of the dam are:

Type - Earthen
Height above lowest foundation - 30.36 m
Length of the dam - 1,261 m
Gross storage capacity - 5,204,000 m^3
Effective storage capacity - 4,540,000 m^3
Volume content of the dam - 354,000 m^3
Year of completion - 1982

53. Dasamanthapur Dam

Dasamanthapur dam is built across the river Godavari near Rayagad in Orissa for irrigation. Salient features of the dam are:

Type	- Earthen
Height above lowest foundation	- 18.2 m
Length of the dam	- 265 m
Gross storage capacity	- 441,000 m^3
Effective storage capacity	- 303,000 m^3
Volume content of the dam	- 71,380 m^3
Year of completion	- 1982

54. Malkangiri Dam

Malkangiri dam is built across the river Godavari near Rayagada in Orissa to assist in irrigation. Main characteristics of the dam are:

Type	- Earthen
Height above lowest foundation	- 16.7 m
Length of the dam	- 122.5 m
Gross storage capacity	- 296,000 m^3
Effective storage capacity	- 250,000 m^3
Volume content of the dam	- 46,290 m^3
Year of completion	- 1982

55. Tegampur Tank

Tegampur tank is constructed across river Godavari near Aurad in Karnataka for irrigation purpose. Salient features of the tank are:

Type	- Earthen
Height above lowest foundation	- 15.18 m
Length of the dam	- 780 m
Gross storage capacity	- 4,040,000 m^3
Effective storage capacity	- 3,630,000 m^3
Year of completion	- 1983

56. Upper Wainganga Dam

Upper Wainganga dam is built across Wainganga river near Seoni in Madhya Pradesh. Salient features of the dam are:

Type	- Earthen
Height above lowest foundation	- 43 m
Length of the dam	- 181 m
Gross storage capacity	- 507,000,000 m^3
Effective storage capacity	- 410,000,000 m^3
Year of completion	- 1984

57. Lower Manair Dam

The Pochampad Project consists of the construction of Lower Manair Dam across the river Manair in Andhra Pradesh. This is a dual purpose project for Drinking Water supply as well as irrigation. Salient features are:

Type	- Masonry and Earth dam
Rainfall	- 75 cm
Area of catchment	- 6,464 Km^2
Gross storage capacity	- 680,458,000 m^3
Effective storage capacity	- 30,000,000 m^3
Height above lowest foundation	- 42 m
Length of the dam	- 10,741 m
Volume content of the dam	- 364,520 m^3
(concrete and masonry)	- 5,405,000 m^3 (earth)
Year of completion	- 1985

58. Lower Thrina Dam

For irrigation purpose in Maharashtra Lower Thrina dam is constructed across the Thrina river, one of the tributaries of Godavari. Salient features are:

Type	- Earthen Gravity dam
Gross storage capacity	- 14,826,000 m^3
Height above lowest foundation	- 19 m
Length of crest	- 3484 m
Volume content of the dam	- 566,000 m^3
Year of completion	- 1988.

59. Majalgaon Dam (Jayakwadi Project)

Majalgaon Dam is constructed across the river Sindphana, one of the tributaries of Godavari. This is an irrigation project. Salient features are:

Type	- Earth dam with gatedogee, masonry spillway in gorge.
Rainfall	- 80 cm
Area of catchment	- 3,840 Km^2
Height above lowest foundation	- 31.19 m
Gross storage capacity	- 453,640,000 m^3
Live storage capacity	- 311,300,000 m^3
Length of the dam	- 6,240 m
Volume content of the dam	- 4,683,000 m^3
Year of completion	- Under construction

60. Wainganga Dam

Wainganga dam is constructed across the river Wainganga near Wara Seoni in Madhya Pradesh. Main features of the dam are:

Type	- Earthen and gravity
Height above lowest foundation	- 11.4 m
Length of the dam	- 2,003 m
Gross storage capacity	- 15,000,000 m^3
Effective storage capacity	- 8,000,000 m^3
Year of completion	- —

61. Lendi Dam

Lendi dam is being built across the river Godavari near Mukhed in Maharashtra for irrigation purpose. Salient features of the dam are:

Type	- Earthen
Height above lowest foundation	- 27 m
Length of the dam	- 2,055 m
Gross storage capacity	- 7,345,000 m^3
Effective storage capacity	- 5,616,000 m^3
Volume content of the dam	- 47,820,000 m^3

Year of completion - Under construction

62. Godavari Barrage

The Godavari Barrage is constructed across the river Godavari in Andhra Pradesh. Salient features are:

Type	- Earthen
Rainfall	- 114.3 cm
Area of catchment	- 3,13,649 Km^2
Purpose	- Irrigation with facility for navigation in canals
Height above lowest foundation	- 51.64 m
Gross storage capacity	- 38,990,000 m^3
Effective storage capacity	- 37,730,000 m^3
Length of the dam	- 728 m
Year of completion	- Under construction

63. Donkarayi Dam

Lower Sileru Hydro Electric Scheme consists of the construction of Donkarayi Dam in Andhra Pradesh. Salient features are:

Type	- Solid Gravity Masonry
Rainfall	- 195 cm
Area of catchment	- 5,770 Km^2
Height above lowest foundation	- 71 m
Gross storage capacity	- 470,000,000 m^3
Effective storage capacity	- 380,000,000 m^3
Length of the dam	- 598 m
Volume content of the dam	- 649,000 m^3
Year of completion	- Under construction

APPROACH TO THE PRESENT SURVEY

THE ASPECTS COVERED

The following aspects were covered in the present survey.

WATER QUALITY

Physico-chemical aspects
Nutrients
Trace metals
Organics
Planktons
Invertebrates
Benthos
Macrophytes
Fisheries
Primary productivity
Rare and endangered aquatic organism
Migratory or native birds

Sediment Quality

Physio-chemical aspects
Nutrients
Organics

Trace metals
Gases

Ground Water Quality/Quantity

Physico-chemical aspects
Nutrients
Trace metals
Organics
Microbiological aspects
Ground water table/Aquifer characteristics

Sedimentation

Sediment concentrations
Annual rate of sediment accumulation

Soil Quality

Nutrients
Salinity
Trace elements
Organics
Other important characteristics

Miscellaneous Studies

Thermal and chemical stratification
Salinity intrusion
Oxygen depletion in hypolimnion
Eutrophication
Incidences of fish kills and toxicity
Rate of loss of storage capacity of reservoir per year
Algal blooms
Weed infestation
Build up of heavy metals in hypolimnetic waters
Incidence of toxic gas generation
Loss of nutrient concentration

Land use

Forests types
Agriculture and cropping pattern

Urban/Rural settlements
Industries

Soil erosion
Soil fertility
Bank Stability
Seismicity
Salinity in irrgated soils
Waterlogging
Public health

Waterborne diseases/parasitic diseases
Diseases due to toxic chemicals

Socio-economic aspects

Agricultural production
Aquaculture
Water supply
Power supply
Flood control
Navigation
Recreation and Tourisms
Industrialization
Employment
Resettlement
Forestry
Archaeological treasures
Landscape

Wild Life

Species of wild animals
Species of rare and endangered animals
Species diversity

Microclimate

Temperature
Humidity
Rainfall
Evaporation loss
Wind speed

SOURCES EXPLORED

The following sources were explored for eliciting information:

Journals

The journals surveyed are listed in Appendix II.

Universities and Autonomous Research Institution

All the universities and research institutions situated in the basins of Krishna, Mahanadi, and Godavari rivers were contacted as also the universities and institutions situated in the capitals of the States through which the rivers flow (listed in Appendix I).

Government Agencies

The State government agencies including the dam authorities functioning in Orissa, Madhya Pradesh, Andhra Pradesh, Maharashtra and Karnataka were approached. The retaled central government agencies were also approached. The list of the agencies contacted is given in Appendix I.

Non-Governmental Organizations

All the non-governmental organizations functioning in the river basins of Krishna, Mahanadi, and Godavari were approached for information. The names and addresses of these organizations (Appendix I) were obtained from the directory published by Ministry of Environment, Government of India.

CONSTRAINTS

Finding the appropriate contact persons or obtaining the correct postal addresses of the dam authorities was the most difficult task. One officer would ask us to contact another who would ask us to contact some other and so on. Many times the chain led us back to the starting point after we had spent a few months approaching one officer after another. As the survey progressed we had an increasing realization that there is a paucity of data and even greater paucity of *analysed* data.

The second major problem was the expected one—tardiness in response. The first three reminders usually went unresponded. At times only the sixth reminder could bring in a reply and that too consisting of a new address to approach.

STATUS OF ENVIRONMENTAL IMPACT ASSESSMENT OF WATER RESOURCES PROJECTS IN KRISHNA RIVER BASIN

UJJANI RESERVOIR

Ujjani reservoir is situated near Ujjani village in Solapur district, Maharashtra. The reservoir is fed by Bhima river and is utilized for irrigation and hydroelectric power generation.

The physical and chemical analysis of the Ujjani reservoir water was conducted by Maharashtra Engineering Research Institute (MERI), Nasik, during 1978-80. The general observations were:

(a) The pH values, free carbon dioxide, total hardness, alkalinity, nitrates, nitrites, chlorides, sulphates, calcium, magnesium, potassium and ammonia were well within the limits acceptable for drinking water. Heavy metals copper and lead were found to be absent. The iron content was relatively high in the rainy season but was still within the maximum allowable concentration. Thus the water of the reservoir was found to be safe for drinking as well as industrial use and fish propogation with respect to its chemical contents.

(b) SAR (sodium adsorption ratio) and conductivity indicated that the Ujjani reservoir water falls in the category C_1S_1 or C_2S_2 which reflect good water quality for irrigational use.

(c) The dissolved oxygen was generally in the range 8.2 to 6.0 ppm; at lower depths it was lesser. Good aerobic condition was reflected in the results. The biochemical oxygen demand and maximum probable number were generally observed higher than the respective desirable ranges but the authors suspected that higher values may be due to the time gap between the collection and the testing of the samples.

Overall, the studies indicated that in 1980, two years after it was commissioned, the Ujjani reservoir had generally acceptable water quality. Unfortunately no data for the subsequent years is available but the MERI studies provide a good body of basic data which will serve as a frame of reference for further studies on the impact of ageing of the Ujjani reservoir on its water quality.

UPPER KRISHNA PROJECT (UKP)

The Upper Krishna Project (UKP) consists of two reservoirs. The main storage reservoir being at Almatti (capacity 6,430 million m^3). The other reservoir at Narayanpur (capacity 1,071 M m^3) is a diversion reservoir. The project includes a pick-up weir at Hippargi to implement a lift irrigation scheme. Phase-I involves completion of the Narayanpur dam, left bank canal and distributaries, and partially building the Almatti dam. An area of 8.43 lakh hectares is irrigated under Phase-I. A considerable fraction of the target has been achieved and over 90 villages are being irrigated. Karnataka's move to raise the level of Alamatti dam had been troubling Andhra Pradesh for sometime. Karnataka is bent on building as high dam as possible so that by the year 2000, when review of the Krishna water dispute tribunal becomes due, it is in a position to show maximum use of the Krishna waters.

The Bachawat award had allocated 700 TMC. ft. (thousand million cubic feet) of water to Karnataka, 800 TMC. ft to Andhra Pradesh and 560 TMC. ft. to Maharashtra. These limits set up by the tribunal and the mega-project centered mindset of the water resources bureaucracy and politicians, seem to be root of the problem. In their haste to show maximum utilization of Krishna waters, all three states are building oversized reservoirs, without taking into consideration social, environmental or financial implications of the projects.

In the haste to complete the dam, the people to be affected by it stand to lose the most. The Alamatti dam—which the Bachawat tribunal called the 'carry over reservoir' has reportedly already reached a height of 507 m. Against the 3m gates as originally envisaged the dam will now have 15.5 m gates.

The UKP command area broadly consists of two types of soils: black and red. Of these black soils, which constitute 86 per cent of the command, have physico-chemical properties which hinder drainage. This is attributed to considerable dispersion and swelling mechanisms by which surface soil aggregates break down impeding infiltration of water into the soil. Swelling and dispersion of black soil clays also affects its water transmission capability by altering the geometry and the continuity of the soil pores.

The intensive irrigation made possible by UKP, faulty irrigation management practices, and seepage from the network of distribution system, are all contributing to waterlogging in the black soil areas. The rise in water table is fast; by 1988, within a period of 4 years (1984-88), the water table on an average had risen by 0.6 to 0.8m in some areas. Often, the rise in water table is alarming and some locations have gone out of cultivation due to waterlogging and development of salinity.

Farmers almost always believe that crop yield increases in direct proportion to the amount of water applied but the excess water percolates into the ground, leading to swelling of the water table. In the beginning the yields are indeed very good, but this lasts only till the water table remains well below the surface. Often the higher lands in the command area do not get waterlogged, because the greater slopes in the upper reaches induce a faster movement of groundwater. But that water moves towards lower lying lands which then get waterlogged.

The second major source of excess water is seepage loss from unlined irrigation canals and reservoirs. Most irrigation canals are not lined because of the high costs involved. Even in rich countries like the USA, only 6 to 8 per cent of the total length of irrigation canals is lined. In some unlined canals, seepage from the bed and sides may be as high as 70 per cent of the water let into them or more. On an average it amounts to about 40 per cent

The other causes of waterlogging are improper levelling of irrigated land, absence of field drains for removing excess surface water, silting up of and weed growth in natural drains, non-exploitation of ground water and adoption of a cropping pattern not best suited to the soil.

Some unique situations in UKP which cause problems in drainage, are:

(a) Red and black soils lying side by side. Areas with red soils having shallow porous nature lying in the upper reaches and black soils with poor drainability occurring in valley portions (anisotropic landscape) as found around Kawadimatti, Kamanatagi, Devatakal and Kodekal villages have caused impediment to drainage. The situation has been accentuated with seepage.

(b) In areas with rock out crops as found around Joganbhavi with irrigation of interspersed land areas, water is wasted causing waterlogging in lower reaches.

(c) Impervious soils such as Tumkur soil series with calcareous lower horizon having high exchangeable sodium percentage (15.9 ESP) easily develop waterlogging and salinity.

Overall the heterogeneity of geology and landscape in UKP are the main causes of waterlogging. In Shorapur and Shahapur taluks (Gulbarga district), close to 1,000 ha. have been affected due to waterlogging and about 500 ha. are suffering due to salinity and sodicity. The affected areas are in small pockets of 15-20 ha. but in few places they extend to more than 100 ha. In Islampur village near Hunasigi, 125-150 ha. have been severely damaged due to waterlogging.

The Agricultural Research Station, Bheemarayonagudi, Dharwad has conducted studies from 1987 onwards on the impact of canal irrigation on groundwater quality.

Water samples from wells as well as from canal (Krishna water) were collected and analysed. Depth of water tables of the wells were also periodically monitored. The studies have clearly indicated that the water table in the wells irrespective of the soil type increased appreciably due to canal irrigation.

The percolating water was found to have a moderating effect on the quality of well waters. In the wells around Hunasigi, the quality of water was not fit for irrigation as it belonged to irrigability class of C_2S_4 . The water contained high levels of carbonates, bicarbonates and sodium with Sodium Absorption Ratio of more than 16. In another well located in slightly waterlogged vertisols of Chennur village, the water had alkaline pH with moderate levels of carbonates and bicarbonates; the EC values were within safer limits and the water was useable for irrigation by providing proper drainage. Irrigation wells situated in red sandy soils of Kawadimatti, Aralahalli, Devatakal and Benakanhalli also contained water suitable for irrigation.

In another study by Subramany (1988), on the chemical quality of groundwater in the command area of UKP, 175 water samples were collected during the post monsoon season (November-December 1987) representing different geological set up and soil conditions. The samples were analysed by the State Groundwater Cell. The main findings were:

(a) Most of the groundwaters from black soils had high TDS (total dissolved solids) concentrations, which ranged from 3,000 to 10,000 ppm, indicating the unfitness of the waters for irrigation.

The TDS of water from areas of red soil was much lower, in the range 310-2,480 ppm, indicating fitness for irrigation.

(b) Three distinct and isolated brackish/saline zones were identified: Yadhalli-Kembhavi Zone, Gonal-Devapur zone and Sagar-Hattigudur-Hayyal K-Zone, where the ground water was not suitable for drinking or irrigation as per the WHO (World Health Organization) standards and USGS (United States Geological Survey) classifications for drinking and irrigation purposes respectively. The brackish/saline zone extended over 26,703 hectares in the command area.

(c) The quality of groundwater vis a vis irrigation in the command area was generally good, Over 70 per cent of the command area fell within the excellent to permissible range, 20 per cent unsuitable and 10 per cent covered by rocky exposures.

(d) The direct use of the groundwater in three isolated brackish/saline zones for irrigation will result in heavy accumulation of salt over the soils. If no canal water is provided urgently for conjunctive use, the entire area may become barren in a couple of years.

Prevalence of Disease

At the instance of Government of Karnataka, Institute for Command Studies and Irrigation Management(ICSM) has conducted a study which indicates the prevalence of water borne diseases like Guinea worm in the command area of UKP attributed to impoundments and stagnation of water. High malaria endemicity is recorded in Upper Krishna Irrigation Project (Jain, 1994).

Displacement

One of the few cases where efforts were made to implement a land-for-land policy was the second of the two dams of the Upper Krishna Irrigation II project in Karnataka.

The World Bank funded part of the project and then realising that pressure for a better plan was building up from local communities who had seen the experience of those displaced by the first dam, withheld its funds.

This led to the involvement of a state based social action group, MYRADA, in two phases of the plan surveys and implementation. While several families were provided plots in the command areas, others were resettled on unirrigated land or given the choice of an income generating project. But even here experience showed that those with assets and power prior to displacement cornered most of the benefits while most of those belonging to poorer communities were left with unproductive lands and a few temporary jobs (Kothari, 1996).

MALAPRABHA PROJECT

This project has a command area of 218,181 hectares. It consists of a dam and canal system to irrigate 212,181 ha., extension of existing Kolchi canal, and 8 lift irrigation schemes to irrigate 24,579 ha.

Surveys have indicated that more than 2,460 ha. is waterlogged or saline; the Soundatty taluk being the worst affected.

In the initial stages of development of the command area, water was being supplied as and when demanded by the irrigators. The cropping pattern was decided by individual farmers without considerations for the soil type and the suitability of the soil for the crop grown. The Warabandi system and night irrigation practices were not followed. Field channels were not maintained properly and the lands were not levelled as required. Silt had collected in natural drains. All these contributed to waterlogging and salinity.

Steps are now being taken for reclaiming the waterlogged areas. A typical drainage scheme for Kapali and Shirol village lands is described below.

The area consists of deep black cotton soils which are impervious, with permeability about 0.35 m per year. The lands are very flat. To enable intensive agriculture, the natural drains have been bunded up for cultivation and weed growth has taken place, obstructing the flow. The result has been a rise in the water table. An area of about 228 ha. is thus affected by waterlogging, rendering the land unfit for agriculture. Also the village itself is affected by the rise leading to unhealthy living conditions and collapse of many houses.

The drainage scheme now prepared to reclaim the land for productive agriculture by lowering the water table, consists of three stages:

(i) Deepening the existing open drains and providing additional drains.
(ii) Providing primary sub-surface drainage by installing perforated pipes with open joints at 60 cm spacing.
(iii) Providing secondary sub-surface drainage, with drainage pipes at closer intervals.

The first stage of the scheme is now underway at an estimated cost of Rs 13,000 per hectare.

Improvements as a result of this scheme are noticeable; there is a lowering of water table by 0.03 m to 0.65 m in the trial pits. Farmers have started growing crops in the area which was previously unproductive.

The Irrigation department, Belgaum, has conducted studies on the physico chemical aspects of the water quality of the reservoir and downstream from 1984 May. From 1981 they have conducted studies on the nutrients of the reservoir and downstream. According to them, the cropping pattern of the command area is: Kharif 40 per cent, two seasonals 20 per cent, Rabi 40 per cent. They have also studied the extent of waterlogging in the command area since 1980 and have reported that an area of 2,729 ha. is waterlogged as on date. The data base generated by them includes different aspects of the microclimate of the reservoir catchment such as temperature, 1974 onwards, humidity, rainfall evaporation losses and wind speed.

GHATAPRABHA PROJECT

This project consists of a storage dam and a canal system for irrigating 317,430 ha. An area of about 2,000 ha. is estimated to have been waterlogged in the command area of the project.

The causes of waterlogging in Ghataprabha command area are similar to the ones in Malaprabha command area. In several areas, particularly in the case of poorly drained soils, salinity has resulted. The problem is particularly bad in the command areas of the Left Bank Canal in Jamkhandi, Mudhol, Raibag and Gokak taluks.

In order to reduce the effect of waterlogging and salinity it is planned to construct a system of drains from each field up to a main drain which in turn would generally follow the natural drainage. The average cost of reclamation of the waterlogged areas works out to Rs 3,300/ha. Upto 20 per cent of the field irrigation canals are proposed to be lined with Murram or stone or concrete slabs.

BHADRA PROJECT

The Command Area Development Authority, Shimoga has jurisdiction over the command areas of Bhadra project, Tunga Anicut and Gondi Anicut. Irrigation in the area is about 30 years old. About 4,300 ha. out of a total irrigated area of 1.24 lakh ha in the CADA area have become waterlogged. Details of the water logged land in Bhadra project are given in the Table 7.1.

The main cause of waterlogging in this area appears to be excess water application due to excessive paddy cultivation. The area notified for paddy by the Bhadra Project authorities is generally around 10,000 ha. in summer and 32,000 ha. in Kharif. Against this the actual area cultivated with paddy is around 50,000 ha. each in summer as well as Kharif. This is mainly at the expense of semi-dry crops, which are grown in an area of only about 20,000 ha. as against the notified area of 55,000 to 70,000 ha. in either season.

TABLE 7.1 DETAILS OF WATERLOGGED LAND IN BHADRA IRRIGATION PRO JECT

Taluk	*District*	*total irrigated aera (Hectare)*	*Area to be reclaimed (Hectare)*
Shimoga	Shimoga	17,198	455
Bhadravathi	Shimoga	21,389	1,185
Honnali	Shimoga	8,659	420
Channagiri	Shimoga	23,809	302
Davangere	Chitradurga	21,374	546
Harihar	Chitradurga	19,200	307
Tarikere	Chikmagalur	11,074	549
Harpanahalli	Bellary	1,689	579
	Total	1,24,392	4,343

It is planned to lower the water table by installing buried clay pipes for subsurface drainage. Semi-broad (10 cm) pipes are being used for lateral drains and broad (15 cm) for main drains. Surface drainage to remove excess irrigation water is also planned with open drains leading to natural drainage pathways. The average cost of reclamation is estimated at Rs 8,079/ha. The amount spent for subsurface drainage is to be recovered by the Revenue Department in 15 annual instalments. Leaching of the excess salts follows installation of subsurface drainage. Block irrigation is being done, wherein 1/6 of the land is kept fallow for one season, thereby taking 5 crops in 3 years. This, it is hoped, would reduce water application by a sixth.

TUNGABHADRA PROJECT

Tungabhadra project is a dual purpose project for power as well as irrigation. The Left Bank Canal irrigates 2,43,900 ha. The Left Bank High Level Canal irrigates 469 ha. The Right Bank Low Level Canal irrigates 37,503 ha., and the Right Bank High Level Canal irrigates 80,908 ha. The total area irrigated thus amounts to 3.63 lakh ha.

In view of the slow pace of land development the ryots were allowed to grow any crop they liked in the earlier stages and there has been a continuous violation of cropping pattern. The trend for growing paddy is ever on the increase. Unauthorized irrigation has also increased. Consequently, the farmers are utilizing more water than stipulated in the higher reaches, thereby making the tailenders suffer.

Water in the wells in the command area is saline. The principal soils of the command area are deep black soils which account for 80 per cent, red soils covering the rest. The clay content in deep black soils is about 76 per cent. Infiltration rate is about 1.2 cm/hour for these soils compared to 3.75 cm/hour for red soil having clay content of 42.5 per cent. Soluble salt content in the soil moisture varies from 0.036 to 0.20 per cent in the root zones and goes beyond 2.5 per cent at the salt concentration zone. The principal salts in the upper layers are sodium and calcium bicarbonates and calcium chlorides, whereas the salt concentration zone contains abundant calcium sulphate and sodium sulphate.

Results of the water analysis reveal that the soils have electrical conductivity higher than 1 m mho/cm at 25° C, pH higher than 8.5 and exchangeable sodium percentage higher than 15, indicating that the soils are predominantly saline. Since the rainfall is low (18 to 23 cm) the salts accumulated on the surface area are not leached out.

After about 35 years of irrigation, it is estimated that waterlogging has occurred in 15,000 ha. under the command of the Left Bank Canal, 6,000 ha under the Right Bank Low Level Canal and 12,000 ha. under the Right Bank High Level Canal, totalling 33,000 ha.

The assessment of waterlogged area is based on the spot visual examination. Salt efflorescence, water stagnation, poor germination and hard soil structures are the symptoms of lands affected by salinity, alkalinity and waterlogging. Also the wells situated in the command area, with their high water table, indicate the predominance of waterlogging (Table 7.2).

TABLE 7.2: RISE OF WATER TABLE IN THE COMMAND AREA OF TUNGABHADRA PROJECTDD

Village	*Period of observation*		*Decrease in depth of water table (m)*		*Net rise in table (m)*	*Average rise in m/year*
			from	*to*		
Paddy & Sugarcane Area						
Kamalapur	Apr 77 to	May 81	2.60	2.05	0.55	0.14
Siruguppe	Jun 78	Jun 81	1.90	1.40	0.50	0.16
Kurugodu						
Well No. 1	Jun 77	Dec 80	1.10	0.75	0.35	0.10
Well No. 2	May 77	May 80	0.80	0.60	0.20	0.07
Chellur						
Well No. 1	May 79	May 81	1.60	1.20	0.40	0.20
Well No. 2	May 77	May 81	1.15	0.95	0.20	0.05
Well No. 3	May 77	May 80	1.65	1.35	0.30	0.10
Dry cum wet crops area						
Lakshmipura	Apr 74	Jun 80	2.45	1.75	0.70	0.12
Sidharagadda	Aug 78	Jul 81	6.60	5.45	1.15	0.29*
Effects due to canal seepage						
Venkatapura	Jul 74	Jul 80	1.70	1.50	0.20	0.03
Somanhal	May 77	Apr 81	2.50	1.90	0.60	0.15

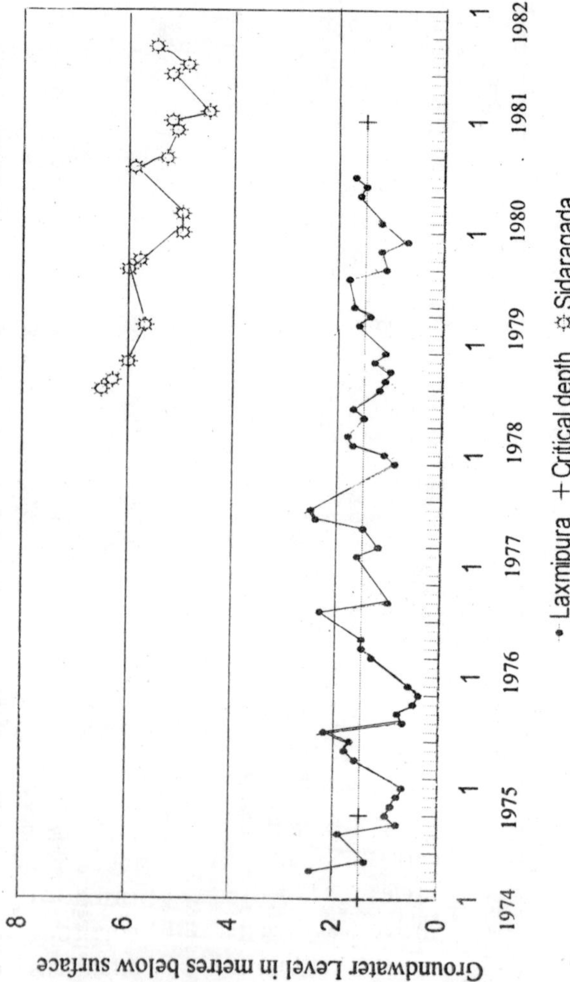

Fig. 7.1: Groundwater level in Tungabhadra Command.

Hydrographs of the wells in the command area have indicated that the average rate of rise in the water table due to irriga tion and canal seepage is about 13 cm per year. (Figure 7.1).

Areas around Yellapura, Genekenal and a few other villages have become swamps, with watertable reaching the surface. Extensive development of saline crusts (2 to 4 cm thick) due to waterlogging has taken place in soils near Kurugodu, Bailur, Gotur, Lakshmipura, Sangankal and other places. Figure 7.1 shows the variations in ground water level at two villages in the Tungabha dra Command. It is seen that at Sidaragadda, although waterlog ging has not yet taken place(water table depth is greater than 1.5 cm) groundwater level shows a rising trend. In Lakshmipura no rising trend is seen, but the land has been waterlogged for several years, with the water table deeper than 1.5 m only during summer months. This is true of many other areas in the command.

*In addition to the dry-cum wet irrigation, the seepage from the nearby pond has contributed to the increased rate of rise in water table.

Tungabhadra project being the first major project where extensive problems due to waterlogging have occurred, and having been in operation for a long time, a more thorough investigation into the causes of waterlogging has been made here than in any other basin of the State. The following causes of waterlogging have been identified.

Irrigation and cropping pattern

Prior to the introduction of irrigation, an extensive soil survey was conducted and soils were classified as Grade I consisting of coarse sandy loams to fine sandy loams, Grade II and II A consisting of deep black cotton soils, Grade III consisting of black cotton soils and Grade IV comprising soils unfit for agriculture. Cropping pattern was planned on the basis of the above classification. But in the initial stages the farmers were allowed and encouraged to grow crops of their choice. Farmers with lands identified for light irrigated crops started growing heavy irrigated crops like paddy without paying any attention to the possible after-effects. Though punitive measures were stipulated to check this unauthorized irrigation at the later stage, they were never imposed strictly (Table 7.3).

Improper land development

Another major reason for waterlogging in the Tungabhadra Command Area is the slow pace of land development. Though irrigation was introduced in 1953, even by 1983 the area developed was only about 60 per cent of the envisaged total. This promoted excessive use of water which was easily available in the absence of demand. Lack of finance seems to be the main impediment in the development of land at the desired pace.

Seepage and drainage

The loss of water due to seepage in field channels is estimated at 22 per cent. The total seepage loss in the conveyance system is estimated at 45 per cent. Subsurface drainage to avoid these losses was not included in the project at the planning and design stage to keep costs down. Even after the start of operations, the provision is not very much (about 0.07 per cent).

TABLE 7.3: AREA PLANNED AND ACTUAL AREA COVERED UNDER HEAVY AND LIGHT IRRIGATION

Type of irrigation	Area planned in hectares	Actual area covered 1971-72	1981-82
Heavy	30,000 (13%)	37,616 (32%)	60,389 (25%)
Light	2,02,000 (87%)	78,135 (68%)	1,86,675 (75%)

Chocking of drainage paths

The natural drainage paths, are cluttered up with vegetation and trapped sediment. As a consequence surface drainage is slow.

Low efficiency of water use

A low efficiency of water use is another cause of waterlogging and soil salinization. The reasons for the poor efficiency of utilization of water, apart from seepage through canals, are,

(i) occurrence of breaches in the embankment of the Left Bank Main Canal
(ii) a mix of crops with very different water demands in an area served by a single outlet;
(iii) the official localization plan of crops to be grown differing from the rational cropping pattern;
(iv) the design of water duty for various crops largely differing from reality;
(v) unauthorized irrigation;
(vi) operation of irrigation system not being attuned to the actual cropping pattern;
(vii) inability of water management officers to make use of powers given to them under Irrigation Act of 1965, to deal with misuse of water crop violation;
(viii) a lack of Organization amongst beneficiaries, with tailenders suffering the most; and
(ix) poor on-farm water mananagement practices.

Extensive reclamation measures have been planned by the Tungabhadra CADA (Command Area Development Authority). The main canals and distributaries are to be lined to block a major source of excess water seepage. Open as well as tile drains are to be constructed to lower the water table and to help leaching. Natural surface drainage paths are to be cleared of weeds and silt. Conjunctive use of groundwater and surface waters for irrigation is also envisaged to help in lowering the water table.

Siltation

In order to overcome the problem of siltation and decreasing water storage capacity, the Central Water Commission (CWC) is examining a proposal to increase the height of Tungabhadra dam in Karnataka.

It assumes greater significance as the farmers of Kurnool, Anantpur and Cuddapah districts in Andhra Pradesh who depend upon the low level and the high level canals of the dam are concerned about the unavoidable cut in their share of water due to silta tion.

DHOM DAM AND RESERVOIR

Dhom Irrigation-Sub Division No. I are conducting studies on the physico chemical aspects of the water quality of the reservoir and the fisheries from 1987. They have also generated data on the groundwater table and aquifer characteristics of wells downstream. They have surveyed about 32,925 ha. for cropping pattern in the command area. Their ongoing studies include flood control, waterlogging, resettlement, and micro-climate.

WARNA PROJECT

Irrigation Division Pune, has studied the concentrations and particle sizes of the sediments of the Warna river from 1966 to 1973. According to them, the annual rate of sediment accumulation in the Warna Reservoir is 0.025306 ha m/km. Warna Project Circle, Kolhapur, believes that the rate of loss of storage capacity of the reservoir is only 0.005 per cent per year. Divisional Forest Office, Kolhapur, have collected information on the forest types and wildlife in the reservoir catchment. Observations on seismicity are also available but they do not point to any adverse impacts. The project area has a wildlife sanctuary called 'Chandoli Abhayaranya' supported by the government of Maharashtra. The construction of a 16 MW power house is in progress and is likely to be completed by 1991. The damming of Warna river has affected 26 villages and 1,262 families. Out of this 25 villages and 1,203 families were shifted to alternative site by June 86. One village Chandoli is yet to be shifted which is on the dam site. To cover the exposed slopes of the catchment 56,500 trees have been planted.

DUDHGANGA IRRIGATIOIN PROJECT

The Irrigation Research Division (IRD), Pune, is conducting studies on the groundwater table in the command area of the dam. According to Warna Project Circle the rate of sedimentation in the reservoir is so low that the likely loss in the live storage capacity after 100 years is only 0.1 per cent. The information on the forests types was collected by Forest Department at the beginning of project only.

HIDKAL DAM AND RESERVOIR

Irrigation Department, Belgaum, has conducted studies on the water quality of the feeder stream and the reservoir covering the physico chemical aspects from 1977 onwards at a frequency of 12 samples per year. The data base being generated by them includes temperature, humidity, rainfall, evaporation lossess and wind speed.

RADHANAGARI RESERVOIR

It is a man-made reservoir over an ephemeral stream 70 km south-west of the Kolhapur city. It is surrounded by hills. The reservoir is fed mainly by run off during the rains. The human activity in the reservoir catchment is insignificant.

Studies by P.K. Goel, R.K. Trivedy and S.V. Bhave of Post-graduate Department of Environmental Pollution, Science College, Karad, reveal the water to be soft and suitable for irrigation:

pH	7.32
Total alkalinity, mg/lit	70.0
Total dissolved solids, mg/lit	397.0
Ammonia, mg/lit	1.68
Nitrate-N, mg/lit	0.31
Inorganic PO-P, mg/lit	0.05
Sulphate, mg/lit	12.00
Chlorides, mg/lit	33.3
Calcium, mg/lit	5.2
Magnesium, mg/lit	2.9

PANSHET DAM AND RESERVOIR

Panshet Dam was designed with the assumption that its annual rate of siltation would be around 2,000 acre feet. But the dam is silting five times more than this mainly due to the deforestation in its catchment.

The Dam has also witnessed long struggle of the people who were displaced from its commissioning. The dam submerged 21 villages affecting over a thousand landowning households and 200 landless families. As no notice of land acquisition was given to the people, the village leaders and local elite took the opportunity to grab all that came their way.

In 1968, their agitation became a focus of the simmering discontent in other parts of the state, and all these movements joined hands to press the state government to meet their demands. Faced with continuous pressure, the government passed the necessary legislation in 1976. But since then the fight is going on for its implementation in a manner that all affected people can be benefitted.

KOYNA DAM AND RESERVOIR

Reservoir-induced seismicity

The seismic activity in the Koyna-Kolkewadi reservoir complex area has been one of the widely accepted cases of reservoir-induced seismicity. Unlike the majority of known reservoir-induced seismicity cases, the seismicity at Koyna has been continuing for the past two and a half decades, though with reduced intensity. Also, it has been observed that the seismicity has shown a trend to migrate in the northwesterly direction towards the recently constructed balancing Kolkewadi reservoir which was impounded in mid-1974 by the water diverted from the Pophali Hydroelectric Power Station.

The Koyna-Kolkewadi reservoir complex, soon after the initiation of water impoundment behind Koyna dam in 1962, started experiencing mild earth tremors accompanied by loud sounds. On

13 September 1967, five significant earthquakes (M 4.0 to 5.8) occurred in the reservoir area. These were followed by a disastrous seismic event, the Koyna earthquake (M 6.5) on 10 December 1967, which caused extensive damage to property and took the lives of about 200 people. Two villages and a number of culverts were totally destroyed. Over 1,500 people were injured and thousends were rendered homeless. More than 80 per cent of the houses in Koynanagar were either completely destroyed or became unhabitable. The city of Bombay and suburds were also rocked. The Koyna dam moved and several cracks apperared in its structure but fortunately the dam did not burst or else the consequences would have been catastrophic. It is evident from the distribution of epicentres of all the earthquakes (over 100,000 of minor intensity upto M 6.5) that have occurred in the region during the period 1963-87 that the epicentres of most of the earthquakes were located in the area around the Koyna dam.

It is significant to note that the weekly frequency of earthquake activity relatively increased with increase in monsoon water level, with some time lag. Also, when water level rose to 650 m above the mean sea level and remained there for a fairly long time, seismic activity increased considerably.

Significant earthquakes in 1967 (M 6.5), 1973 (M 5.3) and 1980 (M 4.8), and increases in earthquake frequency were immediately preceded by high lake-level (L) and high rate of change of lake level (dL/dT).

Studies by S.K. Guha (Department of Geology, University of Poona) reveal that though normally lake-level could be a determining factor in triggering large seismic events, in case of Koyna-Kolkewadi reservoir system high rate of change of lake level (dL/dT) has been found to be more effective in triggering significant earthquakes in 1967, 1973 and 1980. Hence in favourable circumstances, it may be possible to control induced seismicity through the manipulation of dL/dT, though the designed lake level catchment area. There may be a characteristic lake level (L) and rate of change of lake level (dL/dT) for a particular geological situation. This would depend on tectonic stress, fracture pattern, type of faulting, earthquake history of the region, etc. where induced seismicity could be controlled by delimiting lake level (L) or rate of change of lake level (dL/dT) or both. As far as the Koyna reservoir is concerned, the rate of change of lake level (dL/dT) may be the dominant factor, as all the three significant seismic events followed high dL/dT.

The damaged area of the main Koyna earthquake of 10 December 1967 is rather limited as compared to the large area where the earthquake was felt.

Flooding and landslides

After the tail race discharges from Stages I, II and III power houses of Koyna Project began to be let off in the west-flowing river Vashishthi, there have been occasional reports of flooding of low-lying areas at Chiplun, a small town, during high tides.

In June 1983, an area in the upper reaches of Vashishthi suffered massive landslides due to the cumulative effects of Koyna earthquakes. The landlides were accompanied by loud rumbling sounds and occurred during heavy rainfall. Landslides are a rare phenomenon in the geological environment of the area. In 1983, landslides adjacent to Koyna reservoir were investigated by a geologist from the Department of Geology, University of Poona. It is possible that induced seismicity at Koyna had triggered landslides in an unprecedented scale which, in turn, adversely affected the river flow and consequently intensified the flooding of the low-lying area of the Vashishthi river basin. The landslides also deforested significant parts of the affected area.

Siltation of the reservoir and sand bar formation downstream

Rate of deposition of silt as computed from surveys in 1966 and 1977 works out to 1524 $m^3/km^2/yr$ which is equivalent to loss of storage of 0.1 per cent per year. A later survey has shown no excessive siltation following the Koyna earthquake of 10 December 1967. In all Koyna reservoir does not appear to be suffering from excessives siltation.

The depositional characteristics in the Koyna river channel downstream of the dam are due to a reduced flow in the Koyna river following construction of the upstream dam. Thus, the channel geometry of the downstream channel of the river is altered in patches.

Groundwater

It is not been possible to assess any quantitative changes in water levels in these wells following impoundment of Koyna reservoir. This is due to lack of long-term data, though some reports indicate rise in water levels in some nearby wells during post-impoundment periods. Though no information is available, it is possible that due to decreased flow in the downstream channel of the Koyna river, Groundwater potential may have been affected.

Climatic changes

In an attempt to assess any climatic changes brought about by impoundment of Koyna reservoir, temperature and rainfall data available for over 50 years were analysed for climatic changes at Padegaon (long. 18°12' N; lat. 74°10' E), situated near the reservoir. But the results were doubtful and statistically not significant.

Flora and fauna of the Koyna catchment

Forest cover in the catchment is about 41 per cent; about 50 km^2 of forest area was submerged (water spread at maximum flood level being 120.43 km^3) due to impoundment. Considering the physiography and climate of the Koyna valley, most of the forests submerged due to impoundment are of Western (montane) sub-tropical hill type and West Coast semi-evergreen type. Hence, human interference, coupled with submergence, seems to have been responsible for the disappearance of a large tract of dense forest.

There are about 500 species of birds in Maharashtra, including migratory ones. Of these, about 200 abound in Koyna area, out of which about 45 species are more frequently seen in the reservoir area. No large flocks of water birds are seen in the Koyna reservoir area.

Since the Koyna river is only a seasonal one, there was no fishery of commercial importance before the impoundment of the reservoir. However, following dam construction, many zoo-geographical changes have taken place. Faunistic change in Koyna reservoir was attempted by way of direct release of 1.5 lakhs of major carp fish eggs. According to fishery experts, the reservoir, being deep and narrow, with steep hill slopes, is not ideally suited for fishing. Though the reservoir has potential for an annual fish production of 700 Mt, only 200 Mt is produced. The production of fish is steadily increasing. It is estimated that about 200 people are currently engaged in fishing in the reservoir. Though regular fishing was earlier unknown, impoundment of the reservoir has been helpful in the development of employment potential.

Water quality

There is no data available on physical and chemical analysis of Koyna reservoir water, but some information is available on the Krishna river of which Koyna is a tributary. Results of physical, chemical and bacteriological tests of Krishna river water show that it is safe for domestic and industrial use, irrigation as well as pisciculture, but needs conventional treatment before use as drinking water. This is in view of the pollution due to untreated or partly treated sewage and industrial waste being discharged into the main river course or its tributaries. It is worth mentioning here that there is no industrial unit upstream of Koyna reservoir. Its water should be pollution-free, unlike the water of the Krishna downstream.

Public health

The data collected by the Statistics Division of the Department of Public Health, Maharashtra, showed no increase in the incidence of water-borne diseases except jaundice in the Satara district, though separate statistics for Patan Taluka, where Koyna dam is situated, were not available.

Displacement and rehabilitation

In all, 9,424 families from 104 villages have been displaced due to the Koyna reservoir. Most of them have been rehabilitated in 138 places in Satara, Sangli, Thane, Kulaba and Ratnagiri districts. Some of the affected people have accepted cash compensation. Rehabilitation of villagers at distances from their original villages have, at times, caused some distress due to new surroundings and slow adjustments. It is also reported that a small percentage of displaced families could not adjust to new surroundings and actually returned.

SRISAILAM PROJECT

"The problems arising out of the submersion of villages and agri cultural lands by river valley projects affect mostly the poorer sections of the population in the villages". This is one of the conclusions of a report prepared by a fact-finding team sponsored by the Lokayan Research Programme of the Centre for Study of Developing Societies, which surveyed 15 out of the 100 villages affected by the Srisailam dam in Andhra Pradesh.

This gigantic dam across the Krishna river will submerge over 100,000 acres of land, displacing about 100,000 persons 81 per cent of them belong to scheduled and backward castes and about 75 per cent of the households have been marginal farmers or agricultural labourers according to the Lokyan report. While the landowners received some compensation, which they generally described as inadequate, nothing was paid to the weaker sections who had been surviving for years by cultivating government-owned waste lands.

Ninety-five per cent of those surveyed were illiterate and unaware of the provisions of the Land Acquisition Act of 1860. This made them vulnerable to corrupt officials in charge of making compensation payments. On the other hand, many rich and educated persons sued the Government for an increase in compensation. Out of 9,417 cases filed, 416 have been settled and the Government has lost each one of them.

NAGARJUNASAGAR DAM AND RESERVOIR

Centre for Science & Environment reports in its 'The State of India's Environment 1982' (page 135):

The sub-soil environmental changes caused by the construction of the Nagarjunasagar dam are believed to have triggered a chain reaction resulting ultimately in a crippling syndrome of knock-knees (genu valgum) among the poverty-stricken villagers living in the command area of the dam.

Scientists of the National Institute of Nutrition (NIN) at Hyderabad believe that curious but complex and inter-related factors are operating there. Water seepage from the dam's reservoir and canals has increased the level of the sub-soil water. As a result the alkalinity level of the soil has increased. This in turn has changed the fluoride, calcium and trace metals (copper, molybdenum, zinc and magnesium) composition of the soil, thus creating suitable conditions for increased uptake of molybdenum by sorghum plants.

For people living on sorghum as staple, this has meant a high dietary intake of molybdenum and as a consequence, high excretion of copper and thereby copper deficiency. Associated with a high fluoride intake—skeletal fluorosis has been known to be endemic in these parts for almost four decades now this has meant an acute incidence of genu valgum.

Genu valgum can be identified in the people, there, both in standing position and when they walk. In extreme cases the legs are so distorted that the knee joints cross over. In some others, in the standing position the two feet are separated by over a yard while the knees touch each other. In other cases, an s-shaped deformity of legs has resulted in a total incapacity to move.

Apart from the severe physical handicap it has imposed genu valgum has also contributed to serious emotional disturbances and social stress. There are several instances of broken families as a result of married women developing the disease. Affected victims are targets of ridicule, insult and social deprivation. Economic hardships has also visited the affected young men who have been forced to accept lowly paid unskilled occupations having lost their technical occupation. Not merely individuals but the entire community has suffered in the villages studied by the NIN scientists.

Over 75 per cent cases of genu valgum belong to the age group 10-20 years, and detailed history indicated that the deformity sets in at the age between six and seven years. But the skeletal fluorosis is typically found in the adult male beyond the age of 20 years. The old disease of fluorosis has acquired a new dimension in genu valgum because of the environmental changes caused by the Nagarjunasagar dam.

A detailed examination of the diets of those affected by genu valgum shows that the problem is less frequent among people whose staple is rice in comparison with those who eat mainly sorghum. Since the lowest socio-economic strata take sorghum as the their staple, rice being costly, the incidence of genu valgum is higher among the poorest groups of the village populations.

CUMULATIVE IMPACTS

There is no study available on the cumulative impacts of all the dams in the Krishna River basin, which is not surprising in view of the fact that information on even the individual dams in the basin is either unavailable or scanty. It can, however, be estimated that given the frequency and extent of the problem of waterlogging, the cumulative adverse impacts of the dams in this respect must be substantial.

STATUS OF ENVIRONMENTAL IMPACT ASSESSMENT OF WATER RESOURCES PROJECTS IN MAHANADI RIVER BASIN

HIRAKUD DAM AND RESERVOIR

Mahanadi is the biggest river of Orissa. It is called 'the river of happiness and sorrow of Orissa'. It carries 75 million acre feet of mean annual run-off with maximum flood discharge of 1.5 - 2.7 millions cusec. The natural resources of its valley are lush and abundant, while its delta is fertile and prosperous. However the delta is periodically devasted by floods. The economy of the region suffers badly whenever this happens. In order to prevent flood damage, Mahanadi was dammed at Hirakud, 12 Km west of Sambalpur. The other envisaged benefits were power generation (200 MW) and irrigation (1.52 lakh Ha).

The Seonath, the Jonk, the Hasdeo, the Mand and the Ib are the principal tributaries of Mahanadi upstream the Dam.

Deforestation Around the Reservoir

Hirakud reservoir appears to have catalysed deforestration in the areas surrounding it.

TABLE 8.1 : LOSS OF FOREST IN A RADIUS OF 20 MILES AROUND SAMBALPUR AND JHARSUGUDA DURING 1929-1975

	Sambalpur	*Jharsuguda*
Total forest loss (sq mile)	174.46	176.97
Loss rate/year (sq miles)	3.88	3.93
Loss rate/day (hectares)	2.75	2.78
Forest present as percentage of total land area 1929	33.0	30.0
Percentage of total forest area lost 1929-75	43.0	46.0

A comparison of average rates of deforestation between 1950-60, 1960-70 and 1970-75 indicates (Table 8.1) a higher rate during 1970-75 than the other two periods. Mishra and Dash of Department of Sambalpur University, have found significant correlation ($P < 0.02$) between decrease in rainfall and forest loss. The mean rainfall of the decade 1967-76 was 141.15 cm compared to the mean of the periods 1871-40 and 1940-76: 165.1 and 155.97 cm respectively. The authors also found a positive correlation between the loss in storage capacity of Hirakud reservoir during 1957-76 and forest loss ($r = 0.99$, $P < 0.05$). Studies by Mahapatra, G. Panday, N.C and Chari, K.N., have indicated that due to excessive silting, Hirakud reservoir will have a life of 77 years instead of the originally estimated 111 years. If the deforestation continues at this present rate, the life would be still, lesser.

Water Quality of Hirakud Reservoir System

Das and Dash, Department of Life Sciences, Sambalpur University, have studied the water quality of Hirakud Reservoir and its tributary, river Ib. The study includes physico-chemical and biological characteristics. Ib receives effluents of Orient Paper Mills, which is situated on the bank of the river at Brajrajnagar. Ib joins Hirakud reservoir about 20 Km. from the paper mill. The results, summarized in Table 8.2, indicate that Ib is polluted due to the paper mills effluents. The river water downstream has high alkalinity and chemical oxygen demand. The pollution is also reflected in the decreased primary productivity.

TABLE 8.2: WATER QUALITY OF HIRAKUD RESERVOIR AND RIVER IB

Character	*Hirakud Reservoir*	*Upstream Paper Mill*	*Downstream Paper Mill*
Water Temp °C	21 - 30	21 - 28.5	22 - 29
pH	7.3 - 8.5	7.1 - 8.25	8 - 10.8
Transparency (cm)	15 - 250	40 - 180	5 - 115
Conductivity (m mho/cm)	0.11 - 0.29	0.140 - 0.280	0.165 - 0.810
Total hardness (ppm)	57.5 - 80	54 - 85	90 - 260
Total Alkalinity (ppm)	60 - 88	58 - 92	110 - 282
Dissolved oxygen (ppm)	6.8 - 12	6.8 - 11.0	3.8 - 7.2
Chemical oxygen Demand (ppm)	24 - 92	28 - 92	128 - 530
Biochemical oxygen Demand (ppm)	.8 - 4.5	3 - 16	16.9 - 38.0
Phosphate (ppm)	10 - 20.1	11 - 18	12 - 21
Net Primary (Plankton) Production (gmc m, d)	1.2 - 1.87	0.45 - 1.42	0.60 - 0.67

The authors found the water quality of Hirakud Revervoir almost free from pollution except in the rainy season when the high clay content makes the water unsuitable for drinking unless filtered. According to N.K. Choudhary, School of Life Sciences, Sambalpur University, Burla, the amount of bicarbonate in Hirakud reservoir was more during rainy season (August) than the winter (January) and summer (May) because of inflow of mineral salts alongwith water by the rivers. This causes an increase in the alkalinity of the water during the rainy season. After rains, these salts are either carried out by the river when water is released from the reservoir or some mineral salts settle down at the bottom mud. Thus the pH changes from alkaline to neutral and to slightly acidic during winter.

Sedimentation

Remote sensing and echo-soundings have confirmed that the Hirakud Reservoir is subject to heavy silting. The rate of silt deposition in the reservoir is two and half times the anticipated rate out of the total silt inflow 75 per cent is deposited in the reservoir. The reduction of dead storage, live storage and total storage of the reservoir upto 1985 (29 years of existance) was 36.74, 14.01 and 20.36 per cent respectively (Table 8.3). It is estimated that at the present rate of sedimentation, 70 per cent of Hirakud reservoir will be covered with sediments by the next 70 years. According to three survey reports and a warning by a World Bank the heavily silted thirty year old dam is "one of the 25 unsafe dams of the world. The need for an immediate desiltation drive to increase the storage capacity of the dam has been under scored.

TABLE 8.3: LOSS IN STORAGE CAPACITY OF HIRAKUD RESERVOIR

	Original capacity million m^3	*New capacity million m^3*	*Silt deposited million m^3*	*Loss % per year*
Dead storage	2262	1501	753	1.148
Live storage	5843	5106	737	0.435
Gross storage	8105	6615	1490	0.634

Due to the alkalinity and high electrolyte content of river Ib, montmorillonites of the clay may be acquiring ionic charge resulting in the charged particles becoming mutually repulsive and remaining in such a finely dispersed state that they are held in suspension indefinitely in the quiscent waters of the reservoir. This might be causing the confluence of the reservoir with river Ib less chocked. The weighted average rainfalls for Mahanadi and Ib basins are similar thus the likely role of rainfall in causing the difference in chocking at the two confluences can be completely ruled out. Some soil conservation measures adopted by the Government of Orissa in the river Ib basin may be responsible for the less chocking of the Ib confluence.

Another serious concern is the cracks that have developed in the concrete spillway of the Hirakud dam. Experts suspected that it may be due to "Alkali—aggregate reaction" (Expert Committee Report 1983). Some types of silica aggregates slowly react with alkali of cement in the presence of water to form "gels" leading to swelling. Consequently strain develops in the structure. It is possible that the already alkaline character of Hirakud Reservoir water facilitates the alkali aggregate reaction. This is a pure conjecture and nothing definite has been said so far. There are three paper mills situated at Bilaspur (MP), Champa (MP) and Brajrajnagar (Orissa) which discharge their alkaline wastewaters to the tributaries of Mahanadi river (Arpa, Hasdeo and Ib respectively) which eventually come to the reservoir. There are also submerged limestone querries. All these factors with or without any other unknown factor may be contributory towards the alkalinity of the reservoir water.

Degradation of Environment and Climatic Imbalance

Prior to construction of Hirakud dam the average rainfall in Sambalpur and Bolangir districts was 1,526 mm and 1,463 mm respectively as against 1,748 mm in Mayurbhanj and 1,482 mm in the state as a whole. After the construction of Hirakud dam, Padmapur subdivision of Sambalpur district and Patnagarh and Titlagarh subdivisions of Bolangir district are experiencing drought or excessive rainfall. Biswanath Sahu, Department of Agronomy, Bhubaneswar, believes that abberations are likely to be due to the Hirakud reservoir and the deforestation catalysed by it.

Hirakud reservoir lies in the windward side of Barpahar hill ranges which is the path of Bay of Bengal current of the South-West monsoon. The evaporation from the reservoir is about 0.9 million acre feet per year. This influences atmospheric humidity. The cement factory at Bargarh releases calcium carbonate and magnesium carbonate particles into the atmosphere while Rourkela Cement Factory spews fly-ash. These particles provide nuclei for the condensation of water vapour. Ice crystals and cloud condensation nuclei are formed over the reservoir and the windward side of the Barpahar-Harishankar-Gandhamadan hill range which is in the path of the South-West monsoon. Monsoon winds charged with moisture are more often blown away to Madhya Pradesh and Narmada basin causing drought in Padmapur-Patnagarh-Titlagarh-Nawapara belt of Western Orissa. At times this belt gets excessive rainfall.

Flood Control

When Sir Hawthorn Lewis, the then Governor of Orissa, laid the foundation stone of Hirakud Dam on 15th March 1946, he had declared, "The giant Mahanadi is now tamed in the service of common man."

Pandit Jawaharlal Nehru, the first prime minister of independent India, inaugurated the Dam on 13th January, 1956, declaring it 'the modern Konark temple of Orissa'. He hoped that Hirakud Dam will make Orissa the Ukrain of India in grain production by controlling floods and providing irrigation. However now, more than three decades after its commissioning, the dam stands failed in controlling the floods in the Mahanadi delta. The frequency of floods in the delta before the construction of the Dam was 11.8 years but after the construction it has become 3.75 years (Table 8.4).

Present Land Use and Soil Conservation Measures

A survey was conducted by Orissa Soil Conservation Department to assess the main causes for soil erosion in the catchment of Hirakud dam. Based on this assessment and the silt observation reports, priority was fixed for soil conservation treatment of different watersheds. The measures were initiated during the year 1956-57 in a few of the watersheds. During the second plan period the measures were limited to contour bunding, tree plantations and gully control works. During the third plan period emphasis was given on pasture development, stream bank erosion control (SBEC) and water harvesting structures (WHS). Thus the package of treatment measures includes contour bunding, tree plantations of Cashew, Sisal and miscellaneous species, pasture development and erection of engineering structure like WHS, gully controls, farm ponds and silt retention dams.

TABLE 8.4: RECURRENCE OF FLOODS IN MAHANADI

Before Hirakud Dam				*After Hirakud Dam*	
19th Century		*1900-1955*		Year of *flood*	Recurrence *Year*
Year of flood	Recurrence year	Year of flood	Recurrence year		
1834		1926	30	1961	5
1855	21	1933	7	1970	9
1866	11	1937	4	1972	2
1872	6	1940	3	1973	1
1896	24	1955	15	1975	2
				1980	5
				1982	2
				1986	4
Average in 62 years - 15.4		Average in 59 years - 11.8		Average in 30 years - 3.75	

The progress on the soil conservation front appears to be very slow. It is observed that the total coverage is only 54.9 per cent of the treatable area of the priority watersheds. There is a lot yet to be done for the treatment of the identified critical watersheds.

Soil conservation measures delay run-off, encourage infiltration and prevent soil erosion thereby reducing sediment deposit in the river bed and the reservoir. Thus, flood hazard is minimized and flooding of the river bank is prevented. Proper land use according to the land capability in the catchment helps to absorb more rain water and slows release to ensure long supply. Therefore soil conservation needs special attention in the flood control programmes.

Regeneration of Seepage Water and Rice Cropping in Hirakud Command Area

The farmers in the Hirakud command area have been preferring rice on all types of lands ever since the commissioning of Hirakud reservoir in 1957. The area under paddy has exceeded the designed capacity of the canal systems although the drawals from the canals have remained the same in the recent years.

A study by Naik of Indian National Science Academy, New Delhi, in selected portions of Jhaunjore and Danta basins of the Hirakud command showed that about 22.27 per cent of water enters the ayacut as seepage and the rest as surface flow. Out of this total inflow, about 3.8 per cent is lost in evaporation from the uncropped surfaces, 35.18 per cent is lost by deep percolation and 24.48 per cent by way of outflow into the drainage. The balance of 35.54 per cent is only utilized consumptively.

Risk in Water Table

Due to continuous irrigation during the last several years, the water table in the Hirakud command area has consistently risen and has now stabilized within metre of the surface. When water is released through the network of canal distribution system, the entire area becomes re-charged with the transient water table close to the surface.

Several drainage-cum-recycling projects with command area, varying from 15 to 500 acres have been completed by the Command Area Development Authority (CADA) to reduce the drainage congestion and to bring about additional area under irrigation.

Pest Problems

The low-land waterlogged rice crops have been found to be increasingly infested with stem borer during the past few years. The crop becomes heavily infested at earing stage in the month of November resulting in considerable loss in the final yield.

Problems of Aquatic Weeds

The aquatic weed problem is steadily increasing in the waterlogged and submerged areas of the command. The aquatic weeds include both surface floating and submerged weeds like *Nitella, Chara,*

Valisnaria and *Sphenoclea,* in the submerged areas. The floating weeds have also been found to obstruct water-flow in the canal systems in certain areas of the command.

Displacement

Independent studies of the oustees of Hirakud Haeed the figure for those displaced at 1,80,000 while official figures were 1,10,000 (Kothasi, 1996).

UTTEI IRRIGATION PROJECT

This project is situated in the Uttei river, a tributary of river Tel in Mahanadi basin. Uttei Irrigation Division has conducted studies on the agriculture and cropping pattern of the command area from 1976. No information on any other aspect of environmental impact assessment is available.

MAHANADI RESERVOIR PROJECT

Mahanadi Reservoir Project Circle has conducted studies on the physico-chemical aspects of the water quality by collecting samples from six sampling stations six times every year. They have also studied the sediment quality by sampling at forty stations from 1980 onwards at a frequency of four times per year. According to them the catchment areas of both the reservoir and the feeder stream and also the command area are used for mainly paddy cultivation. Eventhough they have not conducted any particular survey on the agricultural production of the catchment area or in the command area, they have claimed some improvement in this aspect.

SONDUR RESERVOIR PROJECT

The Mahanadi Reservoir Project Circle (MRPC) have found that the annual rate of sediment accumulation in Sondur reservoir is about 3-4 acre ft m. Some 2,146 ha. of the reservoir catchment consists of reserved forest and the major cultivation in the command area is paddy. MRPC is also studying bank stability of the reservoir and seismicity but no conclusions have been drawn by them so far.

CUMULATIVE IMPACTS

There is no study on the cumulative impacts of the dams in Mahanadi river basin.

STATUS OF ENVIRONMENTAL IMPACT ASSESSMENT OF WATER RESOURCES PROJECTS IN GODAVARI RIVER BASIN

GANGAPUR RESERVOIR

Gangapur dam is across Godavari near Gangapur village in Nasik District, Maharashtra. The reservoir created by the damming has a gross storage capacity of 203 million m^3. The physical and chemical analysis of the reservoir water samples was conducted by Maharashtra Engineering Research Institute (MERI), Nasik, during 1978-80. The general observations are:

Public Water Supply

The pH values, free CO, total hardness, alkalinity, nitrate, nitrite, chloride, sulphates, calcium, magnesium, potassium, and ammonia contents were generally well within the acceptable limits. Copper, lead and cyanide were found to be nil. Thus with respect to chemical contents the water was found to be fit for public water supply.

Irrigational use

Estimations of sodium, SAR and conductivity showed that the reservoir water falls in the category C_1S_1 and C_2S_2 which is classified as good for irrigational use.

Dissolved Oxygen, BOD and MPN

The DO values of the reservoir water were generally in the range 8.2-6.0 indicating good aerobic conditions.

Thus the studies revealed Gangapur reservoir water to be generally of good quality in 1980. No further information is available.

JAYAKWADI RESERVOIR

Jayakwadi reservoir is also known as Paithan reservoir. It has been developed for providing irrigation. Studies on the physical, chemical and biological quality by Maharashtra Engineering Research Institute (MERI), Nasik, during 1970-80, resulted in findings which were similar to the ones obtained with respect to the Gangapur reservoir.

MULA DAM AND RESERVOIR

Mula Irrigation Division (MID) has studied salinity intrusion and loss of storage capacity of the reservoir per year. Since 1980, they have surveyed weed infestation. From 1976 onwards they are collecting information on the agriculture and cropping pattern, soil fertility, and salinization and waterlogging in the command area.

WILSON DAM AND RESERVOIR

Studies conducted by the Irrigation Wing, Bhandardara Section I, show that sediment concentrations and annual rate of sediment accumulation in the reservoir are negligible. The 45 Km command area is a Deccan trap with tough compact and rocky high hills. Major crops of the catchment area are rice, wheat and groundnut while sugarcane, wheat, jowar, maize, grapes, groundnut and different kinds of fruits are the major crops of the command area. Tigers, monkeys, wolf and snakes are the major wild animals in the catchment area.

UPPER AND LOWER SILERU PROJECTS

In Sileru river there are two hydro electric projects, Upper Sileru Hydro Electric Project (USHE Project) and Lower Sileru Hydro Electric Project (LSHE Project) with installed capacity of 60 MW and 115 MW respectively. There are no ayacuts under these projects.

According to Civil Circle, USHE, no archeological treasure is affected by these projects. They claimed that wild life which wasn't much except one or two tigers, few deers, bucks and bisons before the construction of these projects, now the tiger population has grown, so also the deers, and bucks, as the poaching is strictly prohibited by the government. Among the birds, peacocks and wild fowl are thriving. Wild Minas and doves are also abundant but parrots are not seen as the fruit growing trees are very rare.

PROPOSED POLAVARAM DAM

A barrage, called 'Polavaram Barrage' is due to come up 20 Km upstream Rajamundry. The stretch of Godavari preceding the barrage site is heavily silted owing to deforestation and soil erosion. It is also polluted near Rajamundry by industrial effluents and municipal sewerage. Its water carrying capacity is reduced resulting in frequent floods. If the proposed barrage comes up, it will reduce the river downstream to a canal and aggrevate pollution.

WOHAR RESERVOIR, AURANGABAD

The reservoir is located about 5 kilometres north of Aurangabad city and is the source of drinking water for a part of the city. Studies on seasonal variations in physico-chemical variables were carried out by Masood Ahmed and R. Krishnamurthy (1988). The variables studied were atmospheric temperature, water temperature, humidity, dissolved oxygen, oxidizable organic matter, pH, bicarbonates, chloride, sulphate, total nitrogen, phosphate and total solids.

The samples of water for the analysis were collected from a fixed point from about 15 cm below the surface of water during June 1976 to May 1978. The annual range of atmospheric temperature was 15.8-30.8° C during 76-77 while during 77-78 it was 15.8-32.8° C. The season-wise analysis showed that the average temperature was maximum during summers, slightly lesser during monsoons and least during winters. The water temperature was consistantly lower than the atmospheric temperature by 1-2° C through out. Therefore the pattern of fluctuation was identical with that of the atmospheric temperature. The percentage of humidity was maximum during monsoons being over 75 per cent ; it was around 50 per cent during winters and less than 40 per cent during summers. The DO(dissolved oxygen) showed a range of 6.94-11.34 ppm during 76-77 and 7.83-11.35 ppm during 77-78. It was maximum in summers and minimum in monsoon of both the years. The oxidizable organic matter was 1.83-2.78 ppm during 76-78 and 1.09-2.86 ppm during 77-78. It was maximum and almost in equal quantitites during summer and winter of 76-77 and minimum in monsoon. During 77-78 it was maximum in winter and minimum in monsoon.

The pH indicated an alkaline range (7.0-8.0) throughout. It was relatively more in winters and almost the same during summers and monsoons of both the years. The bicarbonate was in the range 55.57-74.67 ppm and 42.35-90.04 ppm during 76-77 and 77-78 respectively. It was maximum in winter and minimum in summer during the first year, while it was more in monsoon and least in winter during the second year. The chloride ranged between 18.58 to 29.52 ppm and 30.37 to 46.64 ppm during 76-77 and 77-78 respectively. It was more during summers than winters and monsoon of both the years. The range of sulphate during 76-77 and 77-78 was 1.37-2.57 ppm respectively. It was maximum during the monsoon and minimum in summer during the first year, but more in summer and least in winter during the second year. The total nitrogen was in the range 0.30-0.87 ppm during 1976-77 and 0.97-2.46 during 1977-78. It was maximum during monsoons of both the years while minimum during winter of first year and summer of the second year.

Phosphate was in the range 0.01-0.12 ppm and 0.02-0.19 ppm during 76-77 and 77-78 respectively. It was more in winters and less in summers of both the years. The total solids recorded during 76-77 and 77-78 ranged between 355.9-601.2 ppm and 349.8-551.9 ppm respectively. The total solids in general were more in monsoon and less in summers.

The oxidizable organic matter showed a direct relationship with pH but was inversely related to dissolved oxygen. The ionic composition followed from pattern HCO_3>Cl>SO_4.

SRIRAMASAGAR PROJECT

Construction work on this project was started in 1964 with an estimated cost of Rs. 64 crores. By the end of 1987, the money spent on it had amounted to Rs.508 crores and the project was yet to be completed. Meanwhile twenty-five per cent of the project capacity has already been lost due to silting induced by deforestation in upland areas. Thus, even before it would be complete, the project has become unviable—a veritable white elephant. Desilting costs are likely to be prohibitive due to the hugeness of the reservoir.

CUMULATIVE IMPACTS

As in the case with dams in Krishna and Mahanadi river basins, there is no study conducted so far on the cumulative impact of all the dams. One can predict that the cumulative impact would be considerable given the prevalance of the waterlogging and siltation problems.

SUMMARY, CONCLUSIONS AND RECOMMENDATIONS

1. The report presents state-of-the-art of environmental impact assessment of major water resources projects in Krishna, Mahanadi, and Godavari river basins.

For the report some 400 sources were explored (Appendix I and II) comprising of (a) universities and autonomous research institutions; (b) governmental agencies including pollution control boards, electricity boards, irrigation departments, public works departments, command area development authorities, research institutions; (c) non-governmental organizations, and (d) books and journals.

2. The survery explored 75 aspects of environmental impacts covering reservoir catchment, feeder streams, impounded water, and downstream. The entire gamut of physical, chemical, biological and socio-economical impacts were covered (Chapter 6).
3. Of the ninety-one man-made reservoirs, dams, and barrages in these basins, information on environmental aspects was available pertaining to only 28 projects. Of these only Hirakud and Upper Krishna projects appear to have been studied in some detail.
4. The aspect for which quantitative information is often availa able is waterlogging. Of the other 74 aspects only sparse

information is available for some or other aspects and that too is rarely quantitative.

The overall status is as follows:

ASPECT	NAME OF THE PROJECTS (for which information is available relevant pages on which the Information occurs in this report are given in parenthesis).	
Waterlogging	Upper Krishna	218
	Malaprabha	224
	Ghataprabha	226
	Bhadra	227
	Tungabhadra	230
	Hirakud	260
	Koyna	243
	Mula	265
Water Quality	Ujjani	217
Reservoir	Malaprabha	224
	Tungabhadra	230
	Dhom	237
	Hidkal	238
	Mahanadi	252
	Gangapur	264
	Jayakwadi	265
	Koyna	243
	Wohar	267
Feeder stream	Hidkal	238
Cropping Pattern		
Catchment Area	Wilson	265
Command Area		
	Malaprabha	224
	Hirakud	260
	Bhadra	227
	Tungabhadra	232
	Dhom	237
	Mahanadi	262
	Uttei	262
	Wilson	265
	Mula	265
	Sondur	263
Soil Quality		
Command Area	Upper Krishna	219
	Mula	265
	Tungabhadra	230

	Nagarjunasagar	247
Sedimentation	Warna	237
	Dudhganga	238
	Hirakud	254
	Sondur	263
	Mula	265
	Wilson	265
Microclimate		
Reservoir Catchment	Malaprabha	224
	Dhom	237
	Hidkal	238
Forest Types		
Catchment Area	Warna	237
	Dudhganga	238
	Sondur	263
Seismicity	Warna	238
	Koyna	240
	Sondur	263
Siltation	Panshet	239
	Sriramasagar	269
Resettlement	Dhom	237
	Koyna	245
	Panshet	239
	Srisailam	246
Wild Life		
Catchment Area	Warna	237
	Koyna	244
	Wilson	265
	Upper and Lower Sileru	266
Groundwater Quality		
	Koyna	243
Command Area	Upper Krishna	222
Downstream	Malaprabha	226
Prevalence of Disease	Upper Krishna	223
	Nagarjunasagar	247
Nutrient Study		
Reservoir	Malaprabha	226
Downstream	Malaprabha	226
Fisheries	Dhom	237
	Koyna	244
Flora and Fauna	Koyna	244
Flood Control	Dhom	237

	Hirakud	258
	Koyna	242
Deforestation	Hirakud	250
Aquatic Weeds	Hirakud	261
	Mula	265
Cracks developed in the Concrete Spillways	Hirakud	256
	Koyna	242
Climatic Imbalance	Hirakud	257
	Koyna	243
Degradation of Environment	Hirakud	257
Land Use	Hirakud	258
Land slides	Koyna	241
Soil Conservation Measures	Hirakud	258
Past Problems	Hirakud	261
	Koyna	245
Sediment Quality	Mahanadi	262
Archaeological Treasures	Upper and Lower Sileru	262
	Nagarjunasagar	83

5. No single report is found in which environment costs have been quantified and compared with the other costs and benefits of the project.
6. It is recommended that a few studies should be sponsored on selected nature, new, and to-be-commissioned dam-based projects in which the 75 aspects identified by us are all studied and, based on the studies, the environmental costs and benefits are quantified for comparison with the conventionally computed costs and benefits. In summary, attempts should be made to sponsor 'total impact assessment studies' that could provide accurate answers to the raging controversies relating to the dambased projects.

BIBLIOGRAPHY

Bhadra Project

Rama Prasad and Kirti Malhotra (1985). *Waterlogging in the Irrigated Areas of Karnataka,* Karnataka State of Environment Report 1984-85, 31-45.

Dhom Dam and Reservoir

Personal Communication with Dhom Irrigation Sub-division No.: 1, (1989), Wai.

Personal Communication with Dhom Irrigation Division, (1989), Satara.

Dhupdal Weir

Personal Communication with Irrigation Department (1989). Irrigation (North), Belgaum.

Dudhganga Irrigation Project

Personal Communication with Warna Project Circle, 'Warna Bhavan', (1989), Kolhapur.

Ghataprabha Project

Rama Prasad and Kirti Malhotra (1985). *Waterlogging in the Irrigated Areas of Karnataka,* Karnataka State of Environment Report 1984-85, 31-45.

Gangapur Reservoir

Nagarkar, P.K. (1982). *Study of Water Quality of Rivers and Reservoirs in Maharashtra State,* Maharashtra Engineering Research Institute, Nasik - 4, 201.

Hidkal Dam and Reservoir

Personal Communication with Govt. of India, Irrigation Department, Irrigation (North), (1989), Belgaum.

Hirakud Dam and Reservoir

Biswanath Sahu (1988). *Environmental Effects of Dams in Orissa.* Some Case Studies, P (Ed.), Proceedings of the Symposium on Environmental Aspects of Water Resources of Orissa.

Choudhury, N.K., Pradhan, P.K., and Dash, M.C., (1979), Geobios 6(3),104-106.

Das, K.C., (1988). *Extent of Irrigation and Its Environmental Impact in Orissa,* P (Ed.), Proceedings of the Symposium on Environmental Aspects of Water Resources of Orissa.

Das, R.C., Dash, M.C., Mishra, P.C., Choudhury K and Kar, G.K.,(1986). *Pollution Load in the Mahanadi Water System.* I.E. Journal (15), 19-24.

Mahapatra, G., Panday, N.C., and Chari, K.N., (1980). *An Introduction to Watershed Planning,* Part 1, Soil Survey Organization, Orissa.

Mishra, P.C. (1988). *Ecology and Environmental States of Hirakud Reservoir System.* P(Ed.), Proceedings of the Symposium on Environmental Aspects of Water Resources of Orissa.

Mishra, P.C., and Dash, M.C. (1984). *Desertification around Hirakud Reservoir,* The Environmentalist (4), 51-58.

Mohanty, P.B and Mohapatra, G., (1986). *Application of Remote Sensing to Sedimentation Studies in Hirakud Reservoir,* P(Ed.). Central Board of Irrigation and Power Proceedings Volume II, Ground Water, Management of Floods, River Hydraulics and Sediment Transport, Environmental Effects of Water Resources Projects.

Mohanty, R.B., and Mohapatra, G., (1986). *Third Report on Sedimentation Studies in Hirakud Reservoir, Government of Orissa,* Irrigation and Power Department, 1-44.

Pujari, K.L. (1988). *Changes in the Rainfall Pattern in Orissa Following Developmental Activities,* P(Ed.), Proceedings of the Symposium on Environmental Aspects of Water Resources of Orissa, Orissa State Prevention and Control of Pollution Board.

Jayakwadi Reservoir

Nagarkar, P.K. (1982). *Study of Water Quality of Rivers and Reservoirs in Maharashtra State*, Maharashtra Engineering Research Institute, Nasik - 4, 220.

Koyna Dam and Reservoir

Centre for Science and Environment (1982). The State of India's Environment, A Citizens' Report, New Delhi, 59-69.

Guha,S.K.(1991). *Environmental Impact of Koyna and Idukki reservoirs.* Energy and Environment, TERI, New Delhi.

Mahanadi Reservoir Project

Personal Communication with Mahanadi Reservoir Project Dam Circle (1990), Rudri.

Malaprabha Project

Personal Communication with Govt. of India, Irrigation Department (1989). Irrigation (North), Belgaum.

Rama Prasad and Kirti Malhotra (1985). *Waterlogging in the Irrigated Areas of Karnataka,* Karnataka State of Environment Report 1984-85, 31-45.

Nagarjuna Sagar Dam and Reservoir

Personal Communication with Government of Andhra Pradesh, Irrigation and C.A.D (P.W) Department (1989), Vijayapuri North.

Centre for Science and Environment (1982). The State of India's Environment, A Citizens' Report, New Delhi, 127-43.

Nizam Sagar Dam and Reservoir

Centre for Science and Environment (1982), The State of India's Environment, A Citizens' Report, New Delhi, 59-69.

Panshet Dam and Reservoir

Centre for Science and Environment (1985), The State of India's Environment, The Second Citizens' Report, New Delhi, 99-120.

Polavaram Dam and Reservoir

Academy of Gandhian Studies (1990), State of Environment in Andhra Pradesh, Citizens' Report, 19-22.

Radhanagari Reservoir

Goel, P.K., Trivedy, R.K., and Bhave, S.V., (1985). *Studies on the Limnology of a Few Fresh-water Bodies in Southwestern Maharashtra,* Indian Journal of Environmental Protection, (5)19-25.

Sondur Reservoir Project

Personal Communication with Mahanadi Reservoir Project Dam Circle, (1990), Rudri.

Sriramasagar Project

Academy of Gandhian Studies (1990), Status of Environment in Andhra Pradesh, Citizens' Report, 9-22.

Srisailam Project

Centre for Science and Environment (1982), The State of India's Environment, A Citizens' Report, New Delhi, 59-69.

Tungabhadra Project

Rama Prasad and Kirti Malhotra (1985). *Waterlogging in the Irrigated Areas of Karnataka,* Karnataka State of Environment Report 1984-85, 31-45.

Centre for Science and Environment (1982), The State of India's Environment, A Citizens' Report, New Delhi, 59-69.

Ujjani Reservoir

Nagarkar, P.K., (1982). *Study of Water Quality of Rivers and Reservoirs in Maharashtra State,* Maharashtra Engineering Research Institute, Nasik-4, 178-200.

Upper Krishna Project

Personal Communication with Government Karnataka Irrigation Department (1987), Upper Krishna Project Canal Zone, No.2, Kembhavi.

Personal Communication with Government of Karnataka, Command Area Development Authority, (1985), Waterlogging and Soil Salinity in Upper Krishna Project Command Area, Bhimarayanagudi, 1-8.

Personal Communication with Institute for Command Studies and Irrigation Management (1989), Bangalore.

Rama Prasad and Kirti Malhotra (1985). *Water Logging in the Irrigated Areas of Karnataka,* Karnataka State of Environment Report 1984-85, 31-45.

Subramany, M., (1988). *Quality of Groundwater and Scope for Conjunctive Water Resources Development in UKP Stage-I Phase-I Command Area,* Ground Water Survey and Investigation Wing Command Area Development Authority—Upper Krishna Project, Bheemarayanagudi, 1-17.

Upper and Lower Sileru Project

Personal Communication with Civil Circle, Upper Sileru (1982), Sileru.

Personal Communication with Mula Irrigation Division (1989), Ahmednagar.

Uttei Irrigation Project

Personal Communication with Uttei Irrigation Division (1989), Bhavanipatna.

Warna Project

Personal Communication with Warna Dam Division, Warnawati (1989), Sangli.

Personal Communication with Warna Irrigation Project, Salient features, Warna Project Circle (1989), Kolhapur.

Personal Communication with Warna Project Circle, 'Warna Bhavan' (1989), Kolhapur.

Wilson Dam and Reservoir

Personal Communication with Irrigation Wing of Bhandardara Section-1, (1989), Bhadardara.

Wohar Reservoir

Masood Ahmed and Krishnamurthy, R. (1990). *Hydrobiological Studies of Wohar Reservoir Aurangabad (Maharashtra State) India,* Journal of Environmental Biology 11(3), 335-43.

GENERAL

Abbasi, S.A., Nipaney, P.C., (1986). *Infestation of the fern genus Salvinia: Its status and control.* Environmental Conservation, (13), 235-41.

Abbasi, S.A., Nipaney, P.C. and Soni, R., (1988). *Aquatic weeds. Distribution, Impact and Control.* Journal of Scientific and Industrial Research, (47), 650-61.

Barrages in India (1981), P.(Ed.), Central Board of Irrigation and Power, New Delhi.

Biksham, G. and Subramanian, V., (1988). *Elemental Composition of Godavari Sediments (Central and Southern Indian Subcontinent),* Chemical Geology, (70): 275-86.

Biksham, G. and Subramanian, V., (1988). *Nature of Solute Transport in the Godavari Basin.* Journal of Hydrology, (103): 375-92.

Chakrapani, G.J and Subramanian, V., (1990). *Factors Controlling Sediment Discharge in the Mahanadi River Basin, India.* Journal of Hydrology, (117): 169-85.

Chaudhary, R.S., 1978. *Fish and Fisheries of Ranapratap Sagar (RPS) Reservoir, Rajasthan.* Inland Fish. Soc. India, (10): 76-84.

Dam Projects and Environmental Success (1981), P(Ed.) Report prepeard by the Committee on the Environment and Approved by the 48th Executive Meeting, Rome.

Dams and the Environment (1982), P.(Ed.), Members of the Committee on Damming and the Environment.

Dinesh Mohan (1986). *Environmental Guidelines for Planning Water Resources Development Projects.* P.(Ed.). Seminar on Environmental Consideration in Planning of Water Resources Projects, Institution of Engineers, Roorkee Local Centre, Roorkee.

Environmental NGOs in India: A Directory (1989), Envis Centre 07, Environmental Services Group, World wide Fund for Nature, India.

Haws, E.T., (1985). *Dams and the Environment,* P.(Ed.), Committee on the Environment.

Hydroelectric Power Stations in India (1985) P.(Ed.), Central Board of Irrigation and Power, New Delhi.

Hydroelectric Power Stations in India (1987), P.(Ed.), Central Board of Irrigation and Power, New Delhi.

Kanwar Sain,(1985). *Environmental Concern in Rivrer Basin Development in India, (Environmental Impact Assessment of Water Resources Projects),* P.(Ed.), Proceedings of the International Seminar held at Water Resources Development Training Centre University of Roorkee, Vol.III.

Karamchandani, S.J. and Pisolkar, M.D. (1967). *Surney of the fish and fisheries of the Tapti River,* Surv. Rep.Cent. Inl. Fish. Res. Inst., Barrackpore (4), 29P.

Major Canals in India (1986), Central Board of Irrigation and Power.

Major Dams in India (1979), Indian National Committee on Large Dams P.(Ed.), Central Board of Irrigation and Power, New Delhi.

Naik, B. (1979). *Study on Irrigation Efficiency in Selected Portion of Jhaumjote and Danta Basin.* Integrated Agricultural Development in Command Areas of Irrigation Project (Winter School held in 1979), Indian National Science Academy, New Delhi, 64-71.

Proceedings Special Technical Session (1982). P.(Ed.), International Commission on Irrigation and Drainage, (2), New Delhi, India.

Raj, B.S. (1941). *Dams and Fisheries: Mettur and its Lessons for India,* Proc.Indian Acad, Sci., 14, B(5):341-58.

Ramesh, R. and Subramanian, V., (1988). *Nature of the Dissolved Load in the Krishna River Basin, India.* Journal of Hydrology, (103): 139-155.

Register of Water Resources Projects in India (1979) P.(Ed.), Central Board of Irrigation and Power, New Delhi.

Sharma K.P. *Impact of River Basin Development in India with Reference to Fisheries Development.* EIA of W.R. Projects Proceedings, International Seminar held at W.R.D.T.C. University of Roorkee, 1985, Vol.I.

Suhas P. Gurjar, *Discovering Krishna, Report of the Krishna Expedition,* P.(Ed.), River Vally Expedition and Research Society of India.

The Krishna Basin (in Maharashtra), (1987), Basin and Sub-basin Inventory of Water Pollution, P.(Ed.) Maharashtra Pollution Control Board, Mumbai.

APPENDIX–I

ADDRESSES OF AGENCIES/OFFICES/PERSONS CONTACTED

Governmental Agencies

1. Central Water Commission (Govt. of India)
   Office of the Chief Engineer
   Water Resources Organization
   H.No.10-2-8/1, Shanti Nagar
   Hyderabad - 500 028

2. Dr. Md. A. Haque
   Scientist 'C' and Public Relations Officer
   Central Pollution Control Board
   Ministry of Environment and Forests
   Government of India
   5th and 6th Floors, 'Skylark', 60' Nehru Place
   Post Box No. 4364, New Delhi - 110 019

3. Shri K. Ramapathy Rao
   Chief Engineer, A/C
   Central Designs Organzation
   158 Saops Complex, M.J.Road
   Hyderabad - 500 001

4. Shri P. Veerabhadra Swamy
   Assistant Secretary to Government
   Irrigation and CAP (PW) Department
   Secretariat Buildings
   Hyderabad - 500 022

5. Dr. P.T.Cherian
Scientist 'SE'
Zoological Survey of India
Southern Regional Station
100, Santhome High Road
Chennai - 600 028

6. S.R. Choudhari
Sr. Scientific Officer (HQ)
Maharashtra Pollution Control Board,
Army and Navy Building
Gr.Floor, 148, M.G.Road,
Fort, Mumbai- 400 023

7. Dr. (Mrs) Nalini Bhat
Scientist 'SE'
Ministry of Environment and Forests
(Government of India)
Paryavaran Bhavan, C.G.O. Complex
Lodi Road, New Delhi - 110 003

8. Additional Director
Central Water and Power Research Station
P.O. Khadakavasla Research Station
Pune - 411 024

9. R.D. Agrawal
Joint Director
Central Statistical Organization
Government of India, Ministry of Planning
Department of Statistics
Sardar Patel Bhavan
Parliament Street, New Delhi - 110 001

10. N.D. Jayal
Director
The Indian National Trust for Art and Cultural Heritage
71, Lodhi Estate, New Delhi - 110 003

11. R.V. Ranthidevan
    Director General
    National Water Development Agency
    Community Centre
    New Delhi - 110 017

12. Senior Scientist
    Department of Science, Government of Orissa
    Technology and Environment
    Bhubaneswar

13. S.R. Kashyap
    Administrative Officer
    Central Soil and Water Conservation Research and
    Training Institute
    Dehradun - 248 195

14. Executive Engineer
    Maharashtra State Electricity Board
    Office of the Chief Engineer (Hydro)
    Skylark Building
    284, Shahid Bhagat Singh Road,
    Mumbai- 400 001

15. W.A. Smith
    Secretary Action for Water Development
    Mysore Society
    12, Sampangi Ramaswamy Temple Street
    Bangalore - 560 052

16. Dr. G.M. Jazdani
    Scientist SD
    Zoological Survey of India
    Western Regional Station
    1182/2 Fergusson College Road
    Poona - 411 005

17. R. Nagaraj
Deputy Adviser (I and CAD)
Government of India, Planning Commission
Yojana Bhavan, Sansad Marg,
New Delhi-110001.

18. Dr. J. Bahadur
Principal Scientific Officer
Ministry of Science and Technology
Department of Science and Technology
Technology Bhavan
New Mehrauli Road
New Delhi - 110 016

19. B.C. Garg
Secretary
International Commission on Irrigation and Drainage
48 Nyaya Marg. Chanakyapuri
New Delhi - 110 021

20. M.L. Gupta
Under Secretary (Admm.)
Central Board of Irrigation and Power
Malcha Marg, Chanakyapuri
New Delhi - 110 021

21. Officer-in-Charge
Alair Irrigation Dam
PO Medak
Via:Hyderabad, A.P.

22. Superintending Engineer (C & M)
Barma Dam Project (Irrigation)
PO Barj
District Raisen (M.P.)

23. Superintending Engineer (O & M)
Bagh Dam Projct
PO :Gondia
Dist:Bhandara, Mahrashtra.

24. Superintending Engineer (O&M)
Bhima Dam Project
PO Phagna
Dist: Poona, Maharashtra

25. Superintending Engineer (O&M)
Shripuri H.E. Scheme
PO Bhirpuri.

26. Superintending Engineer (O&M)
Bhadra Irrigation Project
PO Lakkavalli
Karnataka

27. Officer-in-charge
Bhatghar Irrigation & Hydropower Projects
Krishna Basin
PO Bhatghar
Dist: Pune, Maharashtra

28. Officer-in-charge
Bhojapur Irrigation Project
PO Dindori
Dist: Nasik, Maharashtra

29. Officer-in-charge
Bhandarodoba Dan
PO Nasik, Maharashtra

30. Officer-in-charge
Balimela Irrigation Dam
PO Vizhag, A.P.

31. Officer-in-charge
Dhom Irrigation Dam
PO Wai
Dist: Satara-415 003
Maharashtra

32. Officer-in-charge
Dowlaiswaram Irrigation Dam
PO Yelleru, A.P.

33. Officer-in-charge
Dudhara Irrigation Tank
PO Kanker, M.P.

34. Officer-in-charge
Donkarayi Dam
Lower Dileru H.E. Scheme
PO Donkarayi
Dist: East Godavari, A.P.

35. Officer-in-charge
Forebay Dam
Lower Sileru H.E. Scheme
Near Forebay Camp
Via Donkarayi, A.P.

36. Chief Engineer
Godavari Delta System (C.E.)
Dowlaiswaram 533 125
Dist. East Godavari (A.P.)

37. Superintending Engineer (O&M)
Ghod Irrigation Project
PO Chinchi
Near Sirpur
Dist: Poona, Maharashtra

38. Superintending Engineer (O&M)
Girna Irrigation Project
PO Banzam
Dist : Nasik, Maharashtra.

39. Superintending Engineer (O&M)
Ghatprabha Weir Project
PO Dhupdal
Dist: Belgaum, Karnataka

40. Officer-in-charge
Gangapur Irrigation Dam
PO Nasik, Maharashtra

41. Shri A. Nagaraj Rao
C.E.
Hasdeo Bango Project
PO Raipur (M.P.)

42. Officer-in-charge
Himayatsagar Irrigation Dam
PO Hydrabad, A.P.

43. Officer-in-charge
Hidkal Irrigation Dam
PO Hidkal
Via: Belgium, Karnataka

44. Officer-in-charge
Hirakund Irrigation Project
PO Burla

45. Superintending Engineer (O&M)
Itiadoh Irrigation Project
PO Wainganga
Dist: Bhadara, Maharashtra

46. Officer-in-charge
Ishtapuri Irrigation Project
PO Nanded
Maharashtra

47. Superintending Engineer (O&M)
Krishna Irrigation Project
PO Borkhal
Dist: Satara, Maharashtra

48. Superintending Engineer (O&M)
Khadakwasla Irrigation Project
PO Khadakwasla
Dist: Poona, Maharashra

49. Superintending Engineer
Kukadi Irrigation Project
PO Yedgaon
Dist: Poona, Maharashtra

50. Officer-in-charge
Kaddam Irrigation Dam
PO Nimal, A.P.

51. Kanher Irrigation Project
(Krishna Irrigation Scheme)
PO Satara, Maharashtra

52. Officer-in-charge
Karamjavan Irrigation Project
PO Nasik, Maharashtra

53. Officer-in-charge
Krishna Irrigation Dam
PO Guntur, A.P.

54. Superintending Engineer (O&M)
Lower Sileru Hydro Electric Scheme
PO Mothugudem - 507 113
Dist: Khammam, A.P.

55. Officer-in-charge
Lendi Irrigation Project
PO Nanded, Maharashtra

56. Officer-in-charge
Lower Thirna Irrigation Project
PO Umerga, Maharashtra

57. Chief Engineer
Mahanadi Godavri Basin
PO Raipur, M.P.

58. Chief Engineer
Mahanadi Reservoir Project
PO Raipur M.P.

59. Superintending Engineer(O&M)
Mula Irrigation Project
PO Goregaon
Via Nandur
Dist: Ahmadnagar, Maharashtra.

60. Executive Engineer (O&M)
Mahanadi Delta Weir Project
PO: Mundali
Dist: Cuttack, Orissa

61. Superintending Engineer (O&M)
Malaprabha Irrigation Project
PO Manoli, Karnataka

62. Officer-in-charge
Majalgaon Irrigation Project
Jayakwadi Scheme
PO Majalgaon
Dist: Beed, Maharashtra

63. Officer-in-charge
Manir Irrigation Dam
PO Kamareddi
Via Hyderabad A.P.

64. Officer-in-charge
Manar Irrigation Project
PO Nanded, Maharashtra

65. Officer-in-charge
Manjara Irrigation Project
PO Kaij-431 123, Maharashtra.

66. Officer-in-charge
Musi Irrigation Project
PO Nalgonda, A.P.

67. Officer-in-charge
Murram Silli Dam
PO Raipur

68. Chief Engineer
Nagarjuna Sagar Project
H.No.3-6-369/B-3
Himayatnagar
Hyderabad-500 029, A.P.

69. Officer-in-charge
Nagarjuna Sagar Irrigation & Power Projects
PO Nandikonda Village
Dist: Nalgonda, A.P.

70. Officer-in-charge
Narayanpur Irrigation Project
PO Siddhapur Village
Dist: Bijapur, Karnataka

71. Officer-in-charge
Nizamsagar Irrigation Project
PO Kamareddi
Via Hyderabad, A.P.

72. Officer-in-charge
Nagarjunasagar Dam
PO Macherla, A.P.

73. Officer-in-charge
Osmansagar Irrigation Project
PO Hyderabad, A.P.

74. Officer-in-charge
Ong Irrigation Project
PO Balangir, Orissa.

75. Divisional Engineer
Pochampad Hydroelectric Project
Post Pochampad
Dist: Nizambad, A.P.

76. Superintending Engineer (O&M)
Purna Irrigation Project
PO Siddheheswar
Dist: Parbhani, Maharashtra

77. Officer-in-charge
Paitham Irrigation & Hydropower Project
Jayakwade Scheme
PO Paithan
Dist: Aurangabad, Maharashtra

78. Officer-in-charge
Pocharam Irrigation Dam
PO Medak
Via Hyderabad, A.P.

79. Officer-in-charge
Penti Pakka Dam
PO Chandrapur, Maharashtra

80. Officer-in-charge
Rudri Pick Up Weir on Mahanadi
PO Dhamtari
Dist: Raipur, M.P.

81. Officer-in-charge
Ravishankar Sagar Multipurpose Reservoir
PO Raipur, M.P.

82. Chief Engineer
Srisailam Project
3-4-417 Cross Road
Kachiguda
Hyderabad, A.P.

83. Chief Engineer
Sree Rama Sagar Project
Mozamjahi Road
Hyderabad, A.P.

84. Officer-in-charge
Siddeswar Irrigation Project
PO Siddheswar Village
Dist: Parbhani, Maharashtra

85. Officer-in-charge
Sindphana Irrigation Project
PO Bhir-431 122, Maharashtra

86. Officer-in-charge
Sonal Irrigation Dam
PO Akola, Maharashtra

87. Officer-in-charge
Sunkesula Irrigation Project
PO Kurnool, A.P.

88. Officer-in-charge
Sondur Irrigation Project
PO Raipur, M.P.

89. The Officer on Special Duty
Telugu Ganga Project
Srikalahasti
Dist: Chittoor, A.P.

90. Superintending Engineer
Tungbhadra Hydro Electric Scheme
PO Tungbhadra Dam-583 225
Via Hospet
Dist: Bellary, Karnataka

91. Officer-in-charge
Tandula Irrigation Project
PO Durg, M.P.

92. Chief Engineer
Upper Krishna Project
Design Org. for UKP
PO Bheemarayangudi,
Dist: Gulbarga-585 287
Karnataka

93. Divisional Engineer Operation
Upper Sileru Project
PO Upper Sileru
Dist: Vizhag, A.P.

94. Superintending Engineer (O&M)
Upper Godavari Irrigation Project
PO Karajvan
Dist: Nasik, Maharashtra

95. Superintending Engineer (O&M)
Upper Godavari Irrigation Project
PO Karajvan
Dist: Nasik, Maharashtra

96. Superintending Engineer (O&M)
Upper Sileru Hydro Power Project
PO Guntawada
Dist: Visakhapatnam, A.P.

97. Officer-in-charge
Uttei Irrigation Project
PO Bharanipatna Project
PO Bharanipatna, Orissa.

98. Superintending Engineer (O&M)
Vir Dam Project
PO Vir
Dist: Poona, Maharashtra

99. Superintending Engineer (O&M)
Varna Dam Project
PO Khujgaon
Near Shirala
Dist: Sangli, Maharashtra

100. Officer-in-charge
Vanivilasa Sagar Dam
PO Vanivilasapura
Dist: Chitradurga, Karnataka

101. Officer-in-charge
Waghed Irrigation Dam
PO Nasik, Maharashtra.

102. Officer-in-charge
Yeldari Irrigation Project
PO Yeldari Village
Dist: Parbhani, Maharashtra

103. Officer on Special Duty
Telugu Ganga Project
Mamillapalli
Cuddapah-516 004, A.P.

104. Sub Divisional Engineer
Manira Irrigation Management
Sub Division Latur
Ausa Road, Dist. Latur
Maharashtra

105. Sub Divisional Engineer
Vir Dam Sub-Dn
Wathar Colony

106. Superintending Engineer
Irrigation Department
Irrigation Circle,
Kurnool-518 002
A.P.

107. Shri B.K. Gangawande
Executive Engineer
Malagaon Project Division
Kesapuri Camp. Tq. Majalgaon
Dist: Beed-431 142

108. Shri B. Achyutareddy
Dy Executive Engineer
Irrigation Department
I.B. Reservoir Sub Division
Nizamsagar

109. The Superintending Engineer
Tungabhadra Hydro Electric Scheme
Tungabhadra Dam-583 225

110. Superintending Engineer
Irrigation Project Investigation Circle
Sincham Sewa Bhavan
Nagpur

111. The Superintending Engineer
Aurangabad Irrigation Circle
Aurangabad

112. The Superintending Engineer
Nanded Irrigation Circle
Nanded, Maharashtra

113. Sub-Divisional Engineer
Irrigation Sub-Division
Nasik-422 002.

114. The Engineer-in-chief cum Project Coordinator
Upper Krishna Project
Almatti

115. The Administrator
CADA, UKP
PO Bheemarayanagudi
Gulbarga, Karnataka

116. The Director of Agriculture
Karnataka, Bangalore

117. The Chief Conservator of Forest
Aranya Bhavan
Bangalore

118. The Director
K.E.R.S.
K.R. Sagar, Dist: Mandya
Karnataka

119. Shri A.V. Appa Rao
Superintending Engineer (A/c)
S.A.C. Barrage Circle
Dowalaiswaram-533 125

120. Executive Engineer
Prachi Division
Bhubaneshwar-12

121. Director
Central Water Commission
Technical Coordination DTE
626, Sewabhavan North
R.K. Puram, New Delhi-1100 66

122. Dy. Executive Engineer
Akola Irrigation Division
Irrigation Department
Akola

123. Shri J.R. Kale
Executive Engineer
Palkhed Irrigation Division
Nasik 2, Maharashtra

124. Executive Engineer
Jalgaon Irrigation Division
Jalgaon

125. Superintending Engineer
A.I. Circle, Aurangabad
P.B. No. 353, Aurangabad

126. Shri V.V. Bapat
Superintending Engineer
Kukadi Project Circle
Sinchan Bhavan, Pune 11

127. Shri M.E. Dalvi
Superintending Engineer
Warna Project Circle
Kolhapur

128. Chief Engineer
Irrigation Department
Seoni, M.P.

129. Chief Engineer
Irrigation Department
Bilaspur

130. Chief Engineer
Mahanadi Godavari Basin
Raipur

131. Chief Engineer
Hasdeo Project
Bilaspur

132. Chief Engineer
Mahanadi Project
Raipur

133. Shri D. Doraswamy
Superintending Engineer
Y.R.P.C. Circle
Karnataka

134. Superintending Engineer
Osmanabad Irrigation Circle
Osmanabad

135. The Chief Engineer & Chief Administrator
Irrigation Department
Command Area Development
Garkheda, Aurangabad

136. Commissioner of Fisheries
Andhra Pradesh
Hyderabad

137. Sri Y. Subbarao
Superintending Engineer A/c
Irrigation Circle
Dowlaiswaram

138. Deputy Conservator of Forests
Bagalkot Division
Bagalkot

139. Sri J. Basav Rao
Superintending Engineer A/c
Govt. of Andhra Pradesh
Irrigation & CAD Department
O&M Circle, Tekulapally, Khammam Post

140. Shri K. Madhava Rao
Superintending Engineer (A/c)
Government of Andhra Pradesh
Irrigation Department
Y.R.P.C. Circle
Kakinada-3

141. Office of the Director
Karanataka Engineering Research Station
Krishnarajsagara

142. Executive Engineer
Ong Canals Division
Sonepur Raj Pin 767 017
Dist: Bolangir, Orissa

143. Office of the Executive Engineer ID
UKP, QC Division No. 1
Almatti 586-201

144. Administrator
CADA, UKP
Bheemarayanagudi

145. Dy. Executive Engineer
Purna Irrigation Division
Basmathnagar-431 512
Dist: Parbhani, Maharashtra

146. Shri S.D. Ketkar
Executive Engineer
Dhom Irrigation Division, Satara

147. Mr Ahmed A/c
Sup. Engg. Civil Circle
A.P.S.E.B. Upper Sileru
Sileru, A.P.

148. Superintending Engineer
L.S.H.E Scheme
Mothugudem-507 113
Kharmmam Dist, A.P

149. Shri Nagendra Rao
Executive Engineer
Dam Maintainance Division
N.S. Dam, Hill Colony
Vijayapuri North-508 202

Universities and Autonomous Research Institutions

150. The Director
Central Inland Capture Fisheries Research Institute
Barrackpore-743 101, West Bengal, India

151. R.A. Altekar
Research Officer
Environmental Engineering Research Division
M.E.R.I., Nashik - 422 004

152. Prof. Rama Prasad
Department of Civil Engineering
Indian Institute of Science
Bangalore - 560 012

153. The Director
A.P. Engineering Research Labs
Aimayatsagar, Hyderabad
Ranga Reddy Districts
Pin- 500 030

154. C. Srinivasa Rao
Deputy Director
Water and Mineral Exploration
Research and Training Institute
Medchal Road
Secunderabad - 500 855

155. Chief Research Officer
Hirakud Research Station.
P.O. Hirakud

156. Dr. A.S. Chawla
Director
Water Resources Development Training Centre
University of Roorkee, Roorkee-247 667
U.P.

157. Professor & Head
Deptartment of Zoology
Srivenkateswaa University
PO Tirupati, A.P.

158. Professor & Head
Deptartment of Chemistry
Srivenkateswa University
PO Tirupati, A.P.

159. Professor & Head
Deptartment of Environmental Studies
Srivenkateswa University
PO: Tirupati, A.P.

160. Professor & Head
Deptartment of Botany
Srivenkateswaa University
PO: Tirupati, A.P.

161. Librarian, Publication & Documentation Division
Srivenkateswa University
PO Tirupati, A.P.

162. Professor & Head
Deptartment of Environmental Science
Andhra University
PO: Waltair, A.P.

163. Head
Library, Publication &
Documentation Division
Andhra University
PO Waltair, A.P.

164. Professor & Head
Deptartment of Botany
Osmania University
PO Hyderabad, A.P.

165. Professor & Head
Deptartment of Zoology
Osmania University
PO Hyderabad, A.P.

166. Professor & Head
Deptartment of Chemistry
Osmania University
PO Hyderabad, A.P.

167. Professor & Head
Deptartment of Environmental Science
Osmania University
PO Hyderabad, A.P.

168. Library, Publication & Documentation Division
Osmania University
PO Hyderabad, A.P.

169. Professor & Head
Deptartment of Botany
Bangalore University
PO Bangalore, Karnataka

170. Professor & Head
Deptartment of Zoology
Bangalore University
PO Bangalore, Karnataka

171. Professor & Head
Deptartment of Chemistry
Bangalore University
PO Bangalore, Karnataka

172. Professor & Head
Deptartment of Environmental Science
Bangalore University
PO Bangalore, Karnataka

173. Library, Publication & Documentation Division
Bangalore University
PO Bangalore, Karnataka

174. Professor & Head
Deptartment of Botany
Karnataka University
Dharwad, Karnataka

175. Professor & Head
Deptartment of Zoology
Karnataka University
Dharwad, Karnataka

176. Professor & Head
Deptartment of Chemistry
Karnataka University
Dharwad, Karnataka

177. Library, Publication & Documentation Division
Karnataka University
Dharwad, Karnataka

178. Professor & Head
Bhopal University
Bhopal, M.P.

179. Professor & Head
Deptartment of Botany
Ravishankar Shukla University
PO Raipur, M.P.

180. Professor & Head
Deptartment of Zoology
Ravishankar Shukla University
PO Raipur, M.P.

181. Professor & Head
Deptartment of Chemistry
Ravishankar Shukla University
PO Raipur, M.P.

182. Professor & Head
Deptartment of Environmental Science
Ravishankar Shukla University
PO Raipur, M.P.

183. Library, Publication & Documentation Division
Ravishankar Shukla University
PO Raipur, M.P.

184. Professor & Head
Deptartment of Botany
Dr Harisingh Gaur University
PO Sagar, M.P.

185. Professor & Head
Deptartment of Zoology
Dr Harisingh Gaur University
PO Sagar, M.P.

186. Professor & Head
Deptartment of Chemistry
Dr Harishingh Gaur University
PO Kolhapur, Maharashtra

187. Professor & Head
Deptartment of Botany
Shivaji University
PO Kolhapur, Maharashtra

188. Professor & Head
Deptartment of Zoology
Shivaji University
PO Kolhapur, Maharashtra

189. Professor & Head
Deptartment of Chemistry
Shivaji University
PO Kolhapur, Maharashtra

190. Professor & Head
Deptartment of Environmental Science
Shivaji University
PO Kolhapur, Maharashtra

191. Library, Publication & Documentation Division
Shivaji University
PO Kolhapur, Maharashtra

192. Professor & Head
Deptartment of Botany
Marathwada University
PO Aurangabad, Maharashtra

193. Professor & Head
Deptartment of Zoology
Marthwada University
PO: Aurangabad, Maharashtra

194. Professor & Head
Deptartment of Chemistry
Marathwada University
PO Aurangabad, Maharashtra

195. Professor & Head
Deptartment of Environmental Science
Marathwada University
PO Aurangabad, Maharashtra

196. Library, Publication & Documentation Division
Marathwada University
PO Aurangabad, Maharashtra

197. Director
Centre for Environmental Studies
Indian Institute of Technology
PO Powai, Mumbai

198. Professor & Head
School of Life Science
Sambalpur University
PO Burla, Orissa

199. Professor & Head
Deptartment of Botany
Sambalpur University
PO Burla, Orissa

200. Professor & Head
Deptartment of Chemistry
Sambalpur University
PO Burla, Orissa

201. Professor & Head
Deptartment of Environmental Studies
Sambalpur University, PO Burla, Orissa

202. Library, Publication & Documentation Division
Sambalpur University

203. Professor & Head
Department of Environmental Sciences
Avadesh Pratap Singh University
PO Rewa, M.P.

204. Professor & Head
Deptartment of Botany
Andhra Pradesh Open University
6-3-645, Somajiguda
Hyderabad-500 482, A.P

205. Professor & Head
Deptartment of Zoology
Andhra Pradesh Open University
6-3-645, Somajiguda
Hyderabad-500 482, A.P.

206. Professor & Head
Deptartment of Chemistry
Andhra Pradesh Open University
6-3-645, Somajiguda
Hyderabad-500 482, A.P

207. Professor & Head
Deptartment of Environmental Science
Andhra Pradesh Open University
6-3-645, Somajiguda
Hyderabad 500,482, A.P.

208. Library, Publication & Documentataion Division
Andhra Pradesh Open University
6-3-645, Somajiguda
Hyderabad-500 482, A.P.

209. Professor & Head
Deptartment of Botany
University of Hyderabad
Central University
PO Hyderabad-500 134

210. Professor & Head
Deptartment of Zoology
University of Hyderabad
Central University
PO Hyderabad-500 134

211. Professor & Head
Deptartment of Chemistry
University of Hyderabad
Central University
PO Hyderabad-500 134

212. Professor & Head
Deptartment of Environmental Science
University of Hyderabad
Central University
PO Hyderabad-500 134

213. Professor & Head
Deptartment of Botany
Utkal University
Vani Vihar, Bhuaneswar-751 004

214. Professor & Head
Deptartment of Zoology
Utkal University
Vani Vihar, Bhuvaneswar-751 004
Orissa

215. Professor & Head
Deptartment of Chemistry
Utkal University
Vani Vihar, Bhuvaneswar-751 004
Orissa

216. Professor & Head
Deptartment of Environnmental Science
Utkal University
Vani Vihar, Bhuvaneswar-751 004
Orissa

217. Head, Library
Utkal University
Vani Vihar, Bhuvaneswar-751 004
Orissa

218. Professor & Head
Deptartment of Botany
Berhampur University
Berhampur-760 007
Orissa

219. Professor & Head
Deptartment of Zoology
Berhampur University
Berhampur-760 007
Orissa

220. Professor & Head
Deptartment of Chemistry
Berhampur University
Berhampur 760 007.
Orissa

221. Professor & Head
Deptartment of Environmental Science
Berhampur University
Berhampur-760 007, Orissa

222. Professor & Head
Deptartment of Botany
Amravati University
Amravati-444 601, Maharashtra

223. Professor & Head
Deptartment of Zoology
Amravati University
Amravati-444 601, Maharashtra

224. Professor & Head
Deptartment of Chemistry
Amravati University
Amravati-444 601, Maharashtra

225. Professor & Head
Deptartment of Environmental Science
Amravati University
Amravati-444 601, Maharashtra

226. Professor & Head
Deptartment of Botany
Gulbarga University
Gulbarga-585106, Karnataka

227. Professor & Head
Deptartment of Zoology
Gulbarga University
Gulbarga-585 106, Karnataka

228. Professor & Head
Dept of Chemistry
Gulbarga University
Gulbarga-585 106, Karnataka

229. Professor & Head
Deptartment of Environmental Science
Gulbarga University
Gulbarga-585 106, Karnataka

230. Professor & Head
Mangalore University
Deptartment of Environmental Sciences
Mangalagangotri-574 199, Karnataka

231. Professor & Head
Deptartment of Botany
Kakatiya University
Vidyaranyapur, Warangal-506 009, A.P.

232. Professor & Head
Deptartment of Zoology
Kakatiya University
Vidyaranyapuri, Warangal-506 009, A.P.

233. Professor & Head
Deptartment of Chemistry
Kakatiya University
Vidyaranyapuri, Warangal-506 009, A.P.

234. Professor & Head
Deptartment of Environmental Science
Kakatiya University
Vidyaranyapuri, Warangal-506 009, A.P

235. Professor & Head
Deptartment of Botany
Nagarjuna University
Nagarjuna Sagar-522 510, A.P.

236. Professor & Head
Deptartment of Zoology
Nagarjuna University
Nagarjuna Sagar-522 510, A.P.

237. Professor & Head
Deptartment of Chemistry
Nagarjuna University
Nagarjuna Sagar-522 510, A.P.

238. Professor & Head
Deptartment of Environmental Science
Nagarjuna University
Nagarjuna Sagar-522 510, A.P.

239. Professor & Head
Deptartment of Botany
Ravindra Nath Tagore Marg
Nagpur-440 001
Maharashtra.

240. Professor & Head
Deptartment of Zoology
Nagpur University
Ravindra Nath Tagore Marg
Nagpur-440 001, Maharashtra

241. Professor & Head
Deptartment of Chemistry
Nagpur University
Ravindra Nath Tagore Marg
Nagpur-440 001, Maharashtra

242. Professor & Head
Deptartment of Environmental Science
Nagpur University
Ravindra Nath Tagore Marg
Nagpur-440 001, Maharashtra

243. The Director
Regional Research Laboratory (RRL)
PO Hyderabad, A.P.

244. Director
Centre for Ecological Studies
Indian Institute of Science,
Bangalore, Karnataka

Non-Governmental Organizations

245. Shri S.G.V. Sharma
Secretary, Academy of Gandhian Studies,
2-2-1133/5/4, New Nallakunter,
Hyderabad 500 044

246. Shri K.M.S. Rao
Asian Academy for Rural Development and Population Studies
1-8-429 Chikadapally
Hyderabad-500 020

247. Dr M. Kurian
Executive Director
Comprehensive Rural Operations Service Society
1-69 Snehapuri
Nacharam, Hyderabad-501 507

248. Dr K.S. Gopal
Executive Director
Deccan Development Society
A-6 Meera Apartments
Basheer Bagh, Hyderabad-500 029

249. Dr K. Sridhar
Executive Director
Development Action for Rural Environment
1-1-770/5 Gandhinagar
Hyderabad-500 380

250. Dr P.V.L.N. Rao
Managing Director
3-5-886/4/A P.O. Box 1067
Himayatnagar, Hyderabad-500 029

251. Dr Brig Lokaranjan
President
The Society for Nature Conservation
593/43-A Gaganmahal Colony
Hyderabad-500 029

252. Dr C. Srinivasa Rao
Director
Water Development Society
Water and Mineral Exploration
Research & Training Institute
Medchel Road, Petbasheerabad
Hyderabad-500 855

253. Honorary Secretary
Wildlife Conservation Society
B-1-471/C-30 Behind Library
Khairatabad 500 004

254. Dr J. Ranga Rao
Director
ASSIST-INDIA
33/379 Adda Road
Chilakaluripet
Guntur-522 616

255. Dr K. Sivavaraprasad
Secretary
Chaitanya Development Society
Akbar Pe, Bapatha
Guntur-522 101

256. Dr A. Prabhakara Rao
GORD
6-10-138-2 and 2A
Near JLB Junior College for Girls
Repalle, Guntur-522 265

257. Dr V. Dakshina Murthy
Guide of Service
Atri Bhavan, Bapatha
District Guntur

258. Dr Nitin Paranjape
Coordinator
Abhivyakti Media for Development
J/2 Shardeshram
Bhavani Shankar Road, Dadar
Mumbai-400 028

259. Dr Saad Ali
Chairman
Bombay Environmental Action Group
Kurla Industrial Estate
LBS Marg
Ghatkopar, Mumbai-400 086

260. Dr A.N.D. Nanavati
Secretary, BNHS
Hornbill House, Opp. Lion Gate
Shahid Bhagat Singh Marg
Mumbai-400 023

261. Coordinator
Centre for Educational and Documentation
3, Suleman Chambers
Behind Regal Cinema
Mumbai-400 039

262. Dr B. Subba Rao
President
Environmental Protection Research Foundation
Arundhai, Near M & EB
Vishrambag, Sangli-416 415

263. Dr P.V.R.C. Panikar
Indian Association for Water Pollution Control
Scientist, NEERI
PO NEERI, Nehru Marg
Nagpur-440 020

264. Dr M.K. Ahmed
General Secretary
National Environment & Ecology Defence Society
Nhava House, 65 M. Karve Road
Mumbai-400 002

265. Dr N.N. Naik
Honorary General Secretary
National Society of the Friends of the Trees
A-2 Anand Nagar
Forgst Street, Mumbai-400 036

266. Dr Kisan Metha
President
Save Bombay Committee
123 Mahatma Gandhi Road
Mumbai-Fort - 400 023

267. General Secretary
Society for Clean Environment
Gorden Resort
606, Sion, Trombay Road, Chembur
Mumbai-400 071

268. Dr R.P. Shetye
Bombay Environment Group
Department of Botany
Mumbai-400 032

269. Dr K.M. Kundnani
Secretary
Bombay Institute of Environmental Technology
Dinnshaw Wacha Road
Churchgate, Mumbai-400 020

270. Dr Prakash Gohe
Ecological Society
Abhimanshree Society
Pashan Road, Pune-411 008

271. Dr Kiran More
Forum for People Oriented Water Utilization
92 Mistry Park
9th Floor, Warden Road
Mumbai-400 036

272. Mr T.D. Singh
No. 812/N2
Sector B, Piplani
Bhopal-462 021

273. Mr S.S. Chitwadgi
Executive Director
Bharat Forestry Consultancy
156/A Indragpuri
Bhopal. 462 022

274. Mr S.K. Choubey
General Secretary
Madhya Pradesh Vigyan Sabha
E-5/44, Arera Colony
Bhopal-462 014

275. P.V. Rajagopal
President
Prayog Samaj Sevi Sanstha
Village Sasaholi
P.O. Tilda-Neora
Raipur District 493 114

276. Yuva Shakti Sanghathan Madhya Pradesh
Parent Organization
Prayog Samaj Sevi Sanstha
Village Tilda-Neora
Raipur-493 114

277. Mr T.R. Sachdev
President
Pathal Gaon
Raigarh-496 118

278. Mr Ramesh Billorey
Campaign Against Indira Sagar
Govinda Garden
Govindpura
Bhopal

279. Mr J.R. Issac
Programme Coordinator
Water Development Project
Evangelical Lutheran Church in Madhya Pradesh
Betul-460 001

280. Administrative Officer
Action for Water Development Mysore Society
124, Palace Road
Bangalore 560 052

281. Mr V.K. Deshpande
Secretary
Dharwad Evironmental Association DEA
Hembli Galli
Hosyellapur, Dharwad-580 001

282. Mr Nagiah
Honorary Secretary
Educator Manufacturer Association EDMA
138, Gangadhara Chetty Road
Bangalore-560 042

283. Mr G.K.Veeresh
Senior Professor and Head
Indian Society of Soil Biology and Ecology
Department of Entomology
University of Agricultural Sciences
Bangalore-560 065

284. Mr K.R. Anand
Honarary Secretary
Life Environment Awareness Foundation LEAF
26-27, 9TH Main
Raja Mahal Vilas
Bangalore-560 080

285. Mr S.R. Hiremath
Coordinator
Samaj Parivartana Samudaya
Jayanagar Cross, Saptapur
Dharwad-580 001

286. Honorary Secretary
The Tree Lovers Karnataka
Edward Road
Bangalore

287. Mr E.A. Naidu
Chief Executive
Wildlife Association of South India WASI
17/1, Victoria Road
Bangalore

288. Mr K.S. Sripada Raju
Water Association for Republic of India
102, Field Marshal K M. Cariappa Road
(Residency Road)
Bangalore 560 025

289. Dr Venkat Rao Centre for Environment Concerns,
14, Jyoti Co-operative Society, Trimulgherry
Post Lecundrobad

290. Mr K. Milan Kumar Patro
Center for Environmental Research and Extension Education
(CEREE), 10 Bapujinagor
Near Medical College, Berhampur, Ganjam-760 004

291. Mr P.K. Sahoo
Chairman
Cente for youth and Social Development
65 Satya Nagar
Bhuvanesvar-751 007

292. Mr Ajoy Kumar Patra
Ecological Society of Orissa
PG Department of Zoology
Utkal University
Vanivihar-751 004

293. Mr S.K. Patnaik
Honorary Secretary
Nature and Wildlife Conservation Society of Orissa
251 Saheed Nagar
Bhuvaneswar-751 007

294. Secretary
Orissa Environmental Consciousness Society (OECS)
School of Life Sciences
Samolpur University
Jyoti Vihar, Burla-768 019

295. Secretary
Orissa Environmental Society
D-39,1 RC Colony
Jayadev Vihar
Bhuvaneswar-751 013

296. B.Ramachandra, Secretary, AMOFOI
AMOFOI Niwas
D/L-7, VSS Nagar
Bhuvaneswar-751 004

297. Mr. C. Manju Prabhadhal
Centre for Action Research and Documentation
Coordination Centre
N/2-133, Lottery Plot
Nayapalli
Bhuvaneswar 751 012

298. R.K. Khare
Member Secretary
Madhya Pradesh Pradushan Niwaran Mandal
Paryawaran Parisar E-5, Azera Colony
Bhopal - 462 016

299. S.N. Patro
Orissa Environmental Society
D-39, 1 RC Village
Jayadev Vihar, Bhavaneswar - 751013

300. Gandhi Peace Foundation
221/3 Deen Dayal Upadhyaya Marg.
New Delhi - 110 002

301. Thomas Mathew
Director
Environmental Services Group
World Wide Fund for Nature-India
B/1, J-Block Local Shopping Centre (First Floor)
Saket, New Delhi - 110 017

APPENDIX–II

JOURNALS

Ambio
Acta hydrochemica
Agricultural Water Management
Applications in Natural Resource Management
Aquaculture
Aquatic Toxicology
Archiv Fur Hydrobiologie
Australian Journal of Marine and Fresh Water Research
Biomass
Bulletin of Environmental Contamination and Toxicology
Catena
California Fish and Game
Chemosphere
Current Science
Ecology
Environment
Environmental Conservation
Environmental Geology and Water Sciences
Environmental Management
Environmental Monitoring and Assessment
Environmental Pollution
Environmental Technology
Environmental Technology Letters
Fisheries
Ground Water
Ground Water Monitoring Review
Hydrobiologie
Hydrological Processes

Hydrological Sciences
Hydrological Sciences Journal
IWEM 1988 Annual Symposium
Internationale Revue Der Gesamten Hydrobiologie
Irrigation Science
Israeli Journal of Aquaculture
Japan Agricultural Research Quarterly
Journal Water Pollution Control Federation
Journal for Water and Waste Water Research
Journal of Applied Ecology
Journal of Environmental Biology
Journal of Environmental Science and Health
Journal of Hydrology
Journal of Institution of Water and Environmental Management
Journal of Irrigation and Drainage Engineering—ASCE
Journal of Water Resources—Planning and Management
Marine Pollution Bulletin
National Geographic Research
Nature
New Scientist
Nordic Hydrology
Northwest Science
Oikos
Proceedings of Watershed 89: A Conference on the Stewardship of Soil, Air and Water Resources
Proceedings of the Indian Academy of Sciences
Science
Search
The Journal of Applied Ecology
The Ohio Journal of Science
Water Engineering and Management
Water Research
Water Resources Bulletin
Water Resources Research
Water S A
Water Science and Technology

APPENDIX-III

PROFORMA FOR SOLICITING INFORMATION

Name of Dam
Name of Feeder River/Tributary
Location of Dam: Village/Town *District* *State*

		Whether any information or data is available yes/no (please strike off what is not applicable)	Information if any, before the construction	during the construction	after the construction
1 *2*	*3*	*4*	*5*	*6*	*7*
1. WATER QUALITY a. Physico-Chemical (Such as pH, DO,	Feeder stream	Yes/no			
EC, TSS, TDS, F turbidity, Na,	Reservoir	Yes/no			
K, Cl, etc.)	Down stream	Yes/no			

{Cont.}...

1	*2*	*3*	*4*	*5*	*6*	*7*
b.	Nutrients (Such as NO, NO, PO, T-N, T-P, SO. etc.)	Feeder stream	Yes/no			
		Reservoir	Yes/no			
		Downstream	Yes/no			
c.	Trace Metals (Such as Fe, Al, B, Zn, Cu, Ni, Co, Hg, etc.)	Feeder stream	Yes/no			
		Reservoir	Yes/no			
		Down stream	Yes/no			
d.	Organics (Such as Pesticides, oils, total carbon)	Feeder stream	Yes/no			
		Reservoir	Yes/no			
		Downstream	Yes/no			
e.	Biological Planktons, Algae, micro invertebrates	Feeder stream	Yes/no			
		Reservoir	Yes/no			

{Cont.}...

1	2	3	4	5	6	7
	and macro-invertebrates	Downstream	Yes/no			
f.	Benthic organisms	Feeder stream	Yes/no			
		Reservoir	Yes/no			
		Downstream	Yes/no			
g.	Macrophyes (including aquatic weeds)	Feeder stream	Yes/no			
		Reservoir	Yes/no			
		Downstream	Yes/no			
h.	Fisheries (including aquatic weeds)	Feeder stream	Yes/no			
		Reservoir	Yes/no			
		Downstream	Yes/no			
i.	Primary productivity	Feeder stream	Yes/no			

{Cont.}...

1	2	3	4	5	6	7
		Reservoir	Yes/no			
		Downstream	Yes/no			
J.	Rare and endangered aquatic organism	Feeder stream	Yes/no			
		Reservoir	Yes/no			
		Downstream	Yes/no			
k.	Migratory or native birds	Reservoir	Yes/no			
2.	SEDIMENT QUALITY					
a.	Physico-Chemical (Such as PH, EC, hardness, etc.)	Feeder stream	Yes/no			
		Reservoir	Yes/no			
		Downstream	Yes/no			
b.	Nutrients (Such as N, P, K, C, S, F)	Feeder stream	Yes/no			
		Reservoir	Yes/no			

{Cont.}...

1	*2*	*3*	*4*	*5*	*6*	*7*
		Downstream	Yes/no			
c.	Organic (Such as Pesticides oils, etc.)	Feeder stream	Yes/no			
		Reservoir	Yes/no			
		Down stream	Yes/no			
d.	Trace metals (Such as Al, B, Si, Cu, Zn, Cd, etc.)	Feeder stream	Yes/no			
		Reservoir	Yes/no			
		Downstream	Yes/no			
e.	Gases (Such as H_2S, CO, NH, DO, CH, etc.)	Feeder stream	Yes/no			
		Reservoir	Yes/no			
		Down stream	Yes/no			
3.	GROUND WATER Quality/Quantity					

{Cont.}...

1	*2*	*3*	*4*	*5*	*6*	*7*
a.	Physico-Chemical (Such as PH, EC, TDS, hardness Cl, Na, K, salinity etc.)	i) Wells near feeder stream	Yes/no			
		ii) Wells near reservoir	Yes/no			
		iii) Wells near downstream	Yes/no			
b.	Nutrients (Such as N, P, C, NO_3, PO_4, NO_2 etc.)	i) Wells near feeder stream	Yes/no			
		ii) Wells near reservoir	Yes/no			
		iii) Wells near downstream	Yes/no			
c.	Trace metals (Such as Al, Fe, B, Zn, Hg, Od, etc.)	i) Wells near feeder stream	Yes/no			
		ii) Wells near reservoir	Yes/no			
		iii) Wells near downstream	Yes/no			
d.	Organics (Such as pesti-	i) Wells near feeder stream	Yes/no			

{Cont.}...

1	*2*	*3*	*4*	*5*	*6*	*7*
	cides, oils, etc.)	ii) Wells near reservoir	Yes/no			
		iii) Wells near downstream	Yes/no			
e.	Microbiological (Such as faecal coliform MPN etc.)	i) Wells near feeder stream	Yes/no			
		ii) Wells near reservoir	Yes/no			
		iii) Wells near downstream	Yes/no			
f.	Ground water table/Aquifer characteristics	i) Wells near feeder stream	Yes/no			
		ii) Wells near reservoir	Yes/no			
		iii) Wells near downstream	Yes/no			
4.	SEDIMENTATION					
a.	Sediment	Feeder stream	Yes/no			

{Cont.}...

1	*2*	*3*	*4*	*5*	*6*	*7*
	concentrations (Such as TSS, TDS, TVS) and particle size	Reservoir	Yes/no			
		Downstream	Yes/no			
b.	Annual rate of sediment accumulation	Reservoir	Yes/no			
5.	SOIL QUALITY					
a.	Nutrients	In catchment of feeder stream	Yes/no			
b.	Salinity	In catchment of reservoir	Yes/no			
c.	Trace elements	In catchment of downstream	Yes/no			
d.	Organics especially pesticides					

{Cont.}...

1	2	3	4	5	6	7
e.	Other important characteristics	In command area	Yes/no			
6.	MISCELLANEOUS STUDIES					
a.	Thermal and Chemical stratification	Reservoir	Yes/no			
b.	Salinity intrusion	Downstream	Yes/no			
c.	Oxygen depletion in hypolimnion	Reservoir	Yes/no			
d.	Eutrophication	Reservoir	Yes/no			
		Downstream	Yes/no			
e.	Incidences of fish kills and	Reservoir	Yes/no			
	toxicity	Downstream	Yes/no			
f.	Rate of loss of	Reservoir	Yes/no			

{Cont.}...

1	2	3	4	5	6	7
	storage capacity of reservoir/yr.					
g.	Algal blooms	Reservoir	Yes/no			
		Downstream river	Yes/no			
h.	Weed infestation	Reservoir	Yes/no			
		Downstream	Yes/no			
		Command area	Yes/no			
i.	Build up of heavy metals in hypo-limnetic waters	Reservoir	Yes/no			
j.	Incidence of toxic gas generation such as H_2S, Methane, ammonia in hypo-limnior and their toxicity	Reservoir	Yes/no			

{Cont.}...

1	*2*	*3*	*4*	*5*	*6*	*7*
k.	Loss of nutrient concentration downstream due to settling of sediments in reservoir bottom	Downstream	Yes/no			
7.	LAND USE					
a.	Forests types	In catchment of feeder stream	Yes/no			
		In reservoir catchment	Yes/no			
		In catchment of downstream	Yes/no			
b.	Agriculture and cropping pattern	In catchment of feeder stream	Yes/no			
		In catchment of reservoir	Yes/no			

{Cont.}...

1	*2*	*3*	*4*	*5*	*6*	*7*
		In catchment of downstream	Yes/no			
		In command areas	Yes/no			
c.	Urban/Rural settlements	In catchment of feeder stream	Yes/no			
		In catchment of reservoir	Yes/no			
		In catchment of downstream	Yes/no			
d.	Industries	In command area	Yes/no			
		In catchment of reservoir	Yes/no			
8.	SOIL EROSION					
		In areas near feeder stream	Yes/no			

{Cont.}...

1	2	3	4	5	6	7
		In reservoir catchment	Yes/no			
		In catchment downstream	Yes/no			
9. SOIL FERTILITY						
		In soils of reservoir catchment	Yes/no			
		In soils of catchment area downstream	Yes/no			
10. BANK STABILITY						
		Cf feeder stream	Yes/no			
		Cf reservoir	Yes/no			
		Cf downstream river	Yes/no			
11. SEISMICITY						
		around reservoir site	Yes/no			

{Cont.}...

1	*2*	*3*	*4*	*5*	*6*	*7*
12. SALINITY IN IRRIGATED SOILS						
		command areas	Yes/no			
13. WATERLOGGING						
		catchment of reservoir	Yes/no			
		catchment of downstream	Yes/no			
		command area	Yes/no			
14. PUBLIC HEALTH						
		In catchment of feeder stream	Yes/no			
a.	Waterborne diseases/ parasitic diseases	In catchment of reservoir	Yes/no			
		In catchment of downstream river	Yes/no			

{Cont.}...

1	*2*	*3*	*4*	*5*	*6*	*7*
		In command areas	Yes/no			
b.	Diseases due to toxic chemicals (like fluoride, nitrate, heavy metals, pesticides, etc.)	In catchment of feeder stream	Yes/no			
		In catchment of reservoir	Yes/no			
		In catchment of downstream river	Yes/no			
		In command areas	Yes/no			
15.	SOCIO-ECONOMIC (Positive or Negative effects)					
a.	Agricultural production	catchment of feeder stream	Yes/no			
		catchment of reservoir	Yes/no			

{Cont.}...

1	*2*	*3*	*4*	*5*	*6*	*7*
		catchment of downstream river	Yes/no			
		command area	Yes/no			
b.	Aquaculture	Reservoir	Yes/no			
		Downstream	Yes/no			
c.	Water supply	Downstream	Yes/no			
		Command area	Yes/no			
		Reservoir of catchment	Yes/no			
d.	Power supply		Yes/no			
e.	Flood control	Downstream	Yes/no			
f.	Navigation	Reservoir	Yes/no			

{Cont.}...

1	*2*	*3*	*4*	*5*	*6*	*7*
g.	Recreation & Tourisms	Reservoir & its catchment	Yes/no			
h.	Industrialization	Command area	Yes/no			
		Reservoir catchment	Yes/no			
i.	Employment	Command area	Yes/no			
		Reservoir catchment	Yes/no			
		Downstream	Yes/no			
j.	Resettlement		Yes/no			
k.	Forestry		Yes/no			
l.	Archeological treasures		Yes/no			
m.	Landscape		Yes/no			

{Cont.}...

1	*2*	*3*	*4*	*5*	*6*	*7*
16.	WILD LIFE					
a.	Species of wild animals		Yes/no			
b.	Species of rare and endangered animals		Yes/no			
c.	Species diversity		Yes/no			
17.	MICROLIMATE					
a.	Temperature	Reservoir catchment	Yes/no			
b.	Humidity	Reservoir catchment	Yes/no			
c.	Rainfall	Reservoir catchment	Yes/no			

{Cont.}...

1	2	3	4	5	6	7
d.	Evaporation losses	Reservoir catchment	Yes/no			
e.	Wind speed	Reservoir catchment				
18.	NOISE POLLUTION		Yes/no			
19.	AIR QUALITY		Yes/no			

INDEX